W9-DIM-331

*Rick Steves*®

SNAPSHOT

# Madrid
# & Toledo

# CONTENTS

**Post-Pandemic Travels: Expect a Warm Welcome...and a Few Changes**
Research for this guidebook was limited by the COVID-19 outbreak, and the long-term impact of the crisis on our recommended destinations is unclear. Some details in this book will change for post-pandemic travelers. Now more than ever, it's smart to reconfirm specifics as you plan and travel. As always, you can find major updates at RickSteves.com/update.

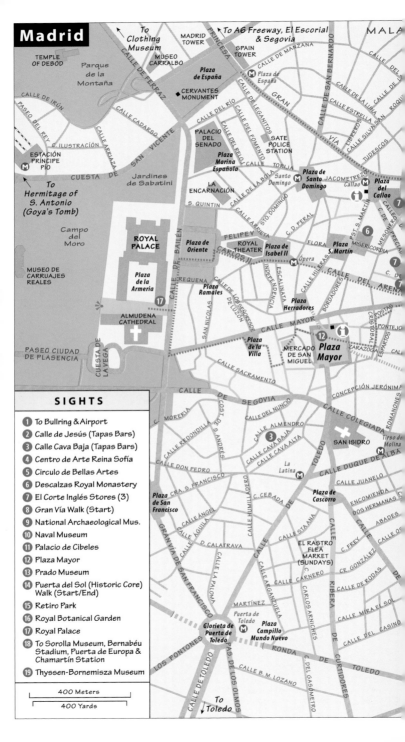

# Madrid

To Clothing Museum

MADRID TOWER

PRINCESA

To A6 Freeway, El Escorial & Segovia

SPAIN TOWER

MALA

TEMPLE OF DEBOD

Parque de la Montaña

MUSEO CARRALBO

CALLE DE FERRAZ

CALLE DE MANZANA

CALLE DE SAN BERNARDO

CALLE DEL

Plaza de España

Plaza de España

CERVANTES MONUMENT

GRAN

CALLE DE LA LUNA

CALLE DE

CALLE ESTRELLA SAN ROQU

CALLE DE IRÚN

CALLE CADARSO

CALLE DEL RÍO

CALLE DE LEGANITOS

VIA

LIBREROS

CALLE SILVA SAN

TUDESCOS

PASEO DEL REY

C. ILUSTRACIÓN

SAN VICENTE

CALLE ARANZA

PALACIO DEL SENADO

CALLE DEL FOMENTO

SATE POLICE STATION

Plaza Marina Española

ESTACIÓN PRÍNCIPE PÍO

CUESTA DE

Jardines de Sabatini

CALLE DE LA BOLA

CALLE

TORIJA

Santo Domingo

Plaza de Santo Domingo

JACOMETREZ

Callao

Plaza del Callao

To Hermitage of S. Antonio (Goya's Tomb)

LA ENCARNACIÓN

S. QUINTIN

CALLE ARRIETA

STO. DOMINGO

C.D. PERAL

ST S. MARTIN

CALLE DE

7

Campo del Moro

ROYAL PALACE

FELIPE V

Plaza de Oriente

CARLOS II

ROYAL THEATER

Plaza de Isabel II

Ópera

FLORA

Plaza S. Martín

MISERICORDIA

6

MESONER

7

MUSEO DE CARRUAJES REALES

Plaza de la Armería

CALLE DE BAILÉN

CALLE DE LOS SENDRES

REQUENA

Plaza Ramales

CALLE DE INDEPENDENCIA

ESCALINATA

CALLE DE HILERAS

CALLE DEL

ARENA

C. DE

7

ALMUDENA CATHEDRAL

17

SAN NICOLAS

Plaza de la Villa

BORDADORES

Plaza Herradores

Plaza de la Villa

CRISTOBAL

PONTEJO

CAL

PASEO CIUDAD DE PLASENCIA

CUESTA DE LA VEGA

CALLE MAYOR

MERCADO DE SAN MIGUEL

12

Plaza Mayor

ZARAGOZA

ESPARTOS

CALLE SACRAMENTO

CALLE

DE

SEGOVIA

CONCEPCIÓN JERÓNIM

C. MORERIA

CALLE DEL NUNCIO

CALLE COLEGIADA

ROMANONES

C. COST P. S. ANDRES

CALLE ALMENDRO

CALLE CAVA BAJA

3

SAN ISIDRO

Tirso de Molina

CALLE REDONDILLA

CALLE CAVA ALTA

TOLEDO

CALLE DON PEDRO

La Latina

CALLE DUQUE DE ALBA

Plaza de San Francisco

CRA. S. FRANCISCO

C. CEBADA DE

Plaza de Cascorro

CALLE JUANELO

GRAN VIA DE SAN FRANCISCO

CALLE ÁNGEL

CALLE AGUILA

CALLE HUMILLADERO

CALLE STA. ANA

ENCOMIENDA

DOS HERMANAS

ABADES

D. CALATRAVA

CALLE

EL RASTRO FLEA MARKET (SUNDAYS)

C. FREY

CALLE DE O

CALLE LA PALOMA

CALLE CARNERO

CE. GONZÁLEZ

CALLE DE RODAS

CARLOS ARNICHES

RIBERA

CALLE MIRA EL SOL

MARTÍNEZ

Puerta de Toledo

Plaza Campillo Mundo Nuevo

CALLE DE CASINO

Glorieta de Puerta de Toledo

LOS PONTONES

PAS. DE LOS OLMOS

CALLE B. M. LOZANO

RONDA

DE

C. DEL GASÓMETRO

CURTIDORES

TOLEDO

To Toledo

## SIGHTS

1. To Bullring & Airport
2. Calle de Jesús (Tapas Bars)
3. Calle Cava Baja (Tapas Bars)
4. Centro de Arte Reina Sofía
5. Circulo de Bellas Artes
6. Descalzas Royal Monastery
7. El Corte Inglés Stores (3)
8. Gran Vía Walk (Start)
9. National Archaeological Mus.
10. Naval Museum
11. Palacio de Cibeles
12. Plaza Mayor
13. Prado Museum
14. Puerta del Sol (Historic Core) Walk (Start/End)
15. Retiro Park
16. Royal Botanical Garden
17. Royal Palace
18. To Sorolla Museum, Bernabéu Stadium, Puerta de Europa & Chamartín Station
19. Thyssen-Bornemisza Museum

400 Meters

400 Yards

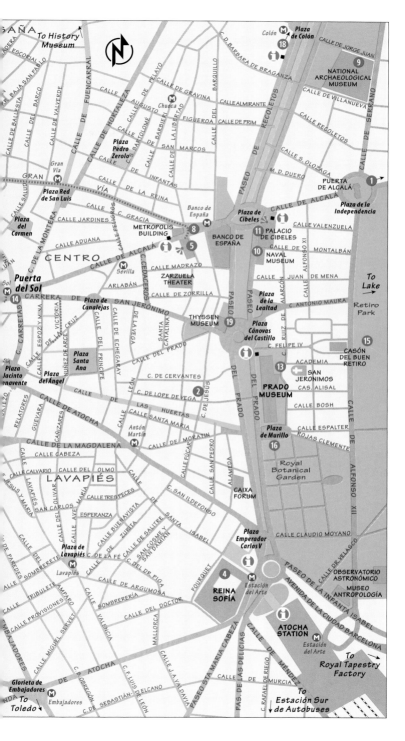

# Central Toledo

1. Army Museum
2. Calle del Comercio
3. El Greco Museum
4. Mezquita del Cristo de la Luz
5. Monastery of San Juan de los Reyes
6. Plaza de Zocodover
7. Plaza del Ayuntamiento
8. Santa Cruz Museum
9. Santa María la Blanca Synagogue
10. Santo Tomé
11. Toledo Cathedral
12. Tránsito Synagogue & Sephardic Jewish Museum
13. Victorio Macho Museum
14. Visigothic Museum

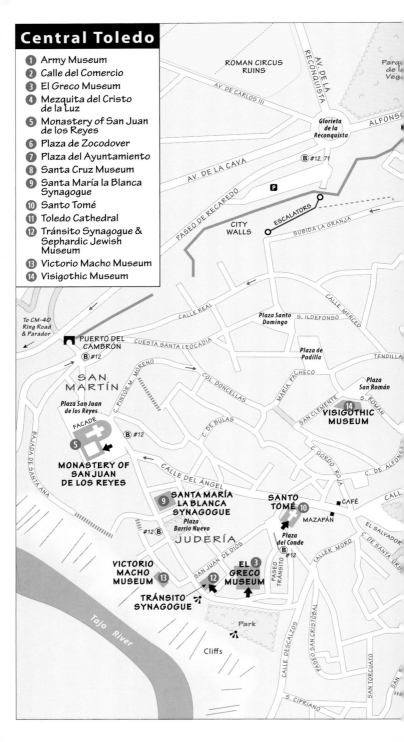

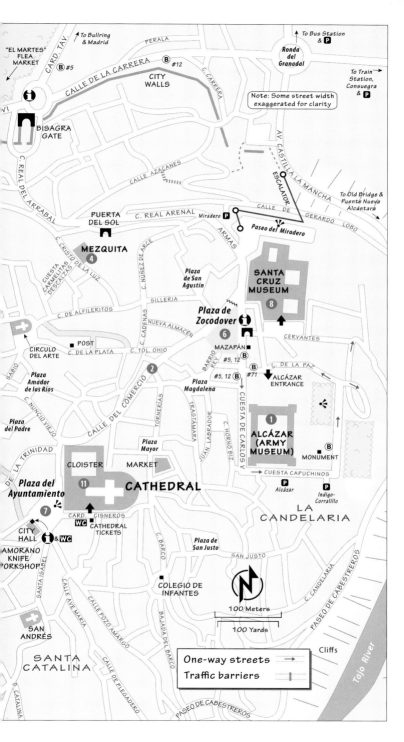

# INTRODUCTION

This Snapshot guide, excerpted from my guidebook *Rick Steves Spain,* introduces you to majestic Madrid. Spain's capital is home to some of Europe's top art treasures (the Prado Museum's collection, plus Picasso's *Guernica* in the Reina Sofía) and a lively selection of characteristic tapas bars, where you can assemble a memorable feast of Spanish specialties. Explore the city's cozy-feeling historic core, tour its lavish Royal Palace, and beat the heat on a rowboat at the lush and inviting Retiro Park.

This book also covers several side-trips from Madrid. Northwest of Madrid, you'll find Spain's grandest palace at the Inquisition-era El Escorial, the powerful monument to victims of the Spanish Civil War at the Valley of the Fallen, and a pair of charming towns: Segovia, with its towering Roman aqueduct, and Ávila, encircled by a medieval wall. Toledo, the hill-capping onetime capital of Spain, features one of the country's most magnificent cathedrals, a medieval vibe, and top paintings by favorite son El Greco.

To help you have the best trip possible, I've included the following topics in this book:

• **Planning Your Time,** with advice on how to make the most of your limited time

• **Orientation,** including tourist information offices (abbreviated as TI), tips on public transportation, local tour options, and helpful hints

• **Sights,** with ratings and strategies for meaningful and efficient visits

• **Sleeping** and **Eating,** with good-value recommendations in every price range

• **Connections,** with tips on trains, buses, and driving

**Practicalities,** near the end of this book, has information on money, staying connected, hotel reservations, transportation, and other helpful hints, plus Spanish survival phrases.

To travel smartly, read this little book in its entirety before you go. It's my hope that this guide will make your trip more meaningful and rewarding. Traveling like a temporary local, you'll get the absolute most out of every mile, minute, and dollar.

*Buen viaje!* Happy travels!

Rick Steves

# MADRID

Today's Madrid is upbeat and vibrant. You'll feel it. Look around—just about everyone has a twinkle in their eyes.

Madrid is the hub of Spain. This modern capital—Europe's second-highest, at more than 2,000 feet above sea level—is home to more than 3 million people, with about 6 million living in greater Madrid.

Like its population, the city is relatively young. In medieval times, it was just another village, wedged between the powerful kingdoms of Castile and Aragon. When newlyweds Ferdinand and Isabel united those kingdoms in 1469, Madrid—sitting at the center of Spain—became the focal point of a budding nation. By 1561, Spain ruled the world's most powerful empire, and King Philip II moved his capital from cramped, medieval Toledo (and the influence of its powerful bishop) to spacious Madrid.

Successive kings transformed the city into a European capital. By 1900, Madrid had 575,000 people, concentrated within a small area. In the mid-20th century, the city exploded with migrants from the countryside, creating modern sprawl. Today Madrid is working hard to make itself more livable. Massive urban-improvement projects—pedestrianized streets, new parks, extended commuter lines, and renovated Metro stations—are transforming the city. Once-dodgy neighborhoods are turning trendy, and the traffic chaos is subsiding. Madrid feels orderly and welcoming.

Fortunately for tourists, the historic core survives intact and is easy to navigate. Dive headlong into the grandeur and intimate charm of Madrid. Feel the vibe in Puerta del Sol, the pulsing heart of modern Madrid and of Spain itself. The lavish Royal Palace, with its gilded rooms and frescoed ceilings, rivals Versailles. The

Prado has Europe's top collection of paintings, and nearby hangs Picasso's chilling masterpiece, *Guernica*. Retiro Park invites you to take a shady siesta and hopscotch through a mosaic of lovers, families, skateboarders, pets walking their masters, and expert bench-sitters. On Sundays, cheer for the bull at a bullfight or bargain like mad at a megasize flea market. Swelter through the hot, hot summers or bundle up for the cold winters. Save some energy for after dark, when Madrileños pack the streets for an evening paseo and *tapeo* (tapas crawl) that can continue past midnight. Lively Madrid has enough street-singing, bar-hopping, and people-watching vitality to give any visitor a boost of youth.

## PLANNING YOUR TIME

Madrid is worth two days and three nights on even the fastest trip. Divide your time among the city's top three attractions: the Royal Palace (worth two hours), the Prado Museum (worth a half-day or more), and the contemporary bar-hopping scene.

Here's a two-day plan that hits Madrid's highlights. If the weather's iffy on Day 1, you can reverse this plan. With more time, Madrid has several days' worth of other museums to choose from (archaeology, city history, tapestries, the cultures of the Americas, clothing, local artists, and so on). Or, for good day-trip possibilities, see the Northwest of Madrid and Toledo chapters.

### Day 1

**Morning:** Get your bearings with my self-guided city walk, which loops from Puerta del Sol to the Royal Palace and back—with a tour through the Royal Palace in the middle.

**Afternoon:** Your afternoon is free for other sights, shopping, or exploring—consider my self-guided walk of the glitzy Gran Vía or self-guided bus tours of the busy Paseo de la Castellana or the funky Lavapiés district. Be out at the golden hour—just before sunset—for the evening paseo, when beautifully lit people fill Madrid.

**Evening:** End your day with a progressive tapas dinner at a series of characteristic bars.

### Day 2

**Morning:** Take a brisk good-morning-Madrid walk along Calle de las Huertas to the Prado, where you'll enjoy some of Europe's best art (purchase your ticket in advance). Art lovers can then head across the street to the Thyssen-Bornemisza Museum.

**Afternoon:** Enjoy an afternoon siesta in Retiro Park. Then tackle modern art at the Reina Sofía, which displays Picasso's *Guernica* (closed Tue).

**Evening:** Take in a flamenco or zarzuela performance.

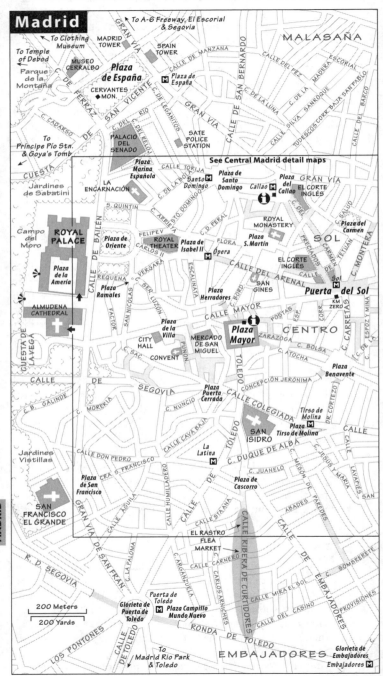

MADRID

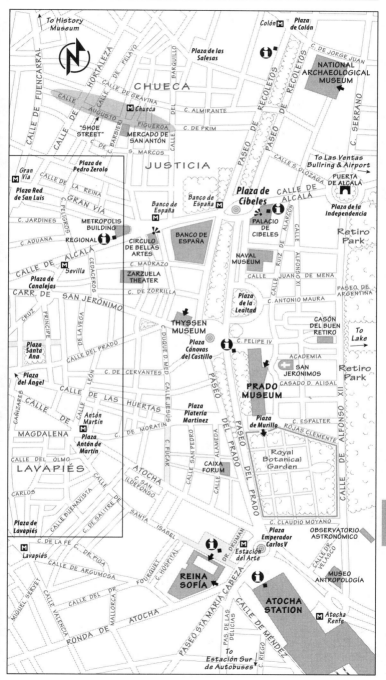

# Orientation to Madrid

While Madrid is a massive city, its historic core—which short-time visitors rarely leave—is compact and manageable. Frame

it off on your map: The square called Puerta del Sol marks the center of Madrid. To the west is the Royal Palace. To the east are the great art museums: Prado, Reina Sofía, and Thyssen-Bornemisza. North of Puerta del Sol is Gran Vía, a broad east-west boulevard bubbling with elegant shops and cinemas. Between Gran Vía and Puerta del Sol is a lively pedestrian shopping zone. And southwest of Puerta del Sol is Plaza Mayor, the center of a 17th-century, slow-down-and-smell-the-cobbles district. Everything described here (roughly the area contained in the "Central Madrid" map in this chapter) is within about a 20-minute stroll or a €10 taxi ride of Puerta del Sol.

For exploring, a wonderful chain of pedestrian streets crosses the city east to west, from the Prado to Plaza Mayor (along Calle de las Huertas) and from Puerta del Sol to the Royal Palace (on Calle del Arenal). Stretching north from Gran Vía, Calle de Fuencarral is a trendy shopping-and-strolling pedestrian street.

## TOURIST INFORMATION

Madrid has city TIs run by the Madrid City Council, and regional TIs run by the privately owned Turismo Madrid. Both are helpful, but you'll get more biased information from Turismo Madrid.

The city-run TIs share a website (www.esmadrid.com), a central phone number (+34 915 787 810), and hours (daily 9:30-20:30 or later). The best and most central city TI is on **Plaza Mayor.** Additional branches are scattered all over the city, often in freestanding kiosks. Look for them near the **Prado** (facing the Neptune fountain), in front of the **Reina Sofía** art museum (across the street from the Atocha train station, in the median of the busy road), along Gran Vía at **Plaza del Callao,** at **Plaza de Colón** (in the underground passage accessed from Paseo de la Castellana and Calle de Goya), inside **Palacio de Cibeles** (up the stairs, and to the right), and at the **airport** (Terminals 2 and 4).

Regional Turismo Madrid TIs share hours and a website (Mon-Sat 8:00-20:00, Sun 9:00-14:00; www.turismomadrid.

es). The main branch is just east of Puerta del Sol at **Calle de Alcalá 31;** branches are also inside the **Sol Metro station** (inside the underground corridor; this branch open daily 8:00-20:00), at **Chamartín train station** (near track 20), at **Atocha train station** (AVE arrivals side; this branch open Sun until 20:00), and at the **airport** (Terminals 1 and 4).

At most TIs, you can get the *Es Madrid* English-language monthly, which includes a map and event listings. Themed *Madrid for You* booklets on various topics (families, museums, viewpoints, gastronomy, and so on) are also available. The regional TIs hand out a handy public transportation map.

**Entertainment Guides:** For arts and culture listings, the TI's printed material is good, but you can also pick up the more practical Spanish-language weekly entertainment guide **Guía del Ocio** (sold cheap at newsstands) or visit www.guiadelocio.com. It lists daily live music *("Conciertos"),* museums (under *"Arte"*—with the latest times, prices, and special exhibits), restaurants (an exhaustive listing), TV schedules, and movies ("V.O." means original version, *"V.O. en inglés sub"* or *"V.O.S.E."* means a movie is played in English with Spanish subtitles rather than dubbed).

## ARRIVAL IN MADRID

For more information on arriving at or departing from Madrid, including stations and connections, see "Madrid Connections," at the end of this chapter.

**By Train:** Madrid's two train stations, Chamartín and Atocha, are on both Metro and *cercanías* (suburban train) lines with easy access to downtown Madrid. Chamartín handles most international trains and the AVE (AH-vay) train to and from Segovia. Atocha generally covers southern Spain, as well as AVE trains to and from Barcelona, Córdoba, Granada, Sevilla, and Toledo. Many train tickets include a *cercanías* connection to or from the train station.

*Traveling Between Chamartín and Atocha Stations:* You can take the Metro (€2, line 1, 30-40 minutes; see "Getting Around Madrid," later), but the *cercanías* trains are faster (€1.70, 6/hour, 13 minutes, Atocha-Chamartín lines C1, C3, C4, C7, C8, and C10 each connect the two stations, lines C3 and C4 also stop at Sol—Madrid's central square). If you have a rail pass or any regular train ticket to Madrid, you can get a free transfer within three hours of your ticket times. At the *Cercanías* ticket machine, choose *combinado cercanías,* then either scan the bar code on your train ticket or punch in a code (labeled *combinado cercanías),* and choose your destination. These trains depart from Atocha's track 6 and generally Chamartín's track 1, 3, 8, or 9—check the *salidas inmediatas* board to be sure).

MADRID

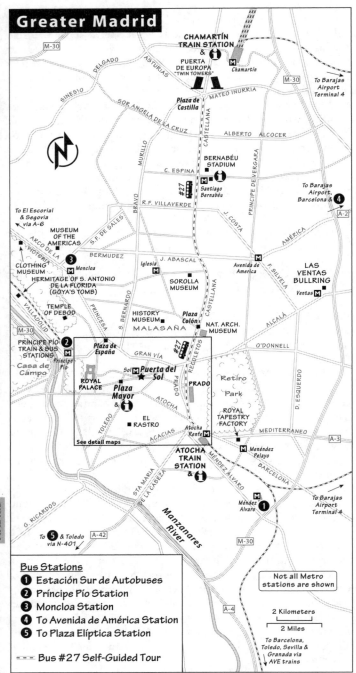

# Greater Madrid

CHAMARTÍN TRAIN STATION &
PUERTA DE EUROPA "TWIN TOWERS"
Chamartín

M-30
DELGADO
ASTURIAS
To Barajas Airport Terminal 4
SINESIO
SOR ANGELA DE LA CRUZ
MATEO INURRIA
Plaza de Castilla
CASTELLANA
ALBERTO ALCOCER
MURILLO

BERNABÉU STADIUM
C. ESPINA
#27
Santiago Bernabéu
PRÍNCIPE DE VERGARA
To Barajas Airport, Barcelona & 4
A-2
BRAVO
R.F. VILLAVERDE
J. COSTA
AMÉRICA
F. SILVELA

To El Escorial & Segovia via A-6
MUSEUM OF THE AMERICAS
ARCO DE LA VICTORIA
S.F. DE SALES
BERMUDEZ
J. ABASCAL
Avenida de América
LAS VENTAS BULLRING
CLOTHING MUSEUM
3 Moncloa
Iglesia
SOROLLA MUSEUM
CASTELLANA
Ventas
HERMITAGE OF S. ANTONIO DE LA FLORIDA (GOYA'S TOMB)
S. BERNARDO
PRINCESA
ALCALÁ
TEMPLE OF DEBOD
HISTORY MUSEUM
Plaza Colón
O'DONNELL
VALLADOLID
MALASAÑA
NAT. ARCH. MUSEUM
D. ESQUERDO
M-30
PRÍNCIPE PÍO TRAIN & BUS STATIONS
2 Plaza de España
GRAN VÍA
#27
REDOTOS
Príncipe Pío
Casa de Campo
Sol Puerta del Sol
PRADO
Retiro Park
ROYAL PALACE
Plaza Mayor &
ATOCHA
PRADO
TOLEDO
EL RASTRO
ACACIAS
ROYAL TAPESTRY FACTORY
MEDITERRANEO
A-3
Atocha Renfe
See detail maps
ATOCHA TRAIN STATION &
MENDEZ ALVARO
Menéndez Pelayo
STA MARIA DE LA CABEZA
BARCELONA
G. RICARDOS
To 5 & Toledo via N-401
A-42
Manzanares River
Méndez Alvaro 1
To Barajas Airport Terminal 4
M-30
To Barcelona, Toledo, Sevilla & Granada via AVE trains
A-4

## Bus Stations
1 Estación Sur de Autobuses
2 Príncipe Pío Station
3 Moncloa Station
4 To Avenida de América Station
5 To Plaza Elíptica Station

--- Bus #27 Self-Guided Tour

Not all Metro stations are shown

2 Kilometers
2 Miles

MADRID

**By Bus:** Madrid has several bus stations, each one handy to a Metro station: Estación Sur de Autobuses (for Ávila, Salamanca, and Granada; Metro: Méndez Álvaro); Plaza Elíptica (for Toledo, Metro: Plaza Elíptica); Moncloa (for El Escorial, Metro: Moncloa); and Avenida de América (for Pamplona and Burgos, Metro: Avenida de América). From any of these, just ride the Metro or a taxi to your hotel.

**By Plane:** Both international and domestic flights arrive at Madrid's Barajas Airport. Options for getting into town include public bus, *cercanías* train, Metro, taxi, and minibus shuttle.

## HELPFUL HINTS

**Sightseeing Tips:** The Prado and Royal Palace are open daily. The Reina Sofía (with Picasso's *Guernica*) is closed on Tuesday, and many other sights are closed on Monday, including the Monasterio de San Lorenzo de El Escorial, a popular day trip outside of Madrid (see next chapter). If you're here on a Sunday, consider visiting the famous El Rastro flea market (year-round) and/or a bullfight (most Sun and holidays in March-mid-Oct plus almost daily during the San Isidro festival in early May-early June).

**Theft Alert:** Be wary of pickpockets—anywhere, anytime, but especially in crowded areas such as Puerta del Sol, the busy street between the Puerta del Sol and the Prado (Carrera de San Jerónimo), El Rastro flea market, Gran Vía (especially the paseo zone: Plaza del Callao to Plaza de España), anywhere on the Metro (especially the Ópera station), bus #27, and at the airport. Be alert to the people around you: Someone wearing a heavy jacket in the summer is likely a pickpocket. Kids may dress like Americans and work the areas near big sights; anyone under 18 can't be charged in any meaningful way by the police. Assume any commotion is a scam to distract people about to become victims of a pickpocket. Wear your money belt. For help if you get ripped off, see the next listing.

**Tourist Emergency Aid:** SATE is an assistance service for tourists who need help with anything from canceling stolen credit cards to reporting a crime (central police station, daily 9:00-24:00, near Plaza de Santo Domingo at Calle Leganitos 19). They can act as an interpreter if you have trouble communicating with the police. Or you can call in your report to the SATE line (24-hour +34 902 102 112, English spoken once you get connected to a person).

**Sex Work:** While it's illegal to make money from someone else selling sex (i.e., pimping), sex workers over 18 can solicit legally. Calle de la Montera (leading from Puerta del Sol to Plaza Red de San Luis) is lined with what looks like a bunch

MADRID

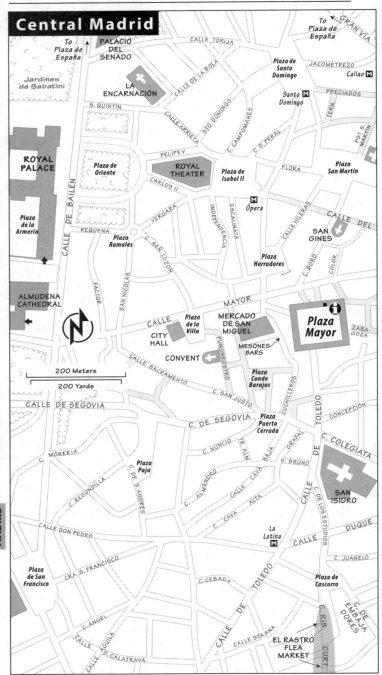

# Central Madrid

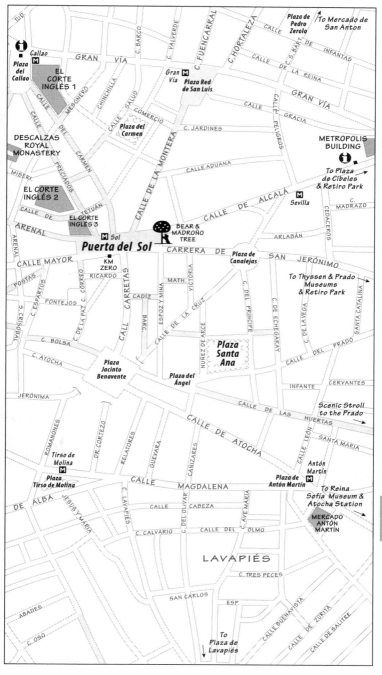

of high-schoolers skipping school for a cigarette break. Don't stray north of Gran Vía around Calle de la Luna and Plaza Santa María Soledad—while the streets may look inviting, this area is bad news.

**One-Stop Shopping at El Corte Inglés:** Madrid's dominant department store, El Corte Inglés, fills three huge buildings in the pedestrian zone just off Puerta del Sol. From groceries and event tickets to fashion and housewares, El Corte Inglés has it all. For a building-by-building breakdown, see "Shopping in Madrid," later.

**Bookstores:** For books in English, try **FNAC Callao** (Calle Preciados 28), **Casa del Libro** (English on basement floor, Gran Vía 29), and **El Corte Inglés** (guidebooks and some fiction, in its Building 3 Books/Librería branch kitty-corner from main store, fronting Puerta del Sol).

**Laundry:** For a self-service laundry, try **Colada Express** at Calle Campomanes 9 (free Wi-Fi, daily 9:00-22:00, mobile +34 657 876 464) or **Lavandería** at Calle León 6 (self-service Mon-Sat 9:00-22:00, Sun 12:00-15:00; full-service Mon-Sat 9:00-14:00 & 15:00-20:00, +34 914 299 545). For locations see the "Madrid Center Hotels" map on page 98.

## GETTING AROUND MADRID

Madrid has excellent public transit. Pick up the Metro map (free at TIs or at Metro info booths in stations with staff); for buses get the

fine, free *Public Transport* map (available at some TIs). The metropolitan Madrid transit website (www.crtm.es) covers all public transportation options (Metro, bus, and suburban rail).

**By Metro:** Madrid's Metro is simple, speedy, and cheap. Distances are short, but the city's broad streets can be hot and exhausting, so a subway trip of even a stop or two saves time and energy. The Metro runs from 6:00 to 1:30 in the morning. At all times, be alert to thieves, who thrive in crowded stations. Metro info: www.metromadrid.es.

*Tickets:* A **single ride ticket** within zone A costs €1.50-2, depending on the number of stops you travel; zone A covers most of the city, but not trains to the airport. A **10-ride ticket** is €12.20 and valid on the Metro and buses; it can be shared by several travelers with the same destination (two people taking five rides should get one).

To buy either a single ride or 10-ride ticket, you'll first buy a rechargeable red **Multi Card** *(tarjeta)* for €2.50 (nonrefundable—consider it a souvenir). The first Metro ticket you buy will cost at least €4 and be issued on the card; thereafter, you can reload the card with additional rides *(viajes)*. Ticket machines ask you to punch in your destination from the alphabetized list (follow the simple prompts) to load up the correct fare. You can also buy or reload Multi Cards at newspaper stands and Estanco tobacco shops.

I'd skip the tourist ticket *(billete turístico)* you may see advertised, which covers all Metro and bus rides for a designated time period; unless you're riding transit like crazy, it's unlikely to save you money over the 10-ride ticket.

*Riding the Metro:* Study your Metro map—the simplified "Madrid Metro" map in this chapter can get you started. Lines are color-coded and numbered; use end-of-the-line station names to choose your direction of travel. When entering the Metro system, touch your Multi Card against the yellow pad to open the turnstile (no need to touch it again to exit). Once in the Metro station, signs direct you to the train line and direction (e.g., Linea 1, *Valdecarros*). To transfer, follow signs in the station leading to connecting lines. Once you reach your final stop, look for the green *salida* signs pointing to the exits. Use the helpful neighborhood maps to choose the right *salida* and save yourself lots of walking.

**By Bus:** City buses, though not as easy as the Metro, can be useful. You can use a **Multi Card** loaded with a 10-ride ticket (see details earlier). But for **single rides,** you'll buy a ticket on the bus, paying the driver in cash (€1.50; bus maps at TI or info booth on Puerta del Sol, poster-size maps usually posted at bus stops, buses run 6:00-24:00, much less frequent *Buho* buses run all night). The EMT Madrid app finds the closest stops and lines and gives accurate wait times (there's a version in English). Bus info: www.emtmadrid.es.

**By Taxi or Uber:** Madrid's taxis are reasonably priced and easy to hail. A green light on the roof and/or the word *Libre* on the windshield indicates that a taxi is available. Foursomes travel almost as cheaply by taxi as by Metro; for example, a ride from the Royal Palace to the Prado costs about €10. After the drop charge (about €3), the per-kilometer rate depends on the time: *Tarifa 1* (€1.05/kilometer) is charged Mon-Fri 6:00-21:00; *Tarifa 2* (€1.20/kilometer) is valid after 21:00 and on Saturdays, Sundays, and holidays. If your cabbie uses anything other than *Tarifa 1* on weekdays (shown as an isolated "1" on the meter), you're being cheated.

Rates can be higher outside Madrid. There's a flat rate of €30 between the city center and any one of the airport terminals. Other legitimate charges include a €3 supplement for leaving any train or bus station, €20 per hour for waiting, and €5 if you call to have the taxi come to you. Make sure the meter is turned on as soon as

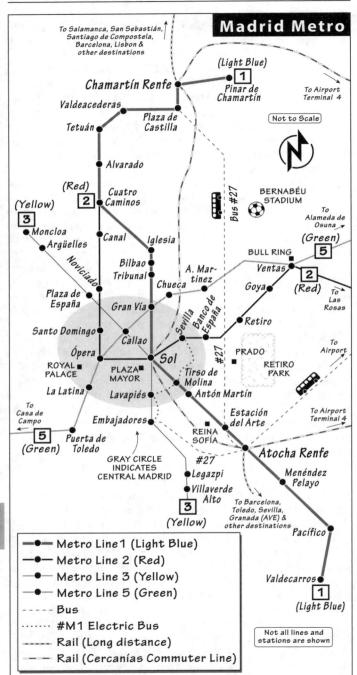

**Madrid Metro**

To Salamanca, San Sebastián, Santiago de Compostela, Barcelona, Lisbon & other destinations

(Light Blue)
1

Chamartín Renfe

Pinar de Chamartín

To Airport Terminal 4

Valdeacederas

Plaza de Castilla

Not to Scale

Tetuán

N

Alvarado

BERNABÉU STADIUM

(Red)
2
Cuatro Caminos

To Alameda de Osuna

(Yellow)
3

(Green)
5

Moncloa

Canal

Iglesia

BULL RING

Argüelles

Ventas

2

Noviciado

Bilbao

Goya

(Red)

Tribunal

A. Martínez

To Las Rosas

Plaza de España

Chueca

Gran Vía

Retiro

To Airport

Santo Domingo

Callao

Ópera

Sol

PRADO

RETIRO PARK

ROYAL PALACE

PLAZA MAYOR

Tirso de Molina

La Latina

Lavapiés

Antón Martín

To Casa de Campo

Embajadores

Estación del Arte

To Airport Terminal 4

5

(Green)

Puerta de Toledo

REINA SOFÍA

Atocha Renfe

GRAY CIRCLE INDICATES CENTRAL MADRID

#27

Menéndez Pelayo

Legazpi

Villaverde Alto

To Barcelona, Toledo, Sevilla, Granada (AVE) & other destinations

3

(Yellow)

Pacífico

Valdecarros

1

(Light Blue)

Not all lines and stations are shown

Bus #27

Sevilla

Banco de España

**Legend**

- ━●━ Metro Line 1 (Light Blue)
- ─●─ Metro Line 2 (Red)
- ─●─ Metro Line 3 (Yellow)
- ─●─ Metro Line 5 (Green)
- ----- Bus
- ········· #M1 Electric Bus
- ----- Rail (Long distance)
- ─ ─ Rail (Cercanías Commuter Line)

MADRID

you get into the cab so the driver can't tack anything onto the official rate. If the driver starts adding up "extras," look for the sticker detailing all legitimate surcharges (it should be on the passenger window).

Uber works in Madrid pretty much like it does at home. Outside of peak times, an Uber ride can be slightly cheaper than a taxi.

# Tours in Madrid

∩ To sightsee on your own, download my free Madrid City Walk audio tour.

## ON FOOT
### Walking Tours

**Across Madrid** is run by Almudena Cros, a well-traveled art history professor. She offers several specialized tours, including one on the Spanish Civil War that draws on her family's history (generally €70/person, maximum 8 people, book well in advance, also gives good tours for children, mobile +34 652 576 423, www.acrossmadrid.com).

**Stephen Drake-Jones,** an eccentric British expat, has led walks of historic old Madrid almost daily for decades. A historian with a passion for the Duke of Wellington (the general who stopped Napoleon), Stephen loves to teach history. For €95 you get a 3.5-hour tour with three stops for drinks and tapas—call it lunch (daily at 11:00, maximum 8 people). He also offers a private version (€190/2 people) and themed tours covering the Spanish Civil War, Hemingway's Madrid, and more (mobile +34 609 143 202, www.wellsoc.org).

### Private Guides

Assemble your own group to share the cost of these tours.

**Federico** and his team of licensed guides lead city walks and museum tours in Madrid and nearby towns. They specialize in family tours and engaging kids and teens in museums, and size their city tours like cups of hot chocolate (small-€150/2 hours, medium-€200/4 hours, large-€250/6 hours, extra large-€300/8 hours, mobile +34 649 936 222, www.spainfred.com).

**Letango Tours** offers private tours, packages, and stays all over Spain with a focus on families and groups. Carlos Galvin, a Spaniard who led tours for my groups for more than a decade, his wife Jennifer from Seattle, and their team of guides in Madrid offer a kid-friendly "Madrid Discoveries" tour that mixes a market walk and history with a culinary-and-tapas introduction (€295/group of up to 5, kids free, 3-plus hours). They also lead tours to Barcelona,

MADRID

# Madrid at a Glance

▲▲▲**Royal Palace** Spain's sumptuous, lavishly furnished national palace. **Hours:** Daily 10:00-20:00, Oct-March until 18:00. See page 40.

▲▲▲**Prado Museum** One of the world's great museums, loaded with masterpieces by Diego Velázquez, Francisco de Goya, El Greco, Hieronymus Bosch, Albrecht Dürer, and more. **Hours:** Mon-Sat 10:00-20:00, Sun until 19:00. See page 53.

▲▲▲**Centro de Arte Reina Sofía** Modern-art museum featuring Picasso's epic masterpiece *Guernica*. **Hours:** Mon and Wed-Sat 10:00-21:00, Sun until 19:00, closed Tue. See page 72.

▲▲▲**Paseo** Evening stroll among the Madrileños. **Hours:** Sundown until the wee hours. See page 91.

▲▲**Puerta del Sol** Madrid's lively central square. See page 21.

▲▲**Plaza Mayor** Historic cobbled square. See page 24.

▲▲**Thyssen-Bornemisza Museum** A great complement to the Prado, with lesser-known yet still impressive works and an especially good Impressionist collection. **Hours:** Mon 12:00-16:00, Tue-Sun 10:00-19:00. See page 69.

▲▲**Retiro Park** Festive green escape from the city, with rental rowboats and great people-watching. **Hours:** Closes at dusk. See page 80.

▲▲**National Archaeological Museum** Traces the history of Iberia through artifacts. **Hours:** Tue-Sat 9:30-20:00, Sun until 15:00, closed Mon. See page 81.

▲▲**Sorolla Museum** Delightful, intimate collection of portraits and landscapes by Spanish artist Joaquín Sorolla. **Hours:** Tue-Sat 9:30-20:00, Sun 10:00-15:00, closed Mon. See page 83.

MADRID

whitewashed villages, wine country, and more (www.letango.com, tours@letango.com).

At **Madridivine,** David Gillison and his team enthusiastically share their passion for Spanish culture through food and walking tours of historic Madrid. They connect you with locals, food, and wine from an insider's perspective (€200/group of up to 6, 3 hours, food and drinks extra—usually around €40, www.madridivine.com, info@madridivine.com).

▲▲**Flamenco** Captivating music and dance performances, at various venues throughout the city. **Hours:** Shows nightly, but some places closed on Sun. See page 94.

▲**Royal Botanical Garden** A relaxing museum of plants, with specimens from around the world. **Hours:** Daily May-Aug 10:00-21:00, April and Sept until 20:00, shorter hours off-season. See page 69.

▲**Naval Museum** Seafaring history of a country famous for its Armada. **Hours:** Tue-Sun 10:00-19:00, until 15:00 in Aug, closed Mon. See page 80.

▲**Museum of the Americas** Pre-Columbian and colonial artifacts from the New World. **Hours:** Tue-Sat 9:30-15:00, Thu until 19:00, Sun 10:00-15:00, closed Mon. See page 82.

▲**Hermitage of San Antonio de la Florida** Church with Goya's tomb, plus frescoes by the artist. **Hours:** Tue-Sun 9:30-20:00, closed Mon. See page 82.

▲**Madrid History Museum** The city's story told through old paintings, maps, fascinating photos, and historic artifacts. **Hours:** Tue-Sun 10:00-20:00, closed Mon. See page 87.

▲**Bullfight** Spain's controversial pastime. **Hours:** Most Sundays and holidays March-mid-Oct, plus almost daily early May-early June. See page 87.

▲**El Rastro** Europe's biggest flea market, filled with bargains and pickpockets. **Hours:** Sun 9:00-15:00, best before 11:00. See page 89.

▲**Zarzuela** Madrid's delightful light opera. **Hours:** Evenings. See page 91.

**MADRID**

Other good, licensed local guides include: **Inés Muñiz Martin** (guiding since 1997 and a third-generation Madrileña, €125-190/2-5 hours, €35 extra on weekends and holidays, mobile +34 629 147 370, www.immguidedtours.com) and **Susana Jarabo** (with a master's in art history, €200/4 hours, tours by bike or Segway possible, available March-Aug, mobile +34 667 027 722, susanjarabo@yahoo.es).

## BY BUS
### Hop-On, Hop-Off Bus
**Madrid City Tour** makes two different hop-on, hop-off circuits through the city: historic and modern (each with 16-21 stops, 1.5 hours, buses depart every 15 minutes). The two routes intersect at the south side of Puerta del Sol and in front of Starbucks across from the Prado. Your ticket covers both loops (€22/1 day, €26/2 consecutive days, pay driver, recorded narration, daily 9:30-22:00, Nov-Feb 10:00-18:00, +34 917 791 888, www.madridcitytour.es).

### Big-Bus City Sightseeing Tours
**Julià Travel** offers bus tours in Madrid and side trips to nearby destinations. Their 2.5-hour Madrid tour is narrated by a live guide in two or three languages (€29, drink stop at Hard Rock Café, one shopping stop, no museum visits, daily at 9:00 and 15:00, no reservation required—just show up 15 minutes before departure). Tours leave from their office at Calle San Nicolás 7 near Plaza de Ramales, just south of Plaza de Oriente (+34 915 599 605, www.juliatravel.com).

### Self-Guided Tours by Bus or Minibus
A ride on public **bus #27** from the museum neighborhood up Paseo del Prado and Paseo de la Castellana to the Puerta de Europa and back gives visitors a glimpse of the modern side of Madrid (see page 84), while a ride on electric **minibus #M1** takes you through the characteristic, gritty old center (see page 85).

# Walks in Madrid

Two self-guided walks provide a look at two sides of Madrid. For a taste of old Madrid, start with my "Historic Core Walk," which winds through the center. My "Gran Vía Walk" lets you glimpse a more modern side of Spain's capital.

⌒ Download my free Madrid City Walk audio tour, which complements this section.

## HISTORIC CORE WALK
Madrid's historic center is pedestrian-friendly and filled with spacious squares, a trendy market, bulls' heads in a bar, and a cookie-dispensing convent. Allow about two hours for this self-guided, mile-long walk that loops from Madrid's central square, Puerta del Sol, to the Royal Palace and back to the square (Metro: Sol).

• *Start in the middle of the square, by the equestrian statue of King Charles III, and survey the scene.*

## ❶ Puerta del Sol

The bustling Puerta del Sol, rated ▲▲, is Madrid's—and Spain's—center. In recent years, the square has undergone a facelift to become a mostly pedestrianized and wide-open gathering place. For Spaniards, this place (with its iconic *Tío Pepe* sign) is probably the most recognizable spot in the country. It's a popular site for political demonstrations and national celebrations. For Madrileños,

Puerta del Sol is a transportation hub for the Metro, *cercanías* (suburban trains), and several main roads. It's also a magnet for strolling locals, sightseers, pickpockets, revelers, and locals dressed as cartoon characters who pose for photos for a fee. In many ways, it's the soul of the city.

The equestrian statue in the middle of the square honors the man who established the Puerta del Sol as an urban hub—**King Charles III** (1716-1788). His enlightened urban policies earned him the affectionate nickname "the best mayor of Madrid." He decorated city squares with beautiful fountains, got those meddlesome Jesuits out of city government, established the public-school system, mandated underground sewers, opened his private Retiro Park to the public, built the Prado, made the Royal Palace the wonder of Europe, and generally cleaned up Madrid. (For more on Charles, see page 45.)

Head to the slightly uphill end of the square and find the **statue of a bear** pawing a tree—not much to look at, but locals love it. This image has been a symbol of Madrid since medieval times. Bears used to live in the royal hunting grounds outside the city. And the *madroño* trees produce a berry that makes the traditional *madroño* liqueur.

Charles III faces a red-and-white building with a bell tower. This was Madrid's first post office, which Charles III founded in the 1760s. Today it's the **county governor's office,** home to the "president" who governs greater Madrid. The building is notorious for having once been dictator Francisco Franco's police headquarters. A tragic number of those detained and interrogated by the Franco police tried to "escape" by jumping out its windows to their deaths.

Appreciate the **harmonious architecture** of the buildings that circle the square—yellow-cream, four stories, balconies of iron, shuttered windows, and balustrades along the rooflines.

Crowds fill the square on New Year's Eve as the rest of Spain

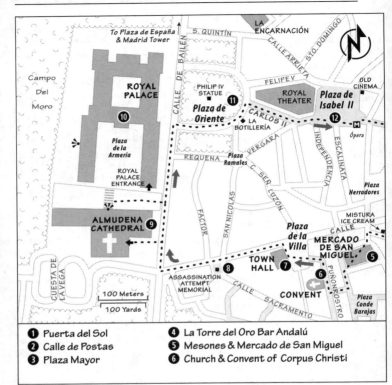

**1** Puerta del Sol
**2** Calle de Postas
**3** Plaza Mayor
**4** La Torre del Oro Bar Andalú
**5** Mesones & Mercado de San Miguel
**6** Church & Convent of Corpus Christi

watches the Times Square-style action on TV. The bell atop the governor's office chimes 12 times, while Madrileños eat one grape for each ring to bring good luck through each of the next 12 months.

• *Cross the square and street to the governor's office.*

Look down at the sidewalk directly in front of the entrance to the governor's office. The plaque marks **"kilometer zero,"** the symbolic center of Spain, from which the country's six main highways radiate (as the plaque shows). Standing on the zero marker with your back to the governor's office, get oriented visually: Directly ahead, at 12 o'clock, is the famous **Tío Pepe sign.** This big neon billboard—25 feet high and 80 feet across—pictures a jaunty Andalusian *caballero* with a sombrero and guitar. He's been advertising a local sherry wine since the 1930s.

Beyond the sign is a thriving **pedestrian commercial zone,** anchored by the huge department store, El Corte Inglés. At two o'clock starts the seedier Calle de la Montera, a street with shady characters and prostitutes that leads to the trendy, pedestrianized Calle de Fuencarral. At three o'clock is a big Apple store; the Prado is about a mile farther to your right. Back over at 10 o'clock is the

# Madrid's Historic Core Walk

⑦ Town Hall
⑧ Assassination Attempt Memorial
⑨ Almudena Cathedral
⑩ Royal Palace
⑪ Plaza de Oriente
⑫ Plaza de Isabel II
⑬ Calle del Arenal

pedestrianized street called Calle del Arenal...where we'll finish this walk.

Now turn around. On the walls flanking the entrance to the governor's office are **two white marble plaques.** These commemorate two important dates, when Madrileños came together in times of dire need. The plaque on the right marks an event from 1808. An angry crowd gathered here to rise up against an invasion by France. Suddenly, French soldiers stormed the square and began massacring the Spaniards. The event galvanized the country, which eventually drove out the French. The painter Francisco de Goya, whose studio was not far from here, captured the event in his famous painting, *The Third of May*, which is now in the Prado museum.

The plaque to the left of the entry remembers a more recent tragedy, on March 11, 2004. That's when brave Spanish citizens helped fellow citizens in the wake of horrific terrorist bombings in the city. We have our 9/11—Spain has its 3/11.

Finally, notice the civil guardsmen at the entry. They may be wearing curious hats with square backs, which it's said were cleverly designed so that the guards can lean against the wall while enjoying a cigarette.

On the corner of Puerta del Sol and Calle Mayor (downhill end of Puerta del Sol) is the busy, recommended *confitería* **La Mallorquina**, *"fundada en 1.894."* Go inside for a tempting peek at racks with goodies hot out of the oven. The crowded takeaway section is in front; the stand-up counter is in back. Enjoy observing the churning energy of Madrileños popping in for a fast coffee and a sweet treat. The shop is famous for its *Napolitana* pastry (like a squashed, custard-filled croissant). Or sample Madrid's answer to doughnuts, *rosquillas* (*tontas* means "silly"—plain, and *listas* means "all dressed up and ready to go"—with icing). Buy something... there's no special system, just order and pay. The café upstairs is more genteel, with nice views of the square.

Before leaving the shop, find the tiles above the entrance door and above the bar with the 18th-century views of Puerta del Sol. This was before the square was widened, when a church stood at its top end. Compare this with today's view out the door.

Puerta del Sol ("Gate of the Sun") is named for a long-gone gate carved with a rising sun, which once stood at the eastern edge of the old city. From here, we begin our walk through the historic town that dates back to medieval times.

• *Head west on busy Calle Mayor, just past McDonald's. Go a few steps up the side-street on the left, then angle right on the pedestrian-only street called...*

## ❷ Calle de Postas

The street sign shows the post coach heading for that famous first post office. Medieval street signs posted on the lower corners of buildings included pictures so the illiterate (and monolingual tourists) could "read" them. Fifty yards up the street on the left, at Calle San Cristóbal, is Pans & Company, a popular Catalan sandwich chain offering lots of healthy choices. While Spaniards tend to consider American fast food unhealthy—both culturally and physically—they love it. McDonald's and Burger King are thriving in Spain.

• *Continue up Calle de Postas, and take a slight right on Calle de la Sal through the arcade, where you emerge into...*

## ❸ Plaza Mayor

This vast, cobbled square (worth ▲▲) dates back to Madrid's glory days, the 1600s. Back then, this—not Puerta del Sol— was Madrid's main square *(plaza mayor)*. The **equestrian statue** (wearing a ruffled collar) honors Philip III, who made this square

the centerpiece of the budding capital in 1619. Philip's dad (Philip II) had founded Madrid, and the son transformed a former marketplace into this state-of-the-art Baroque plaza.

The square is 140 yards long and 100 yards wide, enclosed by four-story buildings with symmetrical windows, balconies, slate roofs, and steepled towers. Each side of the square is uniform, as if a grand palace were turned inside-out. This distinct look, pioneered by architect Juan de Herrera (who finished El Escorial), is found all over Madrid.

This site served as the city's 17th-century open-air theater. Upon this stage, much Spanish history has been played out. The square's lampposts have reliefs on the benches below illustrating major episodes: bullfights fought here, dancers and masked revelers at Carnevale, royal pageantry, a horrendous fire in 1790, and events of the gruesome **Inquisition.** During the Inquisition, many were tried here—suspected heretics, Protestants, Jews, tour guides without a local license, and Muslims whose "conversion" to Christianity was dubious. The guilty were paraded around the square before their executions, wearing placards listing their many sins (bleachers were built for bigger audiences, while the wealthy rented balconies). The heretics were burned, and later, criminals were slowly strangled as they held a crucifix, hearing the reassuring words of a priest as the life was squeezed out of them with a garrote. Up to 50,000 people could crowd into this square for such spectacles.

The square's buildings are mainly private apartments. Want one? Costs run from €400,000 for a tiny attic studio to €2 million and up for a 2,500-square-foot flat. The square is painted a democratic shade of burgundy—the result of a citywide poll. Since the end of decades of dictatorship in 1975, Spain has had a passion for voting. Three different colors were painted as samples on the walls of this square, and the city voted for its favorite.

The building to Philip's left, on the north side beneath the twin towers, was once home to the baker's guild and now houses the **TI,** which is wonderfully air-conditioned.

A stamp-and-coin market bustles at Plaza Mayor on Sundays (10:00-14:00). Day or night, Plaza Mayor is a colorful place to enjoy an affordable cup of coffee or overpriced food. Throughout Spain, lesser *plazas mayores* provide peaceful pools in the whitewater river of Spanish life.

*• Head to #26, which is under the arcade just to the left of the twin towers. This is a bar called...*

### ❹ La Torre del Oro Bar Andalú

For some *Andalú* (Andalusian) ambience, an entertaining (if gruff) staff, and lots of fascinating (if gruesome) bullfighting lore, step inside. Order a drink at the bar and sightsee while you sip. Warning: First check the price list posted outside the door to understand the price tiers: *"barra"* indicates the price at the bar; *"terraza"* is the price at an outdoor table. A *caña* (small draft beer), Coke, or *agua mineral* should cost about €3. Your drink may come with a small, free tapa, per the old Spanish tradition. But to avoid being charged by surprise, clarify, *"Gratis?"*

The interior is a temple to bullfighting, festooned with gory decor. Notice the breathtaking action captured in the many photographs. Look under the stuffed head of Barbero the bull (center, facing the bar). At eye level you'll see a *puntilla*, the knife used to put poor Barbero out of his misery at the arena. The plaque explains: weight, birth date, owner, date of death, which matador killed him, and the location.

Just to the left of Barbero is a photo of longtime dictator Franco with the famous bullfighter Manuel Benítez Pérez—better known as El Cordobés, the Elvis of bullfighters and a working-class hero.

At the top of the stairs going down to the WC, find the photo of El Cordobés and Robert Kennedy—looking like brothers. Three feet to the left of them (and elsewhere in the bar) is a shot of Che Guevara enjoying a bullfight.

Below and left of the Kennedy photo is a picture of El Cordobés' illegitimate son being gored. Disowned by El Cordobés senior, yet still using his dad's famous name after a court battle, the junior El Cordobés is one of this generation's top fighters.

At the end of the bar, in a glass case, is the "suit of lights" the great El Cordobés wore in an ill-fated 1967 fight, in which the bull gored him. El Cordobés survived; the bull didn't. Find the photo of Franco with El Cordobés at the far end, to the left of Segador the bull.

In the case with the "suit of lights," notice the photo of a matador (not El Cordobés) horrifyingly hooked by a bull's horn. For a series of photos showing this episode (and the same matador healed afterward), look to the right of Barbero back by the front door.

Below that series is a strip of photos showing José Tomás—a hero of this generation (with the cute if bloody face)—getting his groin gored. Tomás is renowned for his daring intimacy with the bull's horns—as illustrated here.

Leaving the bull bar, turn right and notice the **La Favorita hat shop** (at #25). See the plaque in the pavement honoring the shop, which has served the public since 1894.

Consider taking a break at one of the tables on Madrid's grandest square. Cafetería Margerit (nearby) occupies Plaza Mayor's sunniest corner and is a good place to enjoy a coffee with the view. The scene is easily worth the extra euro you'll pay for the drink.

• *Leave Plaza Mayor on Calle de Ciudad Rodrigo (at the northwest corner of the square), passing a series of solid turn-of-the-20th-century storefronts and sandwich joints, such as* **Casa Rúa** *(to the left), famous for their cheap* bocadillos de calamares—*fried squid rings on a small baguette.*

*Mistura Ice Cream (across the lane at Ciudad Rodrigo 6) serves fine coffee and quality ice cream. Its cellar is called the "chill zone" for good reason—an oasis of cool and peace, ideal for enjoying your treat.*

*Emerging from the arcade, turn left and head downhill toward the iron-covered market hall. Before entering the market, look downhill to the left, down a street called Cava de San Miguel.*

## ❺ *Mesones* and Mercado de San Miguel

Lining the street called Cava de San Miguel is a series of traditional dive bars called *mesones*. If you like singing, sangria, and sloppy people, come back after 22:00 to visit one. These cave-like bars, stretching far back from the street, get packed with Madrileños out on dates who—emboldened by wine and the setting—are prone to suddenly breaking out in song. It's a lowbrow, electric-keyboard, karaoke-type ambience, best on Friday and Saturday nights. The odd shape of these bars isn't a con-

trivance for the sake of atmosphere—Plaza Mayor was built on a slope, and these underground vaults are part of a structural system that braces the leveled plaza.

For a much more refined setting, pop into the **Mercado de San Miguel** (daily 10:00-24:00). This historic iron-and-glass structure from 1916 stands on the site of an even earlier marketplace. Renovated in the 21st century, the city's oldest surviving market hall

MADRID

now hosts some 30 high-end vendors of fresh produce, gourmet foods, wines by the glass, tapas, and full meals. Locals and tourists alike pause here for its food, natural-light ambience, and social scene.

Go on an edible scavenger hunt by simply grazing down the center aisle. You'll find fish tapas, gazpacho and *pimientos de Padrón* (fried small green peppers), artisan cheeses, and lots of olives. Skewer them on a toothpick and they're called *banderillas*—for the decorated spear a bullfighter thrusts into the bull's neck. The Campo Real olives are a Madrid favorite. You'll find a draft *vermut* (Vermouth) bar with kegs of the sweet local dessert wine, along with sangria and sherry (V.O.R.S. means, literally, very old rare sherry—dry and full-bodied). Finally, the San Onofre bar is for your sweet tooth. You'll probably hear *"Que aproveche!"*—the Spanish version of bon appétit.

• *Exit the market at the far end and turn left, heading downhill on Calle del Conde de Miranda. At the first corner, turn right and cross the small plaza to the brick church in the far corner.*

## ❻ Church and Convent of Corpus Christi

The proud coats of arms over the main entry announce the rich family that built this Hieronymite church and convent in 1607. In 17th-century Spain, the most prestigious thing a noble family could do was build and maintain a convent. To harvest all the goodwill created in your community, you'd want your family's insignia right there for all to see. (You can see the donating couple, like a 17th-century Bill and Melinda Gates, kneeling before the communion wafer in the central panel over the entrance.) Inside is a cool and quiet oasis with a Last Supper altarpiece.

Now for a unique shopping experience. A dozen steps to the right of the church entrance is its associated convent—it's the big brown door on the left, at Calle del Codo 3 (Mon-Sat 9:30-13:00 & 16:30-18:30, closed Sun). The sign reads *Venta de Dulces* (Sweets for Sale). To buy goodies from the cloistered nuns, buzz the *monjas* button, then wait patiently for the sister to respond over the intercom. Say *"dulces"* (DOOL-thays), and she'll let you in. When the lock buzzes, push open the door. It will be dark—look for a glowing light switch to turn on the lights. Walk straight in and to the left, then follow the sign to the *torno*—the lazy Susan that lets the sisters sell their baked goods without being seen. Scan the menu, announce your choice to the sequestered sister (she may tell you she has only one or two of the options available), place your money on the *torno*, and your goodies (and change) will appear. *Galletas* (shortbread cookies) are the least expensive item (a *medio*-kilo costs about €10). Or try the *pastas de almendra* (almond cookies).

• *Continue uphill on Calle del Codo, where, in centuries past, those in* *need of bits of armor shopped (as depicted on the tiled street sign on the building). Bend sharply left with the street—named "Elbow Street"—and head toward the Plaza de la Villa. Before entering the square, notice an **old door** to the left of the **Real Sociedad Económica** sign, made of wood lined with metal. This is considered the oldest door in town on Madrid's oldest building—inhabited since 1480. It's set in a Mudejar keyhole arch. Remember, for many centuries (from 711 to 1492), Spain was largely Muslim, and that influence lived on in its Mudejar craftspeople. Look up to see a tower, once used as a prison.*

*Now continue into the square called Plaza de la Villa, dominated by Madrid's...*

## ❼ Town Hall

The impressive structure features Madrid's distinctive architectural style—symmetrical square towers, topped with steeples and a slate roof...Castilian Baroque.

The building was Madrid's Town Hall. Over the doorway, the three coats of arms sport many symbols of Madrid's rulers: Habsburg crowns on each, castles of Castile (in center shield), and the city symbol— the berry-eating bear (shield on left). This square was the ruling center of medieval Madrid in the centuries before it became an important capital.

Imagine how Philip II took this city by surprise in 1561 when he decided to move the capital of Europe's largest empire (even bigger than ancient Rome) from Toledo to humble Madrid. Madrid proved to be a perfect choice. It was located in the geographical center of the country. It united the two great kingdoms of Philip's great-grandparents, Ferdinand and Isabel. And with plenty of room to grow, Madrid became the ideal spot to administer the growing Spanish empire.

Philip II went on a building spree, and his son Philip III continued it. This particular building reflects the hasty development. It's glorious, yes—but like much of Madrid, it's built with inexpensive brick rather than costly granite.

The venerable Town Hall also bore witness to the decline of Spain's fortunes after the Golden Age. The statue in the little garden is of Philip II's admiral, Don Alvaro de Bazán, who defeated the Turkish Ottomans at the battle of Lepanto in 1571. This was Spain's last great victory. Mere months after Bazán's death in 1588, his "invincible" Spanish Armada was destroyed by England...and Spain's empire began its slow fade.

MADRID

• By the way, a cute little shop selling traditional monk- and nun-made pastries is just down the lane (**El Jardin del Convento**, at Calle del Cordón 1, on the back side of the cloistered convent you dropped by earlier).

From here, walk along busy, bus-lined Calle Mayor, which leads downhill (along the right side of the Town Hall) toward the Royal Palace. You'll pass a fine little shop specializing in books about Madrid (at #80, on the right). A few blocks down Calle Mayor, where the street opens up a bit on the left, is a small plaza in front of a church, where you'll find the...

## ❽ Assassination Attempt Memorial

This statue memorializes a 1906 assassination attempt. The target was Spain's King Alfonso XIII and his bride, Victoria Eugenie, as they paraded by on their wedding day. While the crowd was throwing flowers, an anarchist (as terrorists used to be called) threw a bouquet lashed to a bomb from a balcony at #84 (across the street). He missed the royal newlyweds, but killed 28 people. The king and queen went on to live to a ripe old age, producing many great-grandchildren, including the current king, Felipe VI.

• Continue down Calle Mayor one more block to a busy street, Calle de Bailén. Take in the big, domed...

## ❾ Almudena Cathedral

Madrid's massive, gray-and-white cathedral (Catedral de Nuestra Señora de la Almudena, 110 yards long and 80 yards high) opened

in 1993, 100 years after workers started building it. This is the side entrance for tourists. Climbing the steps to the church courtyard, you'll come to a monument to Pope John Paul II's 1993 visit, when he consecrated Almudena—ending Madrid's 300-year stretch of requests for a cathedral of its own.

Unlike in most Spanish cities, Madrid's churches aren't its most interesting sights. Madrid was built as a capital, so its main landmarks are governmental rather than religious. This cathedral is worthwhile, but if you're running out of steam, it's skippable.

If you go in (€1 donation requested), stop in the center, immediately under the dome, and face the altar. Beyond it, colorful paintings—rushed to completion for the pope's '93 visit—brighten the apse. In the right transept the faithful venerate a 15th-century Gothic altarpiece with a favorite statue of the Virgin Mary—a striking treasure considering the otherwise 20th-century Neo-Gothic interior. Peer down at the glittering 5,000-pipe organ in the rear of the nave.

The church's historic highlight is directly behind the altar: a 13th-century coffin. It's made of painted leather on wood, and depicts scenes of cows, horses, and strolling people. The coffin is now empty, but it once held Madrid's patron saint, Isidro. The story goes that Isidro was only a humble farmer, but he was exceptionally devout. One day, he was visited by angels. They agreed to plow his fields so he could devote himself to praying. When Isidro died, he was buried in this simple coffin. Forty years later, the coffin was opened, and his body was still perfectly preserved. This miracle convinced the pope to canonize Isidro. He is now the patron saint of farmers, and of the city of Madrid.

• *Leave the church from the transept where you entered, go out to the street, and turn left. Hike around the church to its rarely used front door. Climb the cathedral's front steps and face the imposing...*

## ⑩ Royal Palace

Since the ninth century, this spot has been Madrid's center of power: from Moorish castle to Christian fortress to Renaissance palace to the current structure, built in the 18th century. With its expansive courtyard surrounded by imposing Baroque architecture, it represents the wealth of Spain before its decline. Its 2,800 rooms, totaling nearly 1.5 million square feet, make it Europe's largest palace. Stretching toward the mountains on the left is the vast Casa del Campo (a former royal hunting ground, now a city park).

• *You could visit the palace now, using my self-guided tour (see page 43).*

*Or, to follow the rest of this walk back to Puerta del Sol, continue one long block north up Calle de Bailén (walking alongside the palace) toward the **Madrid Tower** skyscraper. This was a big deal in the 1950s when it was one of the tallest buildings in Europe (460 feet) and the pride of Franco and his fascist regime. The tower marks Plaza de España, and the end of my "Gran Vía Walk" (see page 36). To Spaniards, it symbolizes the boom time the country enjoyed when it sided with the West during the Cold War (allowing the US and not the USSR to build military bases in Spain).*

*Walk to where the street opens up and turn right, facing the statue of a king on a horse, the park, and the Royal Theater.*

MADRID

## ⓫ Plaza de Oriente

As its name suggests, this square faces east. The grand yet people-friendly plaza is typical of today's Europe, where energetic govern-

ments are converting car-congested wastelands into inviting public spaces. Where's the traffic? Under your feet. A former Madrid mayor who spearheaded the project earned the nickname "The Mole" for all the digging he did.

Notice the quiet. You're surrounded by more than three million people, yet you can hear the birds, bells, and fountain. The park is decorated with statues of Visigothic kings who ruled from the fifth to eighth century. Romans allowed them to administer their province of Hispania on the condition that they'd provide food and weapons to the empire. The Visigoths inherited real power after Rome fell, but lost it to invading Moors in 711. Throughout Spain's history, the monarchs have traced their heritage back to these distant Visigothic ancestors. The fine bronze equestrian **statue of Philip IV** was a striking technical feat in its day, as the horse rears back dramatically balanced atop its fragile ankles. It was only made possible with the help of Galileo's clever calculations (and by using the tail for extra support).

The king faces the 1,700-seat **Royal Theater** (Teatro Real), built in the mid-1800s and rebuilt in 1997. It hosts traditional opera, ballets, concerts, and that unique Spanish form of light opera called zarzuela.

• *Walk along the right side of the Royal Theater to...*

## ⓬ Plaza de Isabel II

This square is marked by a statue of Isabel II, who ruled Spain in the 19th century and was a great patron of the arts. Although she's immortalized here, Isabel had a rocky reign. She was a conservative out of step with Spain's march toward democracy. A revolution in 1868 forced her to abdicate—bringing Spain its first (brief) taste of self-rule—and Isabel lived out her life in exile. Today, Isabel's statue stands before her most lasting legacy—the Royal Theater she built.

Facing the opera house is an **old cinema** (now closed and under renovation). This grand movie palace from the 1920s is another example of Spain's persistent conservatism. As the rest of the world embraced Hollywood movies and their liberal mores, Spain approached it cautiously. During Franco's conservative rule, many foreign movies were banned. Others were allowed only if they were dubbed into Spanish, so Franco's censors could edit out sexual innuendo or liberal political references.

• *From here, follow Calle del Arenal (on the right side of the square), walking gradually uphill. You're heading straight to Puerta del Sol.*

## ⓭ Calle del Arenal

As depicted on the tiled street signs, this was the "street of sand"—where sand was stockpiled during construction. Each cross street is named for a medieval craft that, historically, was plied along that lane (for example, "Calle de Bordadores" means "Street of the Embroiderers"). Wander slowly uphill. As you stroll, imagine this street as a traffic inferno—which it was until the city pedes-

trianized it a decade ago (and now monitors it with police cameras atop posts at intersections). Notice also how orderly the side streets are. Where a mess of cars once lodged chaotically on the sidewalks, orderly bollards *(bolardos)* now keep vehicles off the walkways. The fancier facades (such as the former International Hotel at #19—look up to see the elaborate balconies) are in the "eclectic" style (Spanish for Historicism—meaning a new interest in old styles) of the late 19th century.

Continue 200 yards up Calle del Arenal to a brick church on the right. As you walk, consider how many people are simply out strolling. The paseo is a strong tradition in this culture—people of all generations enjoy being out, together, strolling. And local governments continue to provide more and more pedestrianized boulevards to make the paseo better than ever.

The brick **St. Ginés Church** (on the right) means temptation to most locals. It marks the turn to the best *chocolatería* in town. From the uphill corner of the church, look to the end of the lane where—like a high-calorie red-light zone—a neon sign spells out *Chocolatería San Ginés*...every local's favorite place for hot chocolate and *churros* (always open). Also notice the charming bookshop clinging like a barnacle to the wall of the church. It's been selling books on this spot since 1650.

Next door is the **Joy Eslava disco,** a former theater famous for operettas in the Gilbert and Sullivan days and now a popular club. In Spain, you can do it all when you're 18 (buy tobacco, drink, drive, serve in the military). This place is an alcohol-free disco for the younger kids until midnight, when it becomes a thriving adult

## Spain's Royal Families:
## From Habsburg to Bourbon

Spain as we know it was born when four long-established medieval kingdoms were joined by the 1469 marriage of Ferdinand, ruler of Aragon and Navarre, and Isabel, ruler of Castile and León. The so-called "Catholic Monarchs" (Reyes Católicos) wasted no time in driving the Islamic Moors out of Spain (the Reconquista)—and expelled the Jews and explored the oceans, to boot. By 1492, Isabel and Ferdinand had conquered a fifth kingdom, Granada, establishing more or less the same borders that Spain has today.

This was an age when "foreign policy" was conducted, in part, by marrying royal children into other royal families. Among the dynastic marriages of their children, Isabel and Ferdinand arranged for their third child, Juana "the Mad," to marry the crown prince of Austria, Philip "the Fair." This was a huge coup for the Spanish royal family. A member of the Habsburg dynasty, Philip was heir to the Holy Roman Empire, which then encompassed much of today's Austria, Czech Republic, Slovakia, Hungary, Transylvania, the Low Countries, southern Italy, and more. When Juana's brothers died, making her ruler of the kingdoms of Spain, it paved the way for her son, Charles, to inherit the kingdoms of his four grandparents—creating a vast realm and famously making him the most powerful man in Europe. He ruled as Charles I (king of Spain, from 1516) and Charles V (Holy Roman Emperor, from 1519).

He was followed by Philip II, Philip III, Philip IV, and finally Charles II. Over this period, Spain rested on its Golden Age laurels, eventually squandering much of its wealth and losing some of its holdings. Arguably the most inbred of an already very inbred dynasty (his parents were uncle and niece), Charles II was weak, sickly, and unable to have children, ending the 200-year Habsburg dynasty in Spain with his death in 1700.

Charles II willed the Spanish crown to the Bourbons of France, and his grandnephew Philip of Anjou, whose granddaddy was the "Sun King" Louis XIV of France, took the throne. But the rest of

space, with the theater floor and balconies all teeming with clubbers. Their slogan: "Go big or go home."

Farther up on the right (at #7) is **Ferpal,** an old-school deli with an inviting bar and easy takeout options. Wallpapered with ham hocks, it's famous for selling the finest Spanish cheeses, hams, and other tasty treats. Spanish saffron is half what you'd pay for it back in the US. While they sell quality sandwiches, cheap and ready-made, it's fun to buy some bread and—after a little tasting—choose a ham or cheese for a memorable picnic or snack. If you're lucky, you may get to taste a tiny bit of Spain's best ham (Ibérico de

Europe feared allowing the already powerful Louis XIV to add Spain (and its vast New World holdings) to his empire. Austria, the Germanic States, Holland, England, and Catalunya backed a different choice (Archduke Charles of Austria). So began the War of Spanish Succession (1700-1714), involving all of Europe. The French eventually prevailed, and with the signing of the Treaty of Utrecht (1713), Philip gave up any claim to the French throne. This let him keep the Spanish crown but ensured that his heirs—the future Spanish Bourbon dynasty—couldn't become too powerful by merging with the French Bourbons.

In 1714, the French-speaking Philip became the first king of the Bourbon dynasty in Spain (with the name Philip V). He breathed much-needed new life into the monarchy, which had grown ineffectual and corrupt under the Habsburgs. After the old wooden Habsburg royal palace burned on Christmas Eve of 1734, Philip (who was born at Versailles) built a new and spectacular late-Baroque-style palace as a bold symbol of his new dynasty. This is the palace that wows visitors to Madrid today. Construction was finished in 1764, and Philip V's son Charles III was the palace's first occupant (you'll see his decorations if you visit the palace's interior). Charles III also renovated the Bourbon Palace rooms at El Escorial.

The Bourbon palace remained the home of Spain's kings from 1764 until 1931, when democratic elections led to the Second Spanish Republic and forced King Alfonso XIII into exile. After Francisco Franco took power in 1939, he sidelined the royals by making himself ruler-for-life. But later he handpicked as his successor Alfonso XIII's grandson, the Bourbon Prince Juan Carlos, whom Franco believed would continue his hardline policies. When Franco died in 1975, Juan Carlos surprised everyone by voluntarily turning power over to Spain's parliament. Today Spain is a constitutional monarchy with a figurehead Bourbon king, Felipe VI, son of Juan Carlos I (who abdicated in 2014).

Bellota). Close your eyes and let the taste fly you to a land of very happy acorn-fed pigs.

Across the street, in a little mall (at #8), are a couple of sights celebrating Spain's answer to Mickey Mouse, called **"Ratón Pérez"**—Perez the Mouse. First, find the six-inch-tall bronze statue of the beloved rodent in the lobby. Ratón Pérez first appeared in a children's book in the late 1800s, and kids have adored him ever since. He also serves as Spain's tooth fairy, leaving money under kids' pillows when they lose a tooth. Upstairs is the fanciful Casita Museo de Ratón Pérez (€3, daily, Spanish only) with a fun window display. A steady stream of adoring children and their parents pour

MADRID

through here to learn about this wondrous mouse.

Just uphill (at #6, on the left) is an official retailer of **Real Madrid** football (soccer) paraphernalia. Many European football fans come to Madrid simply to see its 80,000-seat Bernabéu Stadium. Madrid is absolutely crazy about football. They have two teams: the rich and successful Real Madrid, and the working-class underdog, Atlético. It's like David and Goliath, or the Yankees vs. the Mets. Step inside to see posters of the happy team posing with the latest trophy.

Across the street at #5 is **Pronovias,** a famous Spanish wedding-dress shop that attracts brides-to-be from across Europe. These days, the current generation of Spaniards often just shack up without getting married. Those who do get married are more practical—preferring a down payment on a condo to a fancy wedding with a costly dress.

• *You're just a few steps from where you started this walk, at Puerta del Sol. Back in the square, you're met by a statue popularly known as* **La Mariblanca.** *The statue, which is at least 400 years old, represents a kind of Spanish Venus, possibly a fertility goddess. at her feet, she has Madrid's coat of arms, with our old friend, the bear and the berry tree. today,* La Mariblanca *stands tall amid all the modernity, as she blesses the people of this great city.*

## GRAN VÍA WALK

For a walk down Spain's version of Fifth Avenue, stroll the Gran Vía. Built primarily between 1910 and the 1930s, this boulevard, worth ▲, affords a fun view of

early-20th-century architecture and a chance to be on the street with workaday Madrileños. As you walk, you'll notice that Madrid's main boulevard was renovated with wide sidewalks and traffic is mostly limited to buses and taxis. I've broken this self-guided walk into five sections, each of which was the ultimate in its day, starting near Plaza de Cibeles and ending at Plaza de España.

• *Start at the skyscraper at Calle de Alcalá #42 (Metro: Banco de España).*

### ❶ Circulo de Bellas Artes

This 1920s skyscraper has a venerable café on its ground floor (free entry to enjoy its belle époque-style interior) and the best rooftop view around.

Ride the elevator to the seventh-floor Azotea roof terrace/lounge and bar (€5, daily 11:00-23:00), a fine place to nurse a scenic drink on a sunny day.

On the roof, stand under a black Art Deco statue of Minerva, perhaps put here to associate Madrid with this mythological protectress of culture and high thinking, and survey the city. Start in the far left and work your way around the perimeter for a clockwise tour.

Looking down to the left, you'll see the gold-fringed dome of the landmark Metropolis building (inspired by Hotel Negresco in Nice), once the headquarters of an insurance company. It stands at the start of the Gran Vía and its cancan of proud facades celebrating the good times in pre-civil war Spain. On the horizon, the Guadarrama Mountains hide Segovia. Farther to the right, in the distance, skyscrapers mark the city's north gate, Puerta de Europa (with its striking slanted twin towers peeking from behind other towers). Round the terrace corner. The big traffic circle and fountain below are part of Plaza de Cibeles, with its ornate and bombastic cultural center and observation deck (Palacio de Cibeles—built in 1910 as the post-office headquarters, and since 2006 the Madrid City Hall). Behind that is the vast Retiro Park. Farther to the right (at the next corner of the terrace), the big low-slung building surrounded by green is the Prado Museum.

• *Take the elevator back down and cross the busy boulevard immediately in front of Círculo de Bellas Artes to reach the start of Gran Vía.*

### ❷ 1910s Gran Vía

This first stretch, from the Banco de España Metro stop to the Gran Vía Metro stop, was built in the 1910s as a strip of luxury stores. The Bar Chicote (at #12, on the right, marked *Museo Chicote*) is a classic cocktail bar that welcomed Hemingway and the stars of the day. While the people-watching

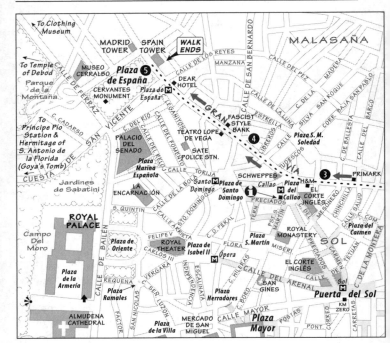

and window-shopping can be enthralling, be sure to look up and enjoy the beautiful facades, too.

By the way, as you stroll along Gran Vía (or anywhere in Madrid), tune into the pedestrian traffic lights. In honor of Pride Day, in 2017 a progressive mayor replaced dozens of these with a version showing two men or two women holding hands as they wait or cross (see photo on previous page).

### ❸ 1920s Gran Vía

The second stretch, from the Gran Vía Metro stop to the Callao Metro stop, starts where two recently pedestrianized streets meet up. To the right, Calle de Fuencarral is the trendiest pedestrian zone in town, with famous brand-name shops and a young vibe. To the left, Calle de la Montera is known for prostitution. The action pulses from the McDonald's down a block or so. Some find it an eye-opening little detour.

The 14-story **Telefónica skyscraper** (on the right) is nearly 300 feet tall. Perched here at the highest point around, it seems even taller. It was one of the city's first skyscrapers (the tallest in Spain until the 1950s) with a big New York City feel—and with a tiny Baroque balcony, as if to remind us we're still in Spain. Telefónica was Spain's only telephone company through the Franco age (and was notorious for overbilling people, with nothing itemized

and no accountability). Today it's one of Spain's few giant blue-chip corporations.

With plenty of money and a need for corporate goodwill, the building houses the free **Espacio Fundación Telefónica** (Tue-Sun 10:00-20:00, closed Mon), with an art gallery, kid-friendly special exhibits, and a fun permanent exhibit telling the story of telecommunications, from telegraphs to iPhones. This exhibit fills the second floor amid exposed steel beams—a space where a thousand "09 girls," as operators were called back then, once worked.

Farther along is a strip of fashion stores, including **Primark** at #32, which occupies the building that held the first modern department store in town. Farther along and just before the Callao Metro station, on the left at #37, step into the **H&M** clothing store for a dose of a grand old theater lobby (don't confuse it with the smaller H&M at the Primark).

## ❹ 1930s Gran Vía

The final stretch, from the Callao Metro stop to Plaza de España, is considered the "American Gran Vía," built in the 1930s to emulate the buildings of Chicago and New York City. The **Schweppes** building (Art Deco in the Chicago style, with its round facade and curved windows) was radical and innovative in 1933. This section of Gran Vía is the Spanish version of Broadway, with all the big theaters and plays. These theaters survive thanks to Spanish translations of Broadway shows, productions that get a huge second life here and in Latin America.

Head a few blocks down the street. Across from the Teatro Lope de Vega (on the left, at #60) is a quasi-fascist-style building (on the right, #57). It's a **bank** from 1930 capped with a stern statue that looks like an ad for using a good, solid piggy bank. Looking up the street toward the Madrid Tower, the buildings become even more severe.

The **Dear Hotel** (at #80) has a restaurant on its 14th floor and a rooftop lounge and small bar above that. (Walk confidently through the hotel lobby, ride the elevator to the top, pass through the restaurant, and climb the stairs from the terrace outside to the rooftop.) The views from here are among the best in town.

### ❺ Plaza de España

The end of Gran Vía is marked by Plaza de España (with a Metro station of the same name). While statues of the epic Spanish characters Don Quixote and Sancho Panza (part of a Cervantes monument) are ignored in the park, two Franco-era buildings do their best to scrape the sky above. Franco wanted to show he could keep up with America, so he had the Spain Tower (shorter) and Madrid Tower (taller) built in the 1950s. But they reminded people more of Moscow than the USA. The future of the Plaza de España looks brighter than its past. Major renovations are underway to limit traffic, invite more pedestrians, and link it up with some of the city's bike paths.

## Sights in Madrid

### ▲▲▲ROYAL PALACE

Spain's Royal Palace (Palacio Real) is Europe's third-greatest palace, after Versailles and Vienna's Schönbrunn. It has arguably the

most sumptuous original interior, packed with tourists and royal antiques. For three centuries, Spain's royal family has called this place home.

The palace is the product of many kings over several centuries. Philip II (1527-1598) made a wooden fortress on this site his governing center when he established Madrid as Spain's capital. When that palace burned down, the current structure was built by King Philip V (1683-1746). Philip V wanted to make it his own private Versailles, to match his French upbringing: He was born in Versailles—the grandson of Louis XIV—and ordered his tapas in French. His son, Charles III (whose statue graces Puerta del Sol), added interior decor in the Italian style, since he'd spent his formative years in Italy. These civilized Bourbon kings were trying to raise Spain to the cultural level of the rest of Europe. They hired foreign artists to oversee construction and established local Spanish porcelain and tapestry factories to copy works done in Paris or Brussels. Over the years, the palace was expanded and enriched, as each Spanish king tried to outdo his predecessor.

Today's palace is ridiculously supersized—with 2,800 rooms, tons of luxurious tapestries, a king's ransom of chandeliers, frescoes by Tiepolo, priceless porcelain, and bronze decor covered in gold leaf. While these days the royal family lives in a mansion a few miles away, this place still functions as the ceremonial palace, used for formal state receptions, royal weddings, and tourists' daydreams.

**Cost and Hours:** €12, €13 with special exhibits; daily 10:00-20:00, Oct-March until 18:00, last entry one hour before closing; from Puerta del Sol, walk 15 minutes down pedestrianized Calle del Arenal (Metro: Ópera); palace can close for royal functions—confirm in advance.

**Information:** +34 914 548 800, www.patrimonionacional.es.

**Crowd-Beating Tips:** The palace is free for EU citizens—and most crowded—Monday-Thursday 18:00-20:00 in summer and 16:00-18:00 in winter. On any day, arrive early or go late to avoid lines and crowds.

**Visitor Information:** Short English descriptions posted in each room complement what I describe in my tour. The museum guidebook demonstrates a passion for meaningless data.

**Tours:** The €3 **audioguide** is good. Or download in advance the helpful Royal Palace of Madrid **app** ($2). The dry English **guided tour** (€4) runs infrequently and is and not worth a long wait.

**Length of This Tour:** Allow 1.5 hours.

**Services:** Free lockers, a WC, and a gift shop are just past the ticket booth. Upstairs you'll find a more serious bookstore with good books on Spanish history.

**Eating:** Though the palace has a refreshing air-conditioned **$ cafeteria** upstairs in the ticket building, I prefer to walk a few minutes and find a place near the Royal Theater or on Calle del Arenal. The recommended **$$$ La Botillería,** boasting good lunch specials and fin-de-siècle elegance, is pricey but memorable, in a delightful park setting opposite the palace off Plaza de Oriente; for location see map on page 106.

MADRID

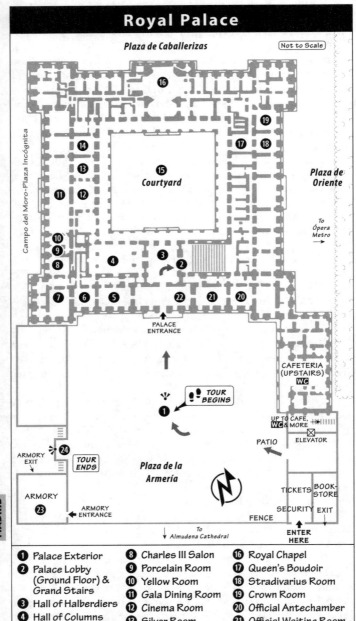

# Royal Palace

*Plaza de Caballerizas*

Not to Scale

*Campo del Moro-Plaza Incógnita*

**15 Courtyard**

*Plaza de Oriente*

To Ópera Metro

PALACE ENTRANCE

TOUR BEGINS

CAFETERIA (UPSTAIRS) WC

UP TO CAFE, WC & MORE

PATIO

ELEVATOR

ARMORY EXIT

TOUR ENDS

*Plaza de la Armería*

ARMORY 23

ARMORY ENTRANCE

TICKETS

BOOK-STORE

SECURITY

EXIT

FENCE

ENTER HERE

To Almudena Cathedral

**MADRID**

| | | |
|---|---|---|
| 1 Palace Exterior | 8 Charles III Salon | 16 Royal Chapel |
| 2 Palace Lobby (Ground Floor) & Grand Stairs | 9 Porcelain Room | 17 Queen's Boudoir |
| | 10 Yellow Room | 18 Stradivarius Room |
| 3 Hall of Halberdiers | 11 Gala Dining Room | 19 Crown Room |
| 4 Hall of Columns | 12 Cinema Room | 20 Official Antechamber |
| 5 Drawing Room | 13 Silver Room | 21 Official Waiting Room |
| 6 Antechamber | 14 Crockery & Crystal Rooms | 22 Throne Room |
| 7 Gasparini Room | 15 Courtyard | 23 Royal Armory |
| | | 24 View of the Gardens |

### ○ Self-Guided Tour

You'll follow a simple one-way circuit on a single floor covering more than 20 rooms.

• *Buy your ticket, proceed outside, stand in the middle of the vast open-air courtyard, and face the palace entrance.*

### ❶ Palace Exterior

The palace sports the French-Italian Baroque architecture so popular in the 18th century—heavy columns, classical-looking statues, a balustrade roofline, and false-front entrance. The entire building is made of gray-and-white local stone (very little wood) to prevent the kind of fire that leveled the previous castle. This became Spain's center of power; notice how the palace of the king faces the palace of the bishop (the cathedral). Now, imagine the place in its heyday, with a courtyard full of soldiers on parade, or a lantern-lit scene of horse carriages arriving for a ball.

• *Enter the palace. Here you'll find an info desk, cloakrooms, and the meeting point for guided tours.*

### ❷ Palace Lobby and Grand Stairs

In the old days, horse-drawn carriages would drop you off inside this covered arcade. Today, stretch limos do the same thing for gala events. When you reach the foot of the Grand Stairs, you'll see a statue of a toga-clad Charles III—the man most responsible for the lavish rooms we're about to see (see the "Charles III" sidebar, later).

Stand at the base of the Grand Stairs and take in the scene. Gazing up the imposing staircase, you can see that Spain's kings wanted to make a big first impression. Whenever high-end dignitaries arrive, fancy carpets are rolled down the stairs (notice the little metal bar-holding hooks).

Begin your ascent, up steps that are intentionally shallow, making your climb slow and regal. At the first landing, the burgundy coat of arms represents the current king, Felipe VI. He's part of a long tradition of kings stretching directly back to the Bourbon King Philip V, and even further back to Ferdinand and Isabel—and (according to legend) all the way back to the Visigothic kings who arrived after the fall of Rome. Overhead, the white-and-blue ceiling fresco opens up to a heavenly host of graceful female Virtues perched on a mountain of clouds, bestowing their favors on the Spanish monarchy.

Continue up to the top of the stairs. Before entering the first

**MADRID**

room, look to the right of the door to find a white marble bust of Felipe VI's great-great-g-g-g-great-grandfather Philip V, who began the Bourbon dynasty in Spain in 1700 and had this palace built. He was a direct descendant of France's "Sun King" Louis XIV...in case you couldn't tell from the curly wig.

• *Now enter the first of the rooms. These were part of King Charles III's apartments, and even today, they belong to Charles' descendants. A big modern portrait of today's royal family seems to welcome visitors to their home:* "Mi casa es su casa."

### ❸ Hall of Halberdiers (Royal Guard)

Immediately you get a sense of the palace's opulence, brought to you by the man portrayed over the fireplace: Charles III. Charles also appears overhead in the ceiling fresco (in red, with his distinctive narrow face) as the legendary hero Aeneas, standing in the clouds of heaven. Charles gazes up at his mother (as Venus), the sophisticated Italian duchess who raised her son to decorate the palace with Italian Baroque splendor. Charles hired the great Venetian painter Giambattista Tiepolo to do this room and others in the palace (see the "Tiepolo's Frescoes" sidebar, later). The fresco's theme, of Vulcan forging Aeneas's armor, relates to the room's function as the palace guards' lounge.

Notice the two fake doors painted on the wall to give the room a more regal symmetry. The old clocks, still in working order, are the first of several we'll see—part of a collection of hundreds amassed as a hobby by Spain's royal family. Throughout the palace, pay attention to the carpets. They're part of a long tradition. Some are from the 18th century and others are new, but all were produced by the same Madrid royal tapestry factory and woven the traditional way—by hand.

The giant **portrait** depicts Spain's royal family: the current king Felipe (right), his dad and mom Juan Carlos I and Sofía (center), and his two sisters (left). It was Juan Carlos who resumed the monarchy in the 1970s after Francisco Franco's dictatorial regime. Rather than end up "Juan the Brief" (as some were nicknaming him), he steered the country toward democracy. (His image appears on older Spanish €1 and €2 coins.) Unfortunately, J. C. showed poor judgment in flaunting his wealth during Spain's recent economic crisis, and was pressured to hand over the crown to his son, Felipe. Juan Carlos had commissioned this family portrait way back in 1993...and it was completed just in time for his abdication in 2014. (You can imagine the artist adding a few more wrinkles with each passing year.) Notice how Felipe stands apart from the rest of his family—a grouping that's open to interpretation. Perhaps he's the baby bird, being nudged from the nest, ready to shoulder the massive responsibility of a proud nation? Felipe's wife

## Charles III (1716-1788)

Of the many monarchs who've enlarged or redecorated the Royal Palace, it was Charles III who set the tone for its Baroque-Rococo interior. Charles' mother was Italian, and he spent his formative years in Italy. When he became Spain's king, he brought along sophisticated Italian artists to decorate his new home—the painter Tiepolo, the architect Sabatini, and the decorator Gasparini. They created some of the most elaborate, jaw-dropping rooms tourists see in the palace today.

Charles was an enlightened ruler who tried to reform Spain along democratic principles. He failed. After his death, Spain dwindled into repressive irrelevance. But over the centuries, each of his successors labored to top Charles in ostentatious decoration, making Madrid's Royal Palace his greatest legacy.

and Spain's current queen, Letizia Ortiz, isn't pictured—when this portrait was begun, they had not yet met.

• *Proceed into the...*

### ❹ Hall of Columns

In Charles III's day, this sparkling, chandeliered venue was the grand ballroom and dining room. The tapestries (like most you'll see in the palace) are 17th-century Belgian, from designs by Raphael. Appropriately, the ceiling fresco (by Jaquinto, following Tiepolo's style) depicts a radiant young Apollo driving the chariot of the sun, while Bacchus enjoys wine, women, and song with a convivial gang. The message: A good king drives the chariot of state as smartly as Apollo, so his people can enjoy life to the fullest.

Today this space is used for intimate concerts as well as important ceremonies. This is where Spain formally joined the European Union in 1985, where Spaniards honored their national soccer team after their 2010 World Cup victory, and where Juan Carlos I signed his abdication in 2014.

• *The next several rooms were the living quarters of King Charles III (r. 1759-1788). First comes his ❺ drawing room (with red-and-gold walls), where the king would enjoy the company of a similarly great ruler—the Roman emperor Trajan—depicted "triumphing" on the ceiling. The heroics of Trajan, one of two Roman emperors born in Spain, naturally made the king feel good. Next, you enter the blue-walled...*

## ❻ Antechamber

This was Charles III's dining room. The gilded decor you see here and throughout the palace is bronze with gold leaf. The furnishings reflect the tastes of various kings and queens who've inhabited this palace. The four paintings are of Charles III's son and successor, King Charles IV (looking a bit like a dim-witted George Washington), and his wife, María Luisa (who wore the pants in the palace). They're by Francisco de Goya, who also made copies of these portraits (now in the Prado) to meet the demand for his work. Velázquez's famous painting, *Las Meninas* (also in the Prado), originally hung in this room.

The 12-foot-tall clock—in porcelain, bronze, and mahogany—sits on a music box. Reminding us of how time flies, it depicts Chronus, the god of time, both as a child and as an old man. The palace's clocks are wound—and reset—once a week to keep them accurate.

## ❼ Gasparini Room

(Gasp!) The entire room is designed, top to bottom, as a single gold-green-rose ensemble: from the frescoed ceiling to the painted stucco figures, silk-embroidered walls, chandelier, furniture, and multicolored marble floor. Each marble was quarried in, and therefore represents, a different region of Spain. Birds overhead spread their wings, vines sprout, and fruit bulges from the surface. With curlicues everywhere (including their reflection in the mirrors), the room dazzles the eye and mind. It's a triumph of the Rococo style, with exotic motifs such as the Chinese people sculpted into the corners of the ceiling. (These figures, like many in the palace, were formed from stucco, or wet plaster, that was molded into shape and painted.) The fabric gracing the walls was recently restored. Sixty people spent three years replacing the rotten silk fabric and then embroidering the original silver, silk, and gold threads back on.

Note the table. The Roman temple, birds, and flowers in the design are a micro-mosaic of teeny stones and glass. This was a typical souvenir from any aristocrat's trip to Rome in the mid-1800s. The chandelier, the biggest in the palace, is mesmerizing, especially with its glittering canopy of crystal reflecting in the wall mirrors.

The mirrors mark this as the king's dressing room. For a divine monarch, dressing was a public affair. The court bigwigs would assemble here as the king, standing on a platform—notice the height of the mirrors—would pull on his leotards and adjust his wig.

• *In the next small room, the silk wallpaper is clearly from modern times—note the intertwined "J. C. S." of the former monarchs Juan Carlos I and Sofía. Pass through the silk room to reach the...*

## Tiepolo's Frescoes

In 1762, King Charles III invited Europe's most celebrated palace painter, Giambattista Tiepolo (1696-1770), to decorate  three rooms in the newly built palace. Sixty-six-year-old Tiepolo made the trip from Italy with his two well-known sons as assistants. They spent four years atop scaffolding decorating in the fresco technique, troweling plaster on the ceiling and quickly painting it before it dried.

Tiepolo's translucent ceilings seem to open up to a cloud-filled heaven, where Spanish royals cavort with Greek gods and pudgy cherubs. Tiepolo used every trick to "fool the eye" (trompe l'oeil), creating dizzying skyscapes of figures tumbling at every angle. He mixes 2-D painting with 3-D stucco figures that spill over the picture frame. His colorful, curvaceous ceilings blend seamlessly with the flamboyant furniture of the room below. Tiepolo's Royal Palace frescoes are often cited as the final flowering of Baroque and Rococo art.

### ❽ Charles III Salon

This was Charles III's grand bedroom, and he died here in his bed in 1788. His grandson, Ferdinand VII, redid the room to honor the great man. The room's color scheme recalls the blue robes of the religious order of monks Charles founded here. A portrait of Charles on the wall shows him also in blue. The ceiling fresco shows Charles (kneeling, in armor) establishing his order, with its various (female) Virtues. Along the bottom edge (near the harp player), find the baby in his mother's arms—that would be Ferdy himself, the long-sought male heir, preparing to continue Charles' dynasty.

The chandelier is in the shape of the fleur-de-lis (the symbol of the Bourbon family) capped with a Spanish crown. As you exit the room, notice the thick walls between rooms. These hid service corridors for servants, who scurried about mostly unseen.

### ❾ Porcelain Room

This tiny but lavish room is paneled with green-white-gold porcelain garlands, vases, vines, babies, and mythological figures. The entire ensemble was disassembled for safety during the civil war. (Find the little screws in the greenery that hides the seams between panels.) Notice the clock in the center with Atlas supporting the world on his shoulders.

## ⑩ Yellow Room

This was a study for Charles III. The chandelier was designed to look like a temple with a fountain inside. Its cut crystal shows all the colors of the rainbow. Stand under it, look up, and sway slowly to see the colors glitter. This brilliantly lit room gives a glimpse of what the entire palace would look like whenever it was lit up for an occasion.

• *And if it were a special occasion, the next room is where everyone would gather and be dazzled.*

## ⑪ Gala Dining Room

This vast venue—perhaps the grandest room in the palace—is the main party room. The parquet floor was the preferred dancing surface when balls were held in this fabulous room. The room is lined with golden vases from China and fine tapestries. The ceiling fresco depicts the historical event that made Spain rich and made this opulent palace possible: Christopher Columbus kneels before Ferdinand and Isabel, presenting exotic souvenirs and his new, native friends (depicted with red skin).

Imagine this hall in action when a foreign dignitary dines here. Up to 12 times a year, the king entertains as many as 144 guests at this bowling lane-size table. If needed, the table can be extended the entire length of the room. The king and queen preside from the center. Find their chairs (slightly higher than the rest, and pulled out from the table a bit). The tables are set with fine crystal and cutlery. And the whole place glitters as the 15 chandeliers (and their 900 bulbs) are fired up.

• *Pass through the next room, originally where the royal string ensemble played for parties next door, but now known as the ⑫ Cinema Room because the royal family once enjoyed Sunday afternoon movies here. From here, move into the...*

## ⑬ Silver Room

Some of this 19th-century silver tableware—knives and forks, bowls, salt and pepper shakers, and the big punch bowl—is used in the Gala Dining Room on special occasions. If you look carefully, you can see quirky royal accessories, including a baby's silver rattle and fancy candle snuffers.

## ⑭ Crockery and Crystal Rooms

Each display case has a different style from a different period and made by a different factory. The oldest and rarest pieces belonged to the man who built this palace—Philip V. His china actually came from China, before that country was opened to the West. Soon, other European royal families were opening their own porcelain works (such as France's Sèvres or Germany's Meissen) to produce high-quality knockoffs (and cutesy Hummel-like figurines). The porcelain technique itself was kept a royal secret. As you leave, check out Isabel II's excellent 19th-century crystal ware.

• *Exit to the hallway and notice the interior courtyard you've been circling one room at a time.*

#### ⓯ Courtyard

Like so many traditional Spanish homes, this palace was built around an open-air courtyard. The royal family lived on this spacious middle floor, staff lived upstairs, and the kitchens, garage, and storerooms were on the ground level. In 2004, this courtyard took on a new use when it was decorated to host King Felipe VI's royal wedding reception. Felipe married journalist Letizia Ortiz, a commoner (for love), and the two make a point to be approachable with their subjects—they're very popular. (But then, so was Juan Carlos I, not long before his abdication. Royal life is fickle.)

• *Between statues of two of the giants of Spanish royal history (Isabel and Ferdinand), you'll enter the...*

#### ⓰ Royal Chapel

This huge domed chapel is best known among Spaniards as the place for royal funerals. When a monarch dies, the royal coffin lies in state here before making the sad trip to El Escorial to join the rest of Spain's past royalty (see next chapter). The glass coffin straight ahead contains the entire body of St. Felix, given to the Spanish king by the pope in the 19th century. Note the glassed-in "crying room" to the left for royal babies. While the royals rarely worship here (they prefer the cathedral adjacent to the palace), the thrones are here just in case.

• *Continue around the courtyard, then pass through the green* ⓱ *Queen's Boudoir—where royal ladies hung out—and into the...*

#### ⓲ Stradivarius Room

Of all the instruments made by the renowned Italian violin maker Antonius Stradivarius (1644-1737), only 300 survive. This is the world's best collection and the only matching quartet set: two violins, a viola, and a cello. Charles III, a cultured man, fiddled around with these. Today, a single Stradivarius instrument might sell for $15 million.

• *The next room (on the left) is the...*

#### ⓳ Crown Room

This room is kind of like the palace's "crown jewels" sanctuary. It displays the precious objects related to the long tradition of crowning a new monarch. In the middle of the room is the scepter of the last Spanish king of the Habsburg family, Charles II, from the 17th century. Alongside is the stunning crown of Charles III, from the succeeding (and current) dynasty, the Bourbons. There's a lion-footed chair, one of Charles III's thrones. Nearby is a golden necklace of the Order of the Golden Fleece, an exclusive club of European royalty (to which all Spanish monarchs belong) that dates back to medieval times. Many of these venerable objects are brought out whenever a new monarch is proclaimed, but today's constitutional monarchs don't go through an elaborate coronation ceremony or don a crown.

There are also more recent royal symbols, such as Juan Carlos I's wooden military baton (a traditional symbol of royal power). There's the 2014 proclamation from when Juan Carlos abdicated, and another from when Felipe VI accepted. Notice which writing implement each man chose to sign with: Juan Carlos' traditional classic pen and Felipe VI's modern one. The fine inlaid marble table in this room was used when King Juan Carlos signed the treaty finalizing Spain's entry into the European Union in 1985.

• *Walk back through the Stradivarius Room and into the courtyard hallway, passing the skippable Stucco Room. Cross over the top of the Grand Stairs, then continue your visit in the blue-wallpapered...*

## ⑳ Official Antechamber

Here, amid royal portraits, ambassadors would wait for their big moment when they met the king in the (upcoming) Throne Room. Tiepolo's ceiling fresco, of Jason returning with the Golden Fleece, would remind them of the exclusive company the Spanish monarch kept, as a Knight of the Golden Fleece. Notice Tiepolo's skill at creating a seemingly three-dimensional space with a two-dimensional painting. He makes a castle tower seem to tower upward, and a trumpeting angel flies directly away from us.

• *After waiting here, the anticipation would build as ambassadors were called into the next room, the red-wallpapered...*

## ㉑ Official Waiting Room

Here dignitaries would have to wait a bit longer—awed by the rich tapestries, paintings, and Tiepolo's reverent ceiling fresco of the Spanish monarchy. It depicts Spain as a woman in white (with her lion and castle symbols), being crowned by wing-footed Mercury and adored by the gods, while an angel plunges dramatically downward. Even today, officials are received in this room by royalty for an official photo op to remember their big moment.

• *And now we've reached the grand finale, as you finally enter the...*

## ㉒ Throne Room

This room, where the Spanish monarchs preside, is one of the palace's most glorious.

The throne stands under a gilded canopy, on a raised platform, guarded by four lions (symbols of power found throughout the palace). The coat of arms above the throne shows the complexity of the Spanish empire across Europe—which, in the early 18th century, included Naples, Sicily, parts of the Netherlands, and more. Though the room was decorated under Charles III (late 18th century), the throne itself dates only from 2014. Traditionally, a new throne is built for each king or queen, complete with a gilded portrait on the back. Felipe VI decided to keep things simple, so his throne has only a crown.

Today, this room is where the king's guests salute him before they move on to state dinners. He receives them relatively informally...standing at floor level, rather than seated up on the throne.

The room holds many of the oldest and most precious things in the palace: silver-and-crystal chandeliers (from Venice's Murano Island), elaborate lions, and black bronze statues from the fortress that stood here before the 1734 fire. The 12 mirrors, impressively large in their day, each represent a different month.

The ceiling fresco (1764) is the last great work by Tiepolo, who died in Madrid in 1770. His massive painting (88 feet by 32 feet) celebrates the vast Spanish empire—upon which the sun also never set. The Greek gods look down from the clouds, overseeing Spain's empire, whose territories are represented by the people and exotic animals ringing the edges of the ceiling. Follow the rainbow to the macho red-caped conquistador who motions toward the big bale of booty and the people he's conquered—feather-wearing Native Americans.

Admire Tiepolo's skill: At the far end of the room, he makes a pillar seem to shoot straight up into the sky. The pillar's pedestal has an inscription celebrating Tiepolo's boss, Charles III ("Carole Magna"). Notice how the painting spills over the gilded wood frame, where 3-D statues recline alongside 2-D painted figures. A woman's painted robe spills over the edge to become a hem made of stucco. Two fish have 2-D bodies but 3-D tails. All of the throne room's decorations—the fresco, gold garlands, mythological statues, wall medallions—unite in a multimedia extravaganza dedicated to the glory of Spain.

• *Your tour of the palace interior is done. Permission granted to call it a tour. But if you want one more interesting collection, you'll find it back outside. Exit the palace down the same grand stairway you climbed at the start. Cross the big courtyard, heading to the far-right corner to the...*

## ㉓ Royal Armory

Here you'll find weapons and armor belonging to many great Spanish historical figures. While some of it was for battle, kings also wore armor for royal hunts, sporting events (such as jousting tournaments), and official ceremonies. Much of this armor dates from

Habsburg times, before this palace was even built. Circle the big room clockwise.

In the three glass cases on the left, you'll see the oldest pieces in the collection. In the central case (case III) are the shield, sword, belt, and dagger of Boabdil, the last Moorish king, who surrendered Granada in 1492. In case IV, the armor and swords belonged to Boabdil's conqueror, King Ferdinand.

The center of the room is filled with knights in armor on horseback. Many of the pieces belonged to the two great kings who ruled Spain at its 16th-century peak, Charles V (a.k.a. the Holy Roman Emperor) and his son, Philip II.

The long wall on the left displays a full array of Charles V's personal armor. At the far end, the mannequin of Charles on horseback wears the same armor and assumes the same pose as in Titian's famous painting of him (in the Prado).

The opposite wall showcases the armor and weapons of Philip II, the king who impoverished Spain with his wars against the Protestants, beginning the country's downward slide. Philip anticipated that debt collectors would ransack his estate after his death and specifically protected his impressive collection of armor by founding this armory.

The tapestries above the armor once warmed the walls of the otherwise stark palace that predated this one. Back when kings had to travel from palace to palace, they packed tapestries to make their home "fit for a king."

Find the stairs near the entrance and head down. You'll see more armor, a mixed collection mostly from the 17th century, plus early guns and Asian armor. The pint-size armor you may see wasn't for children to fight in. Rather, it's training armor for noble youngsters, who as adults would be expected to ride, fight, and play gracefully in these clunky getups. Before you leave, notice the life-saving breastplates dimpled with bullet dents (to right of exit door).

• *Climb the steps from the armory exit to the viewpoint.*

### ㉔ View of the Gardens

Looking down from this high bluff, it's clear why rulers have built on this strategically located spot since the ninth century. The vast palace backyard, once the king's hunting ground, is now a city park, dotted with fountains. Take in this grand vista, as kings and queens have for centuries, and—at least for a moment—you can feel like the ruler of all you survey.

• *Whew. After all those rooms, frescoes, chandeliers, knickknacks, kings, and history, consider a final stop in the palace's upstairs café for a well-deserved rest.*

## BETWEEN THE ROYAL PALACE AND PUERTA DEL SOL
### Descalzas Royal Monastery
### (Monasterio de las Descalzas Reales)

Madrid's most visit-worthy monastery was founded in the 16th century by Philip II's sister, Joan of Habsburg (known to Spaniards as Juana and to Austrians as Joanna). She's buried here. The monastery's chapels are decorated with fine art, Rubens-designed tapestries, and the heirlooms of the wealthy women who joined the order (the nuns were required to give a dowry). Because this is still a working Franciscan monastery, tourists can enter only when the nuns vacate the cloister, and the number of daily visitors is limited. The scheduled tours often sell out, so buy your ticket right at 10:00 for morning tours or 16:00 for afternoon tours (advance tickets available online, but usually for Spanish-language tours only; check www.patrimonionacional.es).

**Cost and Hours:** €6, visits guided in Spanish or English depending on demand, Tue-Sat 10:00-14:00 & 16:00-18:30, Sun 10:00-15:00, closed Mon, last entry one hour before closing, Plaza de las Descalzas Reales 1, near the Ópera Metro stop and just a short walk from Puerta del Sol, +34 914 548 800.

## MADRID'S MUSEUM NEIGHBORHOOD

Three great museums, all within a 10-minute walk of one another, cluster in east Madrid. The Prado is Europe's top collection of paintings. The Thyssen-Bornemisza sweeps through European art from old masters to moderns. And the Centro de Arte Reina Sofía has a choice selection of modern art, starring Picasso's famous *Guernica*.

**Combo-Ticket:** If visiting all three museums, you can skip ticket lines and save a few euros with the **Paseo del Arte** combo-ticket (€31, sold at all three museums, good for a year).

**Free Entry:** The Prado is free to enter every evening, the Thyssen-Bornemisza's permanent collection is free on Monday afternoons, and the Reina Sofía has free hours daily except Tuesday (when it's closed).

## ▲▲▲Prado Museum (Museo Nacional del Prado)

With more than 3,000 canvases, including entire rooms of masterpieces by superstar painters, the Prado (PRAH-doh) is my vote for the greatest collection anywhere of paintings by the European masters. Centuries of powerful Spanish kings (and lots of New World gold) funded art from all across Europe, so you'll see first-class works from the Italian Renaissance (Raphael, Titian) as well as Northern art (Rubens, Dürer, and Bosch's fantastical *Garden of*

# Madrid's Museum Neighborhood

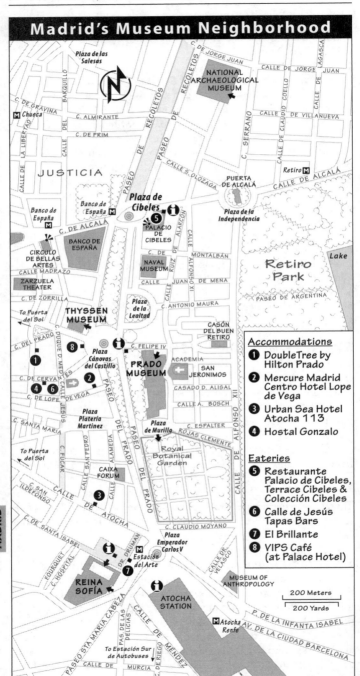

**Accommodations**

1. DoubleTree by Hilton Prado
2. Mercure Madrid Centro Hotel Lope de Vega
3. Urban Sea Hotel Atocha 113
4. Hostal Gonzalo

**Eateries**

5. Restaurante Palacio de Cibeles, Terrace Cibeles & Colección Cibeles
6. Calle de Jesús Tapas Bars
7. El Brillante
8. VIPS Café (at Palace Hotel)

200 Meters
200 Yards

MADRID

*Earthly Delights*). Mainly, the Prado is *the* place to enjoy the holy trinity of Spanish painters—El Greco, Velázquez, and Goya—including Velázquez's *Las Meninas,* considered by many to be the world's finest painting, period. Because the Prado is so huge, my tour zeroes in on a "Top Ten" list of only the very best stops. Allow at least two hours to speed through these highlights—but many spend three hours or more.

**Cost and Hours:** €15/1 day, €22/2 days, additional (obligatory) fee for occasional temporary exhibits, free Mon-Sat 18:00-20:00 and Sun 17:00-19:00, temporary exhibits discounted during free hours, under age 18 always free; open Mon-Sat 10:00-20:00, Sun until 19:00.

**Information:** +34 913 302 800, www.museodelprado.es.

**Crowd-Beating Tips:** The only place to buy tickets on-site is the ground level of the Goya Entrance, where ticket-buying lines can be long. To save time, **buy your ticket online in advance** (€0.50/ticket fee, ticket good all day, same-day tickets may be available—if the ticket line is long, try purchasing from your phone). You'll receive an email with a voucher which you'll then need to exchange for a paper ticket at the Goya Entrance (use shorter online-ticket line), then join the line for security at the Jerónimos Entrance.

Those with a **Paseo del Arte combo-ticket** (described earlier) must also exchange their voucher for a ticket at the Goya Entrance, then line up at the Jerónimos Entrance. To save time, buy the Paseo del Arte online or at the less-crowded Thyssen-Bornemisza or Reina Sofía museums.

The Prado is generally less crowded at lunchtime (13:00-16:00) and on weekdays. It's busiest on free evenings and weekends. Big spenders can pay €50 for a one-day ticket that allows entry one hour before the museum officially opens.

**Getting There:** It's on Paseo del Prado. The nearest **Metro** stops are Banco de España (line 2) and Estación del Arte (line 1), each a 10-minute walk from the museum.

It's a 15-minute **walk** from Puerta del Sol on traffic-and-pickpockets-clogged Carrera de San Jerónimo. For a more pleasant approach (which takes a few minutes longer), use your map to follow this route: From Puerta del Sol, head south to Plaza de Jacinto Benavente, then a block east, to Plaza del Ángel. From here, Calle de Las Huertas (with limited traffic) leads characteristically to Paseo del Prado, between the main Jerónimos Entrance and the Reina Sofía.

**Getting In:** The **Jerónimos Entrance,** where our tour begins, is the main entry (with all services except ticket sales/voucher exchange). It's tucked around behind the north end of the building (to the left, as you face the Prado from the main road).

The nearby **Goya Entrance,** also at the north end of the building, has the ticket office—go here first to exchange your voucher or buy a ticket.

The Murillo Entrance (south/right end of the building, as you face it) is mostly for student groups. All entrances have airport-type security checkpoints. The Velázquez Entrance—in the middle of the building—is typically closed to the public.

**Tours:** The audioguide is a helpful supplement to my self-guided tour, allowing you to wander and dial up commentary on 250 masterpieces as you come across them (€4-6 depending on if there's a temporary exhibit). Skip the Prado's Second Canvas app.

**Services:** The Jerónimos Entrance has an information desk, bag check, audioguides, bookshop, WCs, and café. Larger bags must be checked.

**No-no's:** No photos, drinks, food, backpacks, or large umbrellas are allowed inside.

**Cuisine Art:** The museum's self-service **$ cafeteria/restaurant** is just inside the Jerónimos Entrance (Mon-Sat 10:00-19:30, Sun until 18:30, hot dishes served only 12:30-16:00). Across the street from the Goya Entrance, you'll find **$$ VIPS,** a popular but characterless chain restaurant, handy for a cheap and filling salad or sandwich, with some outdoor tables facing the Neptune fountain (daily 9:00-24:00, across the boulevard from northern end of Prado at Plaza de Canova del Castillo, under Palace Hotel). Next door is Spain's first Starbucks, opened in 2001. A strip of wonderful **$$ tapas bars** is just a few blocks west of the museum, lining Calle de Jésus (see page 104). If you plan to reenter the museum, get your ticket stamped at the desk marked *"Educación"* near the Jerónimos Entrance before you leave for lunch.

## ❷ Self-Guided Tour

Thanks to Gene Openshaw for writing the following tour.

The vast Prado Museum sprawls over four floors. This tour is designed to hit the highlights with a minimum of walking and in a (roughly) chronological way. We'll see altarpieces of early religious art, the rise of realism in the Renaissance, the royal art of Spain's Golden Age, and the slow decline of Spain—bringing us right up to the cusp of the modern world.

Paintings are moved around frequently, and rooms may be renumbered—if you can't find a particular work, ask a guard or at information desks.

• *Enter at the Jerónimos Entrance. Pick up a museum map—you'll need it. Locate where you are on the map—on Level 0, at the Jerónimos Entrance. Our first stop should be nearby, in Room 56A.*

To get there, find the corridor (near the security checkpoint) to the Edificio Villanueva. *Head down the corridor about 30 yards and turn right into Room 55, then immediately right again (into 55A), then left into Room 56A. Let's kick off this tour of artistic delights with a large three-panel painting of* The Garden of Earthly Delights.

### ❶ Hieronymus Bosch

In his cryptic triptych *The Garden of Earthly Delights* (*El Jardín de las Delicias*, c. 1505), the early Flemish painter Bosch (c. 1450-1516) paints a wonderland of eye-pleasing details. The message is that the pleasures of life are fleeting, and we'd better avoid them or we'll wind up in hell. Take your time here to unpack this dense masterpiece.

This altarpiece has a central scene and two hinged outer panels. All the images work together to teach a religious message. Imagine the altarpiece closed (showing the back side). The world is gray and

bare, before God's creation. Now open it up, bring on the people, and splash into this colorful *Garden of Earthly Delights*.

The left panel is Paradise, showing naked Adam and Eve before original sin. Everything is in its place, with animals behaving virtuously. Innocent Adam and Eve get married, with God himself performing the ceremony.

The central panel is a riot of naked men and women, black and white, on a perpetual spring break—eating exotic fruits, dancing, kissing, cavorting with strange animals, and contorting themselves into a *Kama Sutra* of sensual positions. In the background rise the fantastical towers of a medieval Disneyland. It's seemingly a wonderland of pleasures and earthly delights. But where does it all lead? Men on horseback ride round and round, searching for but never reaching the elusive Fountain of Youth. Humankind frolics in earth's "Garden," oblivious to where they came from (left) and where they may end up...

Now, go to hell (right panel). It's a burning Dante's *Inferno*-inspired wasteland where genetic-mutant demons torture sinners. Everyone gets their just desserts, like the glutton who is eaten and re-eaten eternally, the musician strung up on his own harp, and the gamblers with their table forever overturned. In the center, hell is literally frozen over. A creature with a broken eggshell body

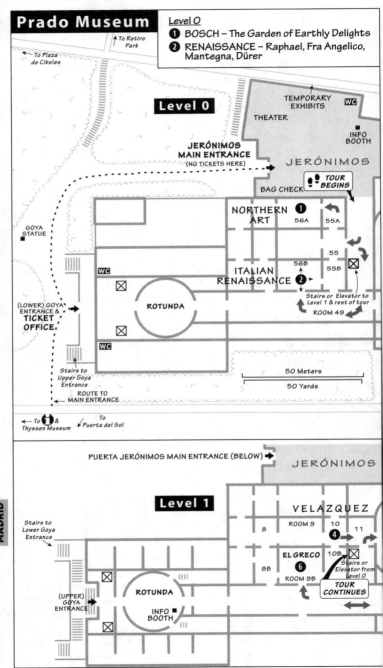

**Prado Museum**

↑ To Retiro Park

<u>Level 0</u>
❶ BOSCH – The Garden of Earthly Delights
❷ RENAISSANCE – Raphael, Fra Angelico, Mantegna, Dürer

← To Plaza de Cibeles

**Level 0**

TEMPORARY EXHIBITS

THEATER

WC

INFO BOOTH

JERÓNIMOS MAIN ENTRANCE (NO TICKETS HERE)

JERÓNIMOS

BAG CHECK

👣 TOUR BEGINS

NORTHERN ART ❶ 56A 55A

GOYA STATUE

WC

ITALIAN RENAISSANCE ❷ 56B 55B 55

ROTUNDA

Stairs or Elevator to Level 1 & rest of tour

(LOWER) GOYA ENTRANCE & **TICKET OFFICE**

WC

ROOM 49

Stairs to Upper Goya Entrance

50 Meters

50 Yards

ROUTE TO MAIN ENTRANCE

← To ❶ & Thyssen Museum

↓ To Puerta del Sol

PUERTA JERÓNIMOS MAIN ENTRANCE (BELOW) ➡ JERÓNIMOS

**Level 1**

VELAZQUEZ

Stairs to Lower Goya Entrance

8 ROOM 9 10 11

❹

EL GRECO ❻ 10B

8B ROOM 9B

Stairs or Elevator from Level 0

(UPPER) GOYA ENTRANCE

ROTUNDA

INFO BOOTH

TOUR CONTINUES

MADRID

Sights in Madrid 59

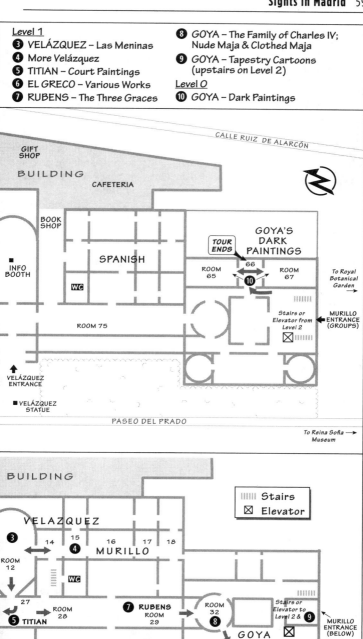

**Level 1**
❸ VELÁZQUEZ – Las Meninas
❹ More Velázquez
❺ TITIAN – Court Paintings
❻ EL GRECO – Various Works
❼ RUBENS – The Three Graces

❽ GOYA – The Family of Charles IV;
Nude Maja & Clothed Maja
❾ GOYA – Tapestry Cartoons
(upstairs on Level 2)

**Level 0**
❿ GOYA – Dark Paintings

CALLE RUIZ DE ALARCÓN

GIFT SHOP

BUILDING

CAFETERIA

BOOK SHOP

GOYA'S DARK PAINTINGS

TOUR ENDS

■ INFO BOOTH

SPANISH

ROOM 65   66   ROOM 67

❿

To Royal Botanical Garden

WC

ROOM 75

Stairs or Elevator from Level 2

MURILLO ENTRANCE (GROUPS)

↑ VELÁZQUEZ ENTRANCE

■ VELÁZQUEZ STATUE

PASEO DEL PRADO

To Reina Sofía Museum →

BUILDING

|||||| Stairs
⊠ Elevator

VELAZQUEZ

❸   14   15   16   17   18
❹ MURILLO

ROOM 12

WC

27

ROOM 28
❺ TITIAN

❼ RUBENS ROOM 29

ROOM 32
❽

GOYA

Stairs or Elevator to Level 2 & ❾

MURILLO ENTRANCE (BELOW)

36 "MAJAS"
34   35   37   38

MADRID

hosting a tavern, tree-trunk legs, and a hat featuring a bagpipe (symbolic of hedonism) stares out—it's the face of Bosch himself.

If you want more Bosch, check out the nearby table featuring his **Seven Deadly Sins** (*Los Pecados Capitales*, late 15th century). Each of the four corners has a theme: death, judgment, paradise, and hell. The fascinating wheel, with Christ in the center, names the sins in Latin (lust, envy, gluttony, and so on), and illustrates each with a vivid scene that works as a slice of 15th-century Dutch life.

Nearby, another Bosch triptych, **The Haywain** (*El Carro de Heno*, c. 1516), has still more vivid imagery about the consequences of sin and the transience of earthly life.

• *The clock is ticking to see the rest of this museum's delights, so let's move on. We're going to the source of European painting as we know it: the Italian Renaissance.*

*Backtrack the way you came. Reaching the corridor, turn right and go past the elevators (remember them—we'll use the elevators later). About 30 yards along, turn right into Room 49—a large, long, sage-green hall labeled* XLIX *above the door you've just entered. You've reached...*

## ❼ The Renaissance

During its Golden Age (the 1500s), Spain may have been Europe's richest country, but Italy was still the most cultured. Spain's kings loved how Italian Renaissance artists captured a three-dimensional world on a two-dimensional canvas, bringing Bible scenes to life and celebrating real people and their emotions.

• *Start midway down Room 49, on the right-hand wall, with a guy in red painted by Raphael.*

**Raphael** (1483-1520) was the undisputed master of realism. When he painted *Portrait of a Cardinal* (*El Cardenal*, c. 1510-11), he showed the sly Vatican functionary with a day's growth of beard and an air of superiority, locking eyes with the viewer. The cardinal's slightly turned torso is as big as a statue. Nearby are several versions of *Holy Family* and other paintings by Raphael.

• *Now climb the four stairs in the middle of the room, up to Room 56B.*

**Fra Angelico's** *The Annunciation* (*La Anunciación*, c. 1426) is half medieval piety, half Renaissance realism. In the crude Garden of Eden scene

(on the left), a scrawny, sinful First Couple hovers unrealistically above the foliage, awaiting eviction. The angel's Annunciation to Mary (right side) is more Renaissance, both with its upbeat message (that Jesus will be born to redeem sinners like Adam and Eve) and in the budding photorealism, set beneath 3-D arches. (Still, aren't the receding bars of the porch's ceiling a bit off? Painting three dimensions wasn't that easy.)

Also in Room 56B, the tiny *Dormition of the Virgin (El Tránsito de la Virgen)*, by **Andrea Mantegna** (c. 1431-1506), shows his mastery of Renaissance perspective. The apostles crowd into the room to mourn the last moments of the Virgin Mary's life. The receding floor tiles and open window in the back create the subconscious effect of Mary's soul finding its way out into the serene distance.

• *To see how the Italian Renaissance spread to northern lands, step into the adjoining Room 55B (to the left, as you face the main hall).*

**Albrecht Dürer's** *Self-Portrait (Autorretrato)*, from 1498, is possibly the first time an artist depicted himself. The artist, age 26, is German, but he's all dolled up in a fancy Italian hat and permed hair. He'd recently returned from Italy and wanted to impress his countrymen with his sophistication. Dürer (1471-1528) wasn't simply vain. He'd grown accustomed, as an artist in Renaissance Italy, to being treated like a prince. Note Dürer's signature, the pyramid-shaped "A. D." (D inside the A), on the windowsill.

Nearby are Dürer's 1507 panel paintings of *Adam* and *Eve*—the first full-size nudes in Northern European art. Like Greek statues, they pose in their separate niches, with three-dimensional, anatomically correct bodies. This was a bold humanist proclamation that the body is good, man is good, and the things of the world are good.

• *The down-to-earth realism of Renaissance art soon spread to Europe's richest country—Spain.*

Backtrack down the four steps into Room 49, and make a U-turn to the left, to reach those elevators we saw earlier. Take the elevator up to level 1, and turn left into Room 11. A painting here (by Velázquez) of a radiant Apollo surprising the cuckold Vulcan and a gang of startled workmen introduces us to the main feature of Spanish art—unflinching realism.

Let's begin next door, in the large, lozenge-shaped Room 12.

### ❸ Velázquez, *Las Meninas*

Diego Velázquez (vel-LAHTH-keth, 1599-1660) was the photo-journalist of court painters, capturing the Spanish king and his court in formal portraits that take on aspects of a candid snapshot. Room 12 is filled with the portraits Velázquez was called on to produce. Kings and princes prance like Roman emperors. Get up close and notice that his remarkably detailed costumes are nothing but a few messy splotches of paint—the proto-Impressionism Velázquez helped pioneer.

The room's centerpiece, and perhaps the most important painting in the museum, is Velázquez's *Maids of Honor* (*Las Meninas*, c. 1656). It's a peek at nannies caring for Princess Margarita and, at the same time, a behind-the-scenes look at Velázquez at work. One hot summer day in 1656, Velázquez (at left, with paintbrush and Dalí moustache) stands at his easel and stares out at the people he's painting—the king and queen. They would have been standing about where  we are, and we see only their reflection in the mirror at the back of the room. Their daughter (blonde hair, in center) watches her parents being painted, joined by her servants *(meninas)*, dwarves, and the family dog. At that very moment, a man happens to pass by the doorway at back and pauses to look in. Why's he there? Probably just to give the painting more depth.

This frozen moment is lit by the window on the right, splitting the room into bright and shaded planes that recede into the distance. The main characters look right at us, making us part of the scene, seemingly able to walk around, behind, and among the characters. Notice the exquisitely painted mastiff—annoyed by the little girl, but staying put...for now.

If you stand in the center of the room, the 3-D effect is most striking. This is art come to life.

• *Let's see more of Velázquez, whose work covers a wide range of subjects and emotions. Facing this painting, leave to the left, pass through Room 11, and enter Room 10.*

### ❹ More Velázquez

Velázquez enjoyed capturing light—and capturing the moment. *The Feast of Bacchus* (*Los Borrachos,* c. 1628-29) is a group selfie in a blue-collar bar. A couple of peasants mug for a photo-op with a Greek god—Bacchus, the god of wine. This was an early work, before Velázquez got his court-painter gig, and shows off his admiration for "real" people. Hardworking farmers enjoying the fruit of their labor deserved portraits, too. Notice the almost-sacramental presence of the ultrarealistic bowl of wine in the center, as Bacchus, with the honest gut, crowns a fellow hedonist.

• *Backtrack through the big gallery with* Las Meninas, *and continue straight ahead into Room 14.*

Velázquez's boss, King Philip IV, had an affair, got caught, and repented by commissioning **The Crucified Christ** (*Cristo Crucificado*, c. 1632). Christ hangs his head, humbly accepting his punishment. Philip would have been left to stare at the slowly dripping blood, contemplating how long Christ had to suffer to atone for Philip's sins. This is an interesting death scene. There's no anguish, no tension, no torture. Light seems to emanate from Jesus as if nothing else matters. The crown of thorns and the cloth wrapped around his waist are particularly vivid. Above it all, a sign reads in three languages: *"Jesus of Nazareth, King of the Jews."*

• *Continue on through Room 15 (with Velázquez's insightful portraits of the royal court* **dwarves***) and detour into Rooms 16 and 17.*

Take a moment to appreciate these paintings by one of Velázquez's admirers: Bartolomé Murillo. **Murillo** (1618-1682) soaked up Velazquez's unflinching photorealism, but added a spoonful of sugar. In his most famous works—called *The Immaculate Conception*—Murillo put a human face on the abstract Catholic doctrine that Mary was conceived and born free of original sin. His "immaculate" virgins float in a cloud of Ivory Soap cleanliness, radiating youth and wholesome goodness. Mary wears her usual colors—white for purity and blue for divinity. Murillo's sweet and escapist work must have been very comforting to the wretched people of his hometown of Sevilla, which was ravaged by plague in 1647-1652.

• *Backtrack to the* Meninas *room (12) and turn left. You'll exit into the museum's looooong grand gallery (Rooms 25-29) and come face-to-face with a large canvas of a knight on horseback.*

### ❺ Titian's Court Paintings

Spain's Golden Age kings Charles V and Philip II both hired Europe's premier painter—Titian the Venetian (c. 1485-1576)—to paint their portraits.

In *The Emperor Charles V at Mühlberg* (*Carlos V en la Batalla de Mühlberg*, 1548), the king rears on his horse, points his lance at a jaunty angle, and rides out to crush an army of Lutherans. Charles, having inherited many kingdoms and baronies through his family connections, was the world's most powerful man in the 1500s. (You can see the suit of armor depicted in the painting in the Royal Palace.)

In contrast (just to the right), Charles I's son, **Philip II** (*Felipe II*, c. 1550-1551), looks pale, suspicious, and lonely—a scholarly and complex figure. He moved Spain's capital from Toledo to Madrid and built the austere, monastic palace at El Escorial. These are the faces of the Counter-Reformation, as Spain took the lead in battling Protestants. Both father and son had one thing in common: underbites, a product of royal inbreeding (which Titian painted...delicately).

• *The ultra-Catholic Philip II amassed a surprisingly large collection of Titian's Renaissance playmates, which you could seek out elsewhere on this floor. But let's turn to a quite different painter that Philip hired—El Greco.*

*Facing Charles and Philip, turn right, walk about 30 yards, and turn right at the first door, into Room 9B.*

## ❻ El Greco

El Greco (1541-1614) was born in Greece (his name is Spanish for "The Greek"), trained in Venice, then settled in Toledo—60 miles from Madrid. His paintings are like Byzantine icons drenched in Venetian color and fused in the fires of Spanish mysticism. (For more on El Greco, see page 195.) The El Greco paintings displayed here rotate, but they all glow with his unique style.

In **Christ Carrying the Cross** (*Cristo Abrazado a la Cruz*, c. 1602), Jesus accepts his fate, trudging toward death with blood running down his neck. He hugs the cross and directs his gaze along the crossbar. His upturned eyes (sparkling with a streak of white paint) lock onto his next stop—heaven.

**The Adoration of the Shepherds** (*La Adoración de los Pastores*, c. 1614—likely next door in room 10B), originally painted for El Greco's own burial chapel in Toledo, has the artist's typical two-tiered composition—heaven above, earth below. The long, skinny shepherds are stretched unnaturally in between, flickering like flames toward heaven.

El Greco's portraits of Spanish nobles and saints (such as *The Nobleman with His Hand on His Chest*, *El Caballero de la Mano al*

*Pecho,* c. 1580) focus on their aristocratic expressions. A man's hand with his fingers splayed out, but with the middle fingers touching, was El Greco's trademark way of expressing elegance (or was it the 16th-century symbol for "Live long and prosper"?). Several paintings have El Greco's signature written in faint Greek letters— "Doménikos Theotokópoulos," El Greco's real name.

*• While El Greco was painting austere Christian saints, other European artists were painting sensual Greek gods, in a dramatic new style—Baroque.*

*Return to the main gallery, turn left, pass by Charles and Philip again, and proceed to the gallery's far end (technically Rooms 28 and 29) for the large, colorful, fleshy canvases by...*

### ❼ Rubens

A native of Flanders, Peter Paul Rubens (1577-1640) painted Baroque-style art meant to play on the emotions, titillate the senses,

and carry you away. His paintings surge with Baroque energy and ripple with waves of figures. Surveying his big, boisterous canvases, you'll notice his trademarks: sex, violence, action, emotion, bright colors, and ample bodies, with the wind machine set on full. Gods are melodramatic, and nymphs flee half-human predators. Rubens painted the most beautiful women of his day—well-fed, no tan lines, squirt-gun breasts, and very sexy.

Rubens' *The Three Graces* (*Las Tres Gracias,* c. 1630-1635) celebrates cellulite. The ample, glowing bodies intertwine as the women exchange meaningful glances. The

Grace at the left is Rubens' young second wife, Hélène Fourment, who shows up regularly in his paintings.

*• Rubens, El Greco, Titian, and Velázquez had all made their living working for Europe's royalty. But that world was changing, and revolution was in the air. No painter illustrates the changing times more than our final artist—Goya.*

*From Rubens, continue to the end of the long main gallery and enter the* round Room 32, *where you'll see royal portraits by Goya.*

**MADRID**

### ❽ Goya—Court Painter

Follow the complex Francisco de Goya (1746-1828) through the stages of his life—from dutiful court painter, to political rebel and scandal maker, to the disillusioned genius of his "black paintings." The museum's exciting Goya collection is displayed on three different levels: classic Goya on this level; early cartoons upstairs; and his dark and political work downstairs.

In the group portrait **The Family of Charles IV** (*La Familia de Carlos IV*, 1800), the royals are all decked out in their Sunday best. Goya himself stands at his easel to the far left, painting the court (a tribute to Velázquez in *Las Meninas*) and revealing the shallowness beneath the fancy trappings. Charles, with his ridiculous hairpiece and goofy smile, was a vacuous, henpecked husband. His toothless yet domineering queen upstages him, arrogantly stretching her swan-like neck. The other adults, with their bland faces, are bug-eyed with stupidity.

Surrounding you in this same room are other portraits of the king and queen. Also notice the sketch paintings, quick studies done with the subjects posing for Goya. He used these for reference to complete his larger, more finished canvases.

• *Exit to the right across a small hallway and turn left to find Room 36, where you'll find Goya's most scandalous work.*

Rumors flew that Goya was fooling around with the vivacious Duchess of Alba, who may have been the model for two similar paintings, **Nude Maja** (*La Maja Desnuda*, c. 1800) and **Clothed Maja** (*La Maja Vestida*, c. 1808). A *maja* was a trendy, working-class girl. Whether she's a duchess or a *maja*, Goya painted a naked lady—an actual person rather than some mythic Venus. And that was enough to risk incurring the wrath of the Inquisition. The nude stretches in a Titian-esque pose to display her charms, the pale body with realistic pubic hair highlighted by cool green sheets. (Notice the

artist's skillful rendering of the transparent fabric on the pillow.) According to a believable legend, the two paintings were displayed in a double frame, with the *Clothed Maja* sliding over the front to hide the *Nude Maja* from Inquisitive minds.

• *Just off the next room, you'll find an elevator and a staircase (farther down the hall). Use one of them to head up to level 2, to Rooms 85-87 and 90-94, for more Goya.*

### ❾ Goya—Tapestry Cartoons

These rooms display Goya's designs for tapestries (known as "cartoons") for nobles' palaces. Dressed in their gay "Goya-style" attire, nobles picnic, dance, fly kites, play paddleball and Blind Man's Bluff, or just relax in the sun—as in the well-known *The Parasol* (*El Quitasol*, Room 86). It's clear that, while revolution was brewing in America and France, Spain's lords and ladies were playing, blissfully ignorant of the changing times.

• *Goya's later paintings took on a darker edge. For more Goya, take the stairs or elevator down to level 0, then go up and down the stairs (across the Murillo Entrance) to Room 66. Entering, start to the left, in Room 65, with powerful military scenes.*

### ❿ Goya—Dark Paintings

Despite working for Spain's monarchs, Goya became a political liberal and a champion of the Revolution in France. But that idealism was soon crushed when the supposed hero of the Revolution, Napoleon, morphed into a tyrant and invaded Spain. Goya, who lived on Madrid's Puerta del Sol, captured the chaotic events that unfolded there.

In *The Second of May, 1808* (*El 2 de Mayo de 1808*, 1814), Madrid's citizens rise up to protest the occupation in Puerta del Sol, and the French send in their dreaded Egyptian mercenaries. They plow through the dense tangle of Madrileños, who have nowhere to run. The next day, *The Third of May, 1808* (*El 3 de Mayo de 1808*, 1814), the French rounded up ringleaders and executed them. The colorless firing squad—a faceless machine of death—mows them down, and they fall in bloody, tangled heaps. Goya throws a harsh prison-yard floodlight on the main victim, who spreads his arms Christ-like to ask, "Why?"

Politically, Goya was split—he was a Spaniard, but he knew France was leading Europe into the modern age. His art, while political, has no Spanish or French flags. It's a universal comment on the horror of war. Many consider Goya the last classical and first modern painter...the first painter with a social conscience.

• *Finish the tour with Goya's final, late-in-life paintings. Turn about-face to the "black paintings" in Room 67.*

Depressed and deaf from syphilis, Goya retired to his small home and smeared its walls with his **"black paintings"**—dark in color and in mood. During this period in his life, Goya would paint his nightmares...literally. The style is considered Romantic—emphasizing emotion over beauty—but it foreshadows 20th-century Surrealism with its bizarre imagery, expressionistic and thick brushstrokes, and cynical outlook.

Stepping into Room 67, you are surrounded by art from Goya's dark period. These paintings are the actual murals from the walls of his house, transferred onto canvas. Imagine this in your living room. Goya painted what he felt with a radical technique unburdened by reality—a century before his time. And he painted without being paid for it—perhaps the first great paintings done not for hire or for sale. We know frustratingly little about these works because Goya wrote nothing about them.

Dark forces convened continually in Goya's dining room, where **The Great He-Goat** (*El Aquelarre/El Gran Cabrón*, c. 1820-1823) hung. The witches, who look like skeletons, swirl in a frenzy around a dark, Satanic goat in monk's clothing who presides over the obscene rituals. The black goat represents the devil and stokes the frenzy of his wild-eyed subjects. Amid this adoration and lust, a noble lady (far right) folds her hands primly in her lap ("I thought this was a Tupperware party!"). Or, perhaps it's a pep rally for her execution, maybe inspired by the chaos that accompanied Plaza Mayor executions. Nobody knows for sure.

In **Fight to the Death with Clubs** (*Duelo a Garrotazos*, c. 1820-1823), two giants stand face-to-face, buried up to their knees, and flail at each other with clubs. It's a standoff between superpowers in the never-ending cycle of war.

In **Saturn** (*Saturno*, c. 1820-1823), fearful that his progeny would overthrow him, the god eats one of his offspring. Saturn, also known as Kronus (*Chronus*, or time), may symbolize how time devours us all. Either way, the painting brings new meaning to the term "child's portion."

**The Drowning Dog** (*Perro Semihundido*, c. 1820-1823) is, according to some, the hinge between classical art and modern art. The dog, so full of feeling and sadness, is being swallowed by quicksand...much as, to Goya, the modern age was overtaking a more classical era. And look closely at the dog. It also can be seen as a turning point for Goya. Perhaps he's bottomed out—he's been overwhelmed by depression, but his spirit has survived. With the portrait of this dog, color is returning.

• *Keep that hope alive for one more painting. Head back to Room 65 or 66, and look to your right.*

The last painting we have by Goya is ***The Milkmaid of Bordeaux*** (*La Lechera de Burdeos,* c. 1827). Somehow, Goya pulled out of his depression and moved to France, where he lived until his death at 82. While painting as an old man, color returned to his palette. His social commentary, his passion for painting what he felt (more than what he was hired to do), and, as you see here, the freedom of his brushstrokes explain why many consider Francesco de Goya to be the first modern artist.

• *There's a lot more to the Prado, but there's also a lot more to Madrid. For a nature break from all this art, exit through the Murillo Entrance and you'll run right into the delightful Royal Botanical Garden, described next.*

## ▲Royal Botanical Garden (Real Jardín Botánico)

After your Prado visit, you can take a lush and fragrant break in this sculpted park. Wander among trees from around the world, originally gathered by—who else?—the enlightened King Charles III. This garden was established when the Prado's building housed the natural science museum. A flier in English explains that this is actually more than a park—it's a museum of plants.

**Cost and Hours:** €4, daily May-Aug 10:00-21:00, April and Sept until 20:00, shorter hours off-season, entrance opposite the Prado's Murillo/south entry, Plaza de Murillo 2, +34 914 203 017.

## ▲▲Thyssen-Bornemisza Museum (Museo del Arte Thyssen-Bornemisza)

Locals call this stunning museum simply the Thyssen (TEE-sun). It displays the impressive collection that Baron Thyssen (a wealthy German married to a former Miss Spain) sold to Spain for $350 million. The museum offers a unique chance to enjoy the sweep of all of art history—including a good sampling of the "isms" of the 20th century—in one collection. It's basically

minor works by major artists and major works by minor artists. (Major works by major artists are in the Prado.) But art lovers appreciate how the good baron's art complements the Prado's collection by filling in where the Prado is weak—such as Impressionism, which is the Thyssen's forte.

**Cost and Hours:** €13, includes temporary exhibits, timed ticket required for temporary exhibits, free on Mon; permanent collection open Mon 12:00-16:00, Tue-Sun 10:00-19:00; temporary exhibits open Sat until 21:00; audioguide-€5 for permanent collection, €4 for temporary exhibits, €7 for both; Second Canvas Thyssen is a decent free app that explains major works—use museum's free Wi-Fi to access; +34 917 911 370, www.museothyssen. org.

**Getting There:** It's located kitty-corner from the Prado at Paseo del Prado 8 in Palacio de Villahermosa (Metro: Banco de España).

**Services:** The museum has free baggage storage (bags must fit through a small x-ray machine), a cafeteria and restaurant, and a shop/bookstore.

**Connecting the Thyssen and Reina Sofía:** It's about a 20-minute, slightly downhill walk. You can hail a cab at the gate to zip straight there. Or take bus #27: Catch it in the square with the Neptune fountain in front of the Starbucks, ride to the end of Paseo del Prado, get off at the McDonald's, and cross the street (going away from the Royal Botanical Garden) to reach Plaza Sánchez Bustillo and the museum.

## ● Self-Guided Tour

After purchasing your ticket, continue down the wide main hall past larger-than-life paintings of former monarchs Juan Carlos I and Sofía, and at the end of the hall, paintings of the baron (who died in 2002) and his art-collecting baroness, Carmen. At the info desk, pick up a museum map.

Each of the three floors is divided into two separate areas: the permanent collection (numbered rooms) and additions from baroness Carmen since the 1980s (lettered rooms). The permanent collection has the heavyweight artists, though Carmen's wing is also intriguing. Ascend to the top floor and work your way down, taking a delightful walk through art history. Visit the rooms on each floor in numerical order, from Primitive Italian (Room 1) to Surrealism and Pop Art (Rooms 45-48). Here's a breezy stroll that hits the highlights:

**Level 2:** Start where Western art did—with religious altarpieces from Italy depicting holy people in the golden realm of heaven (Rooms 1-2). Meanwhile, Flemish painters were discovering oil paints, allowing them to give their Virgin Marys more detail and human tenderness (Room 3). The Italians pioneered 3-D realism, to bring heavenly scenes down into the real world (Room 4).

Turn the corner into the long hallway, featuring portraits of famous Europeans circa 1500, including King Henry VIII (Rooms 5-6). Pop into Room 11 for a few fine El Grecos. In Room 13, turn the corner into Rooms 14-18. It's the 1600s, a time of very forgettable canvases, except for Canaletto's views of Venice (Room 16).

• *At Room 18, turn left.*

Portraits by Rubens (Room 19) and a proud self-portrait by Rembrandt (Room 21) stand out.

• *Go downstairs to...*

**Level 1:** While Italians painted myths and goddesses, the practical Dutch enjoyed down-to-earth portraits, group portraits, everyday scenes, landscapes, seascapes, and detailed still-lifes of fruit and flowers (Rooms 22-26).

• *Turn the corner into Room 28.*

In the 1700s, France dominated Europe, with its porcelain-skinned aristocrats and their Rococo fashions. In art, the French pioneered the march toward modernism (Rooms 29-31). Artists painted in the open air to capture rural landscapes and the working poor with increasing spontaneity.

• *Continue to Rooms 32-33, where the movement culminated in Impressionism.*

The museum has a laudable collection of works by Manet, Monet, and their Impressionist contemporaries, who painted landscapes, Parisian street scenes, a night at the ballet with Degas, or Toulouse-Lautrec's backstage scenes of the Moulin Rouge.

• *Turn the corner as Impressionism becomes Post-Impressionism (Rooms 34-37).*

Note the variety of painters who used Impressionist techniques but with brighter colors, thicker paint, and more furious brushwork. Increasingly, they simplified reality and flattened the 3-D, pointing the way to 20th-century art.

• *In Room 37, turn left.*

As a new century dawned, artists like Kandinsky stopped painting reality altogether and began creating beautiful patterns of pure line and color arranged in pleasing patterns—abstract art (Rooms 37-38). As World War I shattered societal norms, and fascism was on the rise, Expressionist artists expressed their fears in lurid colors and grim scenes (Rooms 39-40).

• *Go downstairs to...*

**Level 0:** The Spaniard Picasso and his Parisian roommate Georges Braque invented Cubism—a revolutionary new style many others would imitate (Rooms 41-42). As artists increasingly turned away from photorealism, Cubism reached its textbook example of purely abstract art with Mondrian's simple rectangular grids of the primary colors—red, yellow, blue—on a white canvas (Room 43).

• *Turn the corner into Room 44.*

MADRID

Cubists explored collage, literally gluing things onto the canvas to make it a kind of sculpture. See the many varieties of Cubism and other "isms," including Picasso—the master of many styles (Room 45). Marc Chagall used modern art techniques to create a dreamlike world of weightless lovers and fiddler-on-the-roof villages. Moving into Room 46, see how World War II shifted the art world to America, where artists "expressed" their emotions in big, minimal "abstract" canvases—Abstract Expressionism. Francis Bacon captured the horror of World War II's destruction with his screaming, caged, isolated figures in a barren landscape (Room 47). In Room 48, see how America's 1960s prosperity elevated the elements of everyday pop culture to the level of art, including Roy Liechtenstein's iconic scenes of comic books blown up to ridiculous proportions and presented as masterpieces.

• Whew. That's five centuries of Western Art. Now you're ready for Madrid's museum of modern art, the Reina Sofía.

## ▲▲▲Centro de Arte Reina Sofía

Home to Picasso's *Guernica*, the Reina Sofía is one of Europe's most enjoyable modern-art museums. Its exceptional collection of 20th-century art is housed in what was Madrid's first public hospital. The focus is on 20th-century Spanish artists—Picasso, Dalí, Miró, and Gris—but you'll also find works by Kandinsky, Braque, Magritte, and other giants of modern art. Many works are displayed alongside continuously running films that place  the art into social context. Those with an appetite for modern and contemporary art can spend several delightful hours in this museum.

**Cost and Hours:** €10 (includes most temporary exhibits); open Mon and Wed-Sat 10:00-21:00, Sun until 19:00 (fourth floor not accessible Sun after 15:00), closed Tue.

**Free Entry:** The museum is free—and often crowded—Mon and Wed-Sat 19:00-21:00 and Sun 13:30-19:00 (must pick up a ticket to enter).

**Information:** +34 917 741 000, www.museoreinasofia.es.

**Getting There:** It's a block from the Estación del Arte Metro stop, on Plaza Sánchez Bustillo at Calle de Santa Isabel 52. In the Metro station, follow signs for the Reina Sofía exit. Emerging from the Metro, walk straight ahead a half-block and turn right on Calle de Santa Isabel. You'll see the tall, exterior glass elevators that flank the museum's main entrance.

A second entrance in the newer section of the building some-times has shorter lines, especially during the museum's free hours. To get there, face the glass elevators and walk left around the old building to the large gates of the red-and-black Nouvel Building.

**Tours:** The hardworking audioguide is €5.50.

**Services:** Bag storage is free. The *librería* just outside the Nou-vel wing has a larger selection of Picasso and Surrealist reproduc-tions than the main gift shop at the entrance.

**Cuisine Art:** The museum's **$$ café** (a long block around the left from the main entrance) is a standout for its tasty cuisine. The square immediately in front of the museum is ringed by fine places for a simple meal or drink. My favorite is **$$ El Brillante,** a classic dive offering pricey tapas and baguette sandwiches. But everyone comes for the fried squid sandwiches. Sit at the simple bar or at an outdoor table (long hours daily, two entrances—one on Plaza Sánchez Bustillo, the other at Plaza del Emperador Carlos V 8, see the "Madrid's Museum Neighborhood" map earlier in this chapter, +34 915 286 966). And just a 10-minute walk north is my favorite strip of **tapas bars,** on Calle de Jesús (see page 104).

### ● Self-Guided Tour

The permanent collection is divided into three groups: art from 1900 to 1945 (second floor, including *Guernica*), art from 1945 to 1968 (fourth floor), and art from 1962 to 1982 (adjoining Nouvel wing). Temporary exhibits are scattered throughout. While the collection is roughly chronological, it's displayed thematically, with each room clearly labeled with its theme.

For a good first visit, ride the fancy glass elevator to level 2 and tour that floor counterclockwise (Modernism, Cubism, Picasso's *Guernica*, Surrealism), then see post-WWII art on level 4, and fi-nally descend to the Nouvel wing for the finale.

• *Pick up a free map and take an elevator (slow, hot, and crowded, so be patient) to level 2. Begin in Room 201—located between the two eleva-tors—which introduces you to the dawn of the 20th century.*

### Modernism (Room 201)

You could make a good case that the changes in society in the year 1900 were more profound than those we lived through in 2000. Trains and cars brought speed to life. Electricity brought light. Revolutions were toppling centuries-old regimes. Einstein intro-duced mind-bending ideas. Photography captured reality, and movies set it in motion. The 20th century—accelerated by technol-ogy and shattered by war—would produce the exciting and turbu-lent modern art showcased in this museum.

The collection kicks off with engravings by the 19th-century artist Goya, often considered the first "modern" painter (and the Reina Sofía's one point of overlap with the Prado). He used art to express his inner feelings and address social injustice, and his dynamic style anticipated the formless chaos of Modern Art.

You may also see early works by young Pablo Picasso—a precocious teenager who skipped his art classes to sketch works by Goya, Velázquez, and El Greco in the Prado. In the year 1900, 19-year-old Picasso moved to the world's art capital, Paris, where the Modern Art revolution was about to begin.

• *We'll tour this floor counterclockwise (in reverse order to how the rooms are numbered). Start in Room 210.*

### Cubism (Rooms 210, 208, 207)

In Paris, Picasso and his roommate Georges Braque invented a new way of portraying the world on a canvas—Cubism. They shattered the world into a million pieces, then reassembled the shards and "cubes" onto a canvas. The things they painted—bottles, fruit, dead birds, playing cards, guitars, a woman's head—are vaguely recognizable, but composed of many different geometrical pieces. It was a way of showing a three-dimensional object on a two-dimensional surface. (Imagine walking around a statue to take in all the angles, and then attempting to put it on a 2-D plane.)

Room 210 makes it clear that Cubism was very much a Spaniard-driven movement. Picasso was soon joined in Paris by Madrid's own Juan Gris. Gris adored Picasso (the feeling wasn't mutual) and added his own spin on the Cubist style. Gris used curvier lines, brighter colors, and more recognizable images, composing his paintings as if he were pasting paper cutouts on the canvas to make a collage.

In the same room, watch Georges Méliès' film *The Extraordinary Dislocation* (1901), where a man's head and limbs become fantastically detached from his body. It scrambles expectations—juxtaposing the familiar and the impossible—in much the same way as Cubist paintings.

Proceed through the rest of the Cubism exhibit (Rooms 208 and 207), tracing the development of this cornerstone of Modernism. You'll see how various artists expressed this same idea in different ways. The techniques they pioneered—deconstructing reality and reassembling the pieces into a collage of arresting images—would reach its culmination in the world's most famous Cubist work: *Guernica.*

• *Continuing counterclockwise, you enter Room 206 ("Guernica and the 1930s"). This "room" is actually a series of sub-rooms (206.01, 206.02, and so on) offering context and a setup for the main attraction. Absolutely no photos are allowed in this area. Make your way through this wing and find the big room with a movie screen-size, black-and-white canvas. You've reached what is likely the reason for your visit...*

### Picasso's *Guernica* (Room 206)

Perhaps the single most impressive piece of art in Spain is Pablo Picasso's *Guernica* (1937). The monumental canvas—one of Europe's must-see sights—is not only a piece of art but a piece of history, capturing the horror of modern war in a modern style.

While it's become a timeless classic representing all war, it was born in response to a specific conflict—the Spanish Civil War (1936-1939), which pitted the democratically elected Second Republican government against the fascist general Francisco Franco. Franco won and ended up ruling Spain with an iron fist for the next 36 years. At the time Franco cemented his power, *Guernica* was touring internationally as part of a fundraiser for the Republican cause. With Spain's political situation deteriorating and World War II looming, Picasso in 1939 named New York's Museum of Modern Art as the depository for the work. It was only after Franco's death, in 1975, that *Guernica* ended its decades of exile. In 1981 the painting finally arrived in Spain (where it had never before been), and it now stands as Spain's national piece of art.

**Guernica—The Bombing:** On April 26, 1937, Guernica—a Basque market town in northern Spain and an important Republican center—was the target of the world's first saturation-bombing raid on civilians. Franco gave permission to his fascist confederate Adolf Hitler to use the town as a guinea pig to try out Germany's new air force. The raid leveled the town, causing destruction that was unheard of at the time (though by 1944, it would be commonplace).

News of the bombing reached Picasso in Paris, where coincidentally he was just beginning work on a painting commission awarded by the Republican government. Picasso scrapped his earlier plans and immediately set to work sketching scenes of the destruction as he imagined it. In a matter of weeks, he put these bomb-shattered shards together into a large mural (286 square

feet). For the first time, the world could see the destructive force of the rising fascist movement—a prelude to World War II.

*Guernica*—**The Painting:** The bombs are falling, shattering the quiet village. ❶ A woman howls up at the sky (far right), ❷ horses scream (center), and ❸ a man falls from a horse and dies, while ❹ a wounded woman drags herself through the streets. She tries to escape, but her leg is too thick, dragging her down, like trying to run from something in a nightmare. ❺ On the left, a bull—a symbol of Spain—ponders it all, watching over ❻ a mother and her dead baby...a modern pietà. ❼ A woman in the center sticks her head out to see what's going on. The whole scene is lit from above by the ❽ stark light of a bare bulb. Picasso's painting threw a light on the brutality of Hitler and Franco, and suddenly the whole world was watching.

Picasso's abstract, Cubist style reinforces the message. It's as if he'd picked up the shattered shards and pasted them onto a canvas. The black-and-white tones are as gritty as the black-and-white newspaper photos that reported the bombing. The drab colors create a depressing, almost nauseating mood.

Picasso chose images with universal symbolism, making the work a commentary on all wars. Picasso himself said that the central horse, with the spear in its back, symbolizes humanity succumbing to brute force. The fallen rider's arm is severed and his sword is broken, more symbols of defeat. The bull, normally a proud symbol of strength and independence, is impotent and frightened. Between the bull and the horse, the faint dove of peace can do nothing but cry.

The bombing of Guernica—like the entire civil war—was an exercise in brutality. As one side captured a town, it might systematically round up every man, old and young—including priests—line them up, and shoot them in revenge for atrocities by the other side.

Thousands of people attended the Paris exhibition, and *Guernica* caused an immediate sensation. They could see the horror of modern war technology, the vain struggle of the Spanish Republicans, and the cold indifference of the fascist war machine. Picasso vowed never to return to Spain while Franco ruled (the dictator outlived him).

With each passing year, the canvas seemed more and more prophetic—honoring not just the hundreds or thousands who died in Guernica, but also the estimated 500,000 victims of Spain's bitter civil war and the 55 million worldwide who perished in World War II. Picasso put a human face on what we now call "collateral damage."

• *After seeing* Guernica, *view the additional exhibits here and in ad-*

*joining rooms that put the painting in its social context. No photos allowed here either.*

### Other Picasso Exhibits

On the back wall on the *Guernica* room is a line of **photos** showing the evolution of the painting, from Picasso's first concept to the final mural. The photos were taken in his Paris studio by Dora Maar, Picasso's mistress-du-jour (and whose portrait by Picasso hangs in the adjoining Room 206.10). Notice how his work evolved from the defiant fist in early versions to a broken sword with a flower.

The room in front of *Guernica* (206.6) contains **studies** Picasso did for the painting. These studies are filled with motifs that turn up in the final canvas—iron-nail tears, weeping women, and screaming horses. Picasso returned to these images in his work for the rest of his life. He believed that everyone struggles internally with aspects of the horse and bull: rationality and brutality, humanity and animalism. Notice the etching *Minotauromachy* (from 1935). The Minotaur—half-man and half-bull—powerfully captures Picasso's poet/rapist vision of man. Having lived through the brutality of the age—World War I, the Spanish Civil War, and World War II—his outlook is understandable. The adjoining room plays newsreel footage of the civil war and of Franco's fascist regime that kept Picasso from ever returning home.

In the next room (206.7), you'll also find a **model of the Spanish Pavilion** at the 1937 Paris exposition where *Guernica* was first displayed (look inside to see Picasso's work). Picasso originally toyed with painting an allegory on the theme of the artist's studio for the expo. But the bombing of Guernica jolted him into the realization that Spain was a country torn by war. Thanks to *Guernica*, the pavilion became a vessel for propaganda and a fundraising tool against Franco. (Notice the pavilion flies the flag of the Republicans: red, yellow, and purple.)

Near the Spanish Pavilion, you'll see posters and political cartoons that are pro-communist and anti-Franco. Made the same year as *Guernica* and the year after, these touch on timeless themes related to rich elites, industrialists, agricultural reform, and the military industrial complex versus the common man, as well as promoting autonomy for Catalunya and the Basque Country.

The remaining rooms display pieces from contemporary artists reacting to the conflict of the time, whether through explicit commentary or through new, innovative styles inspired by the changing political and social culture.

• *Exiting back into the corridor, continue counterclockwise to Room 205.*

### Surrealism and Salvador Dalí (Room 205)

Another Spaniard in Paris—Salvador Dalí (1904-1989)—helped found another groundbreaking Modern Art style, Surrealism. Dalí arrived in Jazz Age Paris in the 1920s, in the wake of World War I. He hung out with his idols, fellow Spaniards Picasso, Gris, and Joan Miró, as well as an international set.

Disillusioned by the irrationality of the war, they rebelled against traditional mores and the shackles of the rational mind. Influenced by Freud's theories about the power of the subconscious, they let their emotions and primal urges speak freely on the canvas. They painted imagery from their dreams (mindscapes, rather than landscapes). They captured the realm beyond the world we see—it was "sur-real."

You'll see Dalí's distinct, melting-object style. Dalí places familiar items in a stark landscape, creating an eerie effect. Figures morph into misplaced faces and body parts. Background and foreground play mind games—is it an animal (seen one way) or a man's face? A waterfall or a pair of legs? It's a wide shot...no, it's a close-up. Look long at paintings like Dalí's *The Endless Enigma* (1938) and *The Invisible Man* (1929-1932); they take different viewers to different places.

***Face of the Great Masturbator*** (1929) is psychologically exhausting, depicting in its Surrealism a lonely, highly sexual genius in love with his muse, Gala (while she was still married to a French poet). This is the first famous Surrealist painting. Like a dream, it mixes and matches seemingly unrelated objects. Swarming ants. A limp earthworm hanging from a hook. Faceless mannequins roaming a desert. A teetering tower of rock, cork, seashell, and olive. What does it mean? What does *any* dream mean? You tell me.

During this productive period, Dalí collaborated with Luis Buñuel on the classic Surrealist film *Un Chien Andalou* (*The Andalusian Dog*, 1928, in the adjoining room). It's hard to overstate how influential this little silent film is in the world of cinema. A cloud cuts across the night sky, slicing across the moon. A man holds a razor to a woman's eye. And then the man slices through...the eye of a dead horse. Buñuel's juxtaposition of images into a montage is something that filmmakers today are still reckoning with. Buñuel and Dalí were members of the Generation of '27, a group of nonconformist Spanish bohemians whose creative interests had a huge influence on art and literature in their era.

Just outside of the screening room are photographs by **Man Ray** (1890-1976). What Dalí did with paint and Buñuel did with film, Man Ray did with photographs—creating surreal and, yes, dreamlike images that are as haunting today as they were nearly a century ago.

• *Head up to level 4, where the permanent collection continues. Start in Room 401 (which may require a bit of searching depending on which elevator you take). From there, circle this floor counterclockwise.*

MADRID

### Post-WWII Art (1945-1968)

The organizing theme in this part of the museum is "Art in a Divided World"—a world upset by war, divided by the Iron Curtain, and under the constant threat of nuclear war. Art, too, shattered into many styles and "isms." As you browse, use the newsreel footage to put these trends in their historical context.

The collection starts in the troubled wake of World War II, with canvases that are often distorted, harsh-colored, and violent-looking. Picasso—still in Paris—continued to invent and reflect many international trends.

With Europe in ruins, the center of the art world was moving from Paris to New York City. As you browse counterclockwise, you'll see the distorted yet recognizable figures of Picasso give way to purely abstract art—the geometrical designs and big empty canvases of Abstract Expressionism. More and more, artists focused on the surface texture of the canvas: thick paint, cutting the canvas, or piling on fibrous substances. The canvas became not a window on the world you look *through,* but a kind of standalone sculpture you look *at.*

Meanwhile (as you'll see in numerous rooms), Spain was still recovering from its devastating civil war and ruled by a dictatorship. Its avant-garde could not be so *avant,* and they lagged a decade behind the trends. But old Spanish "masters" abroad like Picasso and Miró continued to be cutting-edge into the 1960s.

The final rooms (423-429) bring in the 1960s, with its Pop Art—everyday pop-culture objects displayed as art. By now, the lingering aftermath of World War II was coming to an end, and a new, equally revolutionary age was beginning. The one element of continuity through it all is that artists of any age will portray the times in which they live by depicting the human figure.

• *End your visit in the Nouvel wing. The easiest "connection" between the main building and Nouvel wing is to descend to level 2, make your way to Room 206.01, enter the Nouvel wing, descend the stairs to level 1, and start your visit in Room 104.01. But regardless of where you start, the Nouvel wing is made for browsing.*

### Nouvel Wing (1962-1982)

Here you'll see art from the 1960s to the 1980s, with a thematic focus on the complexity and plurality of modern times. As revolutions liberated Third World countries, art became more global. With new technologies, the quaint ideas of art-as-a-painted-canvas give way to multimedia assemblages and installations. While these galleries have fewer household names, the pieces displayed demonstrate the many aesthetic directions of more recent modern art.

And now, having seen this museum and followed the evolution of art over a century, you don't need anyone to explain it to you...right?

## NEAR THE PRADO (AND BEYOND)

Several other worthy sights are located in and around the museum neighborhood (see the "Madrid's Museum Neighborhood" map, earlier). This is also where my self-guided bus tour along Paseo de la Castellana to the modern skyscraper part of Madrid starts (see page 84).

### ▲▲Retiro Park (Parque del Buen Retiro)

Once the private domain of royalty, this majestic park has been a favorite of Madrid's commoners since Charles III decided to share it with his subjects in the late 18th century. Siesta in this 300-acre green-and-breezy escape from the city. At midday on Saturday and Sunday, the area around the lake becomes a street carnival, with jugglers, puppeteers, and lots of local color. These peaceful gardens offer great picnicking and people-watching (closes at

dusk). From the Retiro Metro stop, walk to the big lake (El Estanque), where you can rent a rowboat. Enjoy the 19th-century glass-and-iron Crystal Palace, which often hosts free exhibits and installations. Past the lake, a grand boulevard of statues leads to the Prado.

### ▲Naval Museum (Museo Naval)

This museum tells the story of Spain's navy, from 1492 to today, in a plush and fascinating-to-boat-lovers exhibit. Given Spain's importance in maritime history, there's quite a story to tell. Because this is a military facility, you'll need to show your passport or driver's license to get in. A good English brochure is available. Access to the Wi-Fi-based English audioguide can be unreliable, but give it a try.

**Cost and Hours:** €3, Tue-Sun 10:00-19:00, until 15:00 in Aug, closed Mon, a block north of the Prado, across boulevard from Thyssen-Bornemisza Museum, Paseo del Prado 5, +34 915 238 789, http://fundacionmuseonaval.com.

### CaixaForum

Across the street from the Prado and Royal Botanical Garden, this impressive exhibit hall has sleek architecture and an outdoor hanging garden—a bushy wall festooned with greens designed by a French landscape artist. The forum, funded by La Caixa Bank, features world-class temporary art exhibits—generally 20th-century art, well described in English. Ride the elevator to the top, where you'll find a café with a daily fixed-price meal for around €14 and sperm-like lamps dangling from the ceiling; from here, explore your way down.

**Cost and Hours:** €6, daily 10:00-20:00, audioguide-€2, Paseo del Prado 36, +34 913 307 300.

## Palacio de Cibeles

This former post-office headquarters, now a cultural center, features mostly empty exhibition halls, an auditorium, and public hangout spaces—and is called the CentroCentro Cibeles for Culture and Citizenship. (Say that five times fast!) Skip the temporary exhibits: The real attraction lies in the gorgeous 360-degree rooftop views from the eighth-floor observation deck (ticket office outside to the right of the main entrance). Visit the recommended sixth-floor Restaurante Palacio de Cibeles and bar for similar views from its two terraces. Entering the Palacio itself is free—take advantage of its air-conditioning and free Wi-Fi.

**Cost and Hours:** Building free and open Tue-Sun 10:00-20:00, closed Mon; observation deck-€2, limited number of visitors allowed every half-hour 10:30-13:30 & 16:00-19:00, ticket office opens 30 minutes early, advance tickets available online; Plaza de Cibeles 1, +34 914 800 008, www.centrocentro.org.

## ▲▲National Archaeological Museum (Museo Arqueológico Nacional/MAN)

This well-curated, rich collection of artifacts and tasteful multimedia displays tells the story of Iberia. You'll follow a chronological walk through the wonders of each age: Celtic pre-Roman, Roman, a fine and rare Visigothic section, Moorish, Romanesque, and beyond. A highlight is the Lady of Elche (Room 13), a prehistoric Iberian female bust and a symbol of Spanish archaeology. You may also find underwhelming replica artwork from northern Spain's Altamira Caves (big on bison), giving you a faded peek at the skill of the cave artists who created the originals 14,000 years ago. **Cost and Hours:** €3, free on Sat after 14:00 and all day Sun; open Tue-Sat 9:30-20:00, Sun until 15:00, closed Mon; multimedia guide-€2; 20-minute walk north of the Prado at Calle Serrano 13, Metro: Serrano or Colón, +34 915 777 912, www.man.es.

## Royal Tapestry Factory (Real Fábrica de Tapices)

Take this factory tour for a look at traditional tapestry making. You'll also have the chance to order a tailor-made tapestry (starting at $10,000).

**Cost and Hours:** €5, by tour only, in English at 12:00, in Spanish at 10:00, 11:00, and 13:00; open Mon-Fri 10:00-14:00,

MADRID

closed Sat-Sun and Aug; south of Retiro Park at Calle Fuenterrabia 2, Metro: Menendez Pelayo—take Gutenberg exit, +34 914 340 550, www.realfabricadetapices.com.

## AWAY FROM THE CENTER

To locate these sights, see the "Greater Madrid" map at the beginning of this chapter.

### ▲Museum of the Americas (Museo de América)

Thousands of pre-Columbian and colonial artworks and artifacts make up the bulk of this worthwhile museum, though it offers few English explanations. Covering the cultures of the Americas (North and South), its exhibits focus on language, religion, and art, and provide a new perspective on the cultures of our own hemisphere. Highlights include one of only four surviving Mayan codices (ancient books) and a section about the voyages of the Spanish explorers, with their fantastical imaginings of mythical creatures awaiting them in the New World.

**Cost and Hours:** €3, free on Sun; open Tue-Sat 9:30-15:00, Thu until 19:00, Sun 10:00-15:00, closed Mon; Avenida de los Reyes Católicos 6, Metro: Moncloa, +34 915 492 641, http://museodeamerica.mcu.es.

**Getting There:** The museum is a 15-minute walk from the Moncloa Metro stop: Take the Calle de Isaac Peral exit, cross Plaza de Moncloa, and veer right to Calle de Fernández de los Ríos. Follow that street (toward the shiny Faro de Moncloa tower), and turn left on Avenida de los Reyes Católicos. Head around the base of the tower, which stands at the museum's entrance.

### Clothing Museum (Museo del Traje)

In a cool and air-conditioned chronological sweep, this museum's exhibits illustrate the history of clothing from the 18th century through today. Displays cover regional ethnic costumes, the influence of bullfighting and the French, accessories through the ages, and Spanish flappers. The only downside of this marvelous, modern museum is its remote location.

**Cost and Hours:** €3, free on Sat after 14:30 and all day Sun; open Tue-Sat 9:30-19:00, Thu until 22:30 in July-Aug, Sun 10:00-15:00, closed Mon; Avenida de Juan Herrera 2; Metro: Moncloa and a longish walk, bus #46, or taxi; +34 915 497 150, http://museodeltraje.mcu.es.

### ▲Hermitage of San Antonio de la Florida (Ermita de San Antonio de la Florida)

In this simple little Neoclassical chapel from the 1790s, Francisco de Goya's tomb stares up at a splendid cupola filled with his own proto-Impressionist frescoes. He used the same unique technique that he employed for his "black paintings" (described earlier, under the Prado Museum listing). Use the mirrors to enjoy the drama and energy he infused into this marvelously restored masterpiece.

**Cost and Hours:** Free, Tue-Sun 9:30-20:00, closed Mon, Glorieta de San Antonio de la Florida 5; Metro: Príncipe Pío, then eight-minute walk down Paseo de San Antonio de la Florida; +34 915 420 722, www.esmadrid.com (search for "Ermita de San Antonio de la Florida").

### Temple of Debod (Templo de Debod)

In 1968, Egypt gave Spain its own ancient temple. It was a gift of the Egyptian government, which was grateful for the Spanish dictator Franco's help in rescuing monuments that had been threatened by the rising Nile waters above the Aswan Dam. Consequently, Madrid is the only place I can think of in Europe where you can actually wander through an intact original Egyptian temple—complete with fine carved reliefs from 200 BC. Set in a romantic park that locals love for its great city views (especially at sunset), the temple—as well as its art—is well described.

**Cost and Hours:** Free, open Tue-Fri 10:00-20:00 in summer, shorter hours off-season, closed Mon year-round, north of the Royal Palace in Parque de Montaña, +34 913 667 415, www.esmadrid.com (search for "Templo de Debod").

### ▲▲Sorolla Museum (Museo Sorolla)

The delightful, art-filled home of painter Joaquín Sorolla (1863-1923) is one of Spain's most enjoyable museums. Sorolla is known for his portraits, landscapes, and use of light. Imagine the mansion, back in 1910, when it stood alone—without the surrounding high-rise buildings. With the aid of the essential audioguide, stroll through his home and studio, zeroing in on whichever painting grabs you. Sorolla captured wonderful slices of life—his wife/muse, his family, and lazy beach scenes of his hometown Valencia. He was a late Impressionist—a period called Luminism in Spain. And it was all about nature: water, light, reflection. The collection is intimate, and you can cap it with a few restful minutes in Sorolla's Andalusian gardens. Visit in the morning to experience the works with the best natural light.

**Cost and Hours:** €3, free on Sat 14:00-20:00 and all day Sun; open Tue-Sat 9:30-20:00, Sun 10:00-15:00, closed Mon; last entry 45 minutes before closing, audioguide-€2.50, General Martínez Campos 37, Metro: Iglesia, +34 913 101 584, www.museosorolla.es.

MADRID

### ▲Madrid History Museum (Museo de Historia de Madrid)

This building, a hospital from 1716 to 1910, has housed a city history museum since 1929. The entrance features a fine Baroque door by the architect Pedro de Ribera, with a depiction of St. James the Moor-Slayer. Start in the basement (where you can study a detailed model of the city made in 1830) and work your way up through the four-floor collection. The history of Madrid is explained through old paintings that show the city in action, maps, historic fans, jeweled snuffboxes, etchings of early bullfighting, and fascinating late-19th-century photographs.

Don't miss Goya's *Allegory of the City of Madrid* (c. 1810), an angelic tribute to the rebellion against the French on May 2, 1808. The museum is in the trendy Malasaña district, near the Plaza Dos de Mayo, where some of the rebellion that Goya painted occurred.

**Cost and Hours:** Free, Tue-Sun 10:00-20:00, closed Mon, Calle de Fuencarral 78, Metro: Tribunal, +34 917 011 863, www.esmadrid.com (search for "Museo de Historia").

## Experiences in Madrid

### ▲Self-Guided Bus Tour: Paseo de la Castellana

Many visitors leave Madrid without ever seeing the modern "Manhattan" side of town. But it's easy to find. From the museum neighborhood, bus #27 makes the trip straight north along Paseo del Prado and then Paseo de la Castellana, through the no-nonsense skyscraper part of this city of more than three million. The line ends at the leaning towers of Puerta de Europa (Gate of Europe). This trip is simple and cheap (€1.50 or a single ride on a 10-ride Multi Card ticket, buses run every 10 minutes, see the "Greater Madrid" map at the beginning of this chapter for route). If starting from the Prado, catch the bus from the museum side to head north; from the Reina Sofía, the stop is a couple of blocks away at the Royal Botanical Garden, at the end of the garden fence. You'll joyride for 30-45 minutes to the last stop, get out at the end of the line when everyone else does, ogle the skyscrapers, and catch the Metro for a 20-minute ride back to the city's center (to Puerta del Sol). The ride is particularly enjoyable at twilight, when fountains and facades are floodlit. Possible stops of interest along the way are Plaza de Colon (National Archaeological Museum) and Bernabéu (massive soccer stadium).

**Historic District:** Bus #27 rumbles from the end of the Paseo del Prado at the Royal Botanical Garden (opposite McDonald's) and the Velázquez entrance to the Prado. Immediately after the Prado you pass a number of grand landmarks: a square with a fountain of Neptune (left); an obelisk and war memorial (right, with the stock market behind it); the Naval Museum (right); and Plaza de

Cibeles—with the fancy City Hall and cultural center. From Plaza de Cibeles, you can see the 18th-century Gate of Alcalá (the old east entry to Madrid), the Bank of Spain, and the start of the Gran Vía (left). Then you can relax for a moment while driving along Paseo de Recoletos.

**Modern District:** Just past the National Library (right) is a roundabout and square **(Plaza de Colon)** with a statue of Columbus in the middle and a giant Spanish flag. This marks the end of the historic town and the beginning of the modern city. (Hop out here for the National Archaeological Museum.)

At this point the boulevard changes its name (and the sights I mention are much more spread out). Once named for Franco, this street is now named for the people he no longer rules—*la Castellana* (Castilians). Next, you pass high-end apartments and embassies. Immediately after an underpass with several modern sculptures comes the **American Embassy** (right, hidden behind its fortified wall). Near a roundabout with a big fountain, watch on the left for some circa-1940s buildings that once housed Franco's ministries (typical fascist architecture, with large colonnades). You'll pass under a second underpass and see 1980s business sprawl on the left. One of these is the distinctive **Picasso Tower,** resembling one of New York's former World Trade Center towers with its vertical black-and-white stripes (it was designed by the same architect). Just after the Picasso Tower is the huge **Bernabéu Stadium** (right, home of Real Madrid, one of Europe's most successful soccer teams; bus stops on both sides of the stadium).

Your trip ends at **Plaza de Castilla,** where you can't miss the avant-garde Puerta de Europa, consisting of the twin "Torres Kios," office towers that lean at a 15-degree angle (look for the big green sign *BANKIA,* for the Bank of Madrid). In the distance, you can see the four tallest buildings in Spain. The plaza sports a futuristic golden obelisk by contemporary Spanish architect Santiago Calatrava.

It's the end of the line for the bus—and for you. You can return directly to Puerta del Sol on the Metro, or cross the street and ride bus #27 along the same route back to the Prado Museum or Atocha train station.

**MADRID**

## ▲Electric Minibus Joyride through the Lavapiés District

For a relaxing ride through the characteristic old center of Madrid, hop the little electric **minibus #M1** (€1.50, 5/hour, 20-minute trip, Mon-Sat 8:20-20:00, none on Sun). These are designed especially for the difficult-to-access streets in the historic heart of the city, and are handy for seniors (offer your seat if you see a senior standing).

**The Route:** Catch the minibus near the Sevilla Metro stop at the top of Calle Sevilla, and simply ride it to the end (Metro: Embajadores). Enjoy this gritty slice of workaday Madrid—both people and architecture—as you roll slowly through Plaza Santa Ana, down a bit of the pedestrianized Calle de las Huertas, past gentrified Plaza Tirso de Molina (its junkies now replaced by a faded family-friendly flower market), and through Plaza de Lavapiés and a barrio of African and Bangladeshi immigrants. Jump out along the way to explore Lavapiés on foot, or stay on until you get to Embajadores just a few blocks away. From there, you can catch the next #M1 minibus back to the Sevilla Metro stop (it returns along a different route) or descend into the subway system (it's just two stops back to Sol).

**The Lavapiés District:** In the Lavapiés neighborhood, the multiethnic tapestry of Madrid enjoys seedy-yet-fun-loving life on the streets. Neighborhoods like this typically experience the same familiar evolution: Initially they're so cheap that only immigrants, the downtrodden, and counterculture types live there. The diversity and color they bring attracts those with more money. Businesses erupt to cater to those bohemian/trendy tastes. Rents go up. Those who gave the area its colorful energy in the first place can no longer afford to live there. They move out...and here comes Starbucks.

For now, Lavapiés is still edgy, yet comfortable enough for most. To help rejuvenate the area, the city built the big Centro Dramático Nacional Theater just downhill from Lavapiés' main square.

The district has almost no tourists. (Some think it's too scary.) Old ladies with their tired bodies and busy fans hang out on their tiny balconies, watching the scene. Shady types lurk on side streets (don't venture off the main drag, don't show your wallet or money, and don't linger late on Plaza de Lavapiés).

If you're walking, start from Plaza de Antón Martín (Metro: Antón Martín) or Plaza Santa Ana. Find your way to Calle del Ave María (on its way to becoming Calle del Ave Allah) and on to Plaza de Lavapiés (Metro: Lavapiés), where elderly Madrileños hang out with swarthy drunks and drug dealers; a mosaic of cultures treat this square as a communal living room. Then head up Calle de Lavapiés to the Plaza Tirso de Molina (Metro stop). Once plagued by druggies, this square is now home to flower kiosks and a playground—a good example of Madrid's vision for reinvigorating its public spaces.

For food, you'll find plenty of tapas bars, plus gritty Indian (almost all run by Bangladeshis) and Moroccan eateries lining Calle de Lavapiés. For Spanish fare, try **$ Bar Melos,** a thriving, dinner-only dive jammed with a hungry and nubile crowd. It's famous for its giant patty melts called *zapatillas de lacón y queso* (because they're the size and shape of a *zapatilla,* or slipper—feeds at least two, Tue-Sat 20:00-late, closed Sun-Mon, Calle del Ave María 44).

### ▲Bullfight

Madrid's Plaza de Toros hosts Spain's top bullfights on most Sundays and holidays from March through mid-October, and nearly

every day during the San Isidro festival (early May-early June—often sold out long in advance). Fights start between 17:00 and 19:00 (early in spring and fall, late in summer). The bullring is at the Ventas Metro stop (a 25-minute Metro ride from Puerta del Sol, +34 913 562 200, www.las-ventas.com). **Tickets:** Bullfight tickets range from €5 to €150. There are no bad seats at Plaza de Toros; paying more gets you in the shade and/or closer to the gore. (The action often intentionally occurs in the shade to reward the expensive-ticket holders.) To be close to the bullfighters, choose areas 8, 9, or 10; for shade: 1, 2, 9, or 10; for shade/sun: 3 or 8; for the sun and cheapest seats: 4, 5, 6, or 7. Note these key words: *corrida*—a real fight with professionals; *novillada*—rookie matadors, younger bulls, and cheaper tickets.

Two booking offices sell tickets online and in person. When buying online, read conditions carefully: The purchase voucher usually must be exchanged for a ticket at the booking office. The easiest place is **Bullfight Tickets Madrid** at Plaza del Carmen 1 (Mon-Sat 9:00-13:00 & 16:30-19:00, Sun 9:30-14:00, +34 915 319 131, www.bullfightticketsmadrid.com; run by José and his English-speaking son, also José, who also sells soccer tickets; will deliver tickets to your hotel). A second option is **Toros La Central** at Calle Victoria 3 (Mon-Fri 10:00-14:30 & 16:30-20:00, Sat-Sun 10:00-13:00, +34 915 211 213, www.toroslacentral.es).

Getting tickets through your hotel or a booking office is convenient, but they add 20 percent or more and don't sell the cheapest seats. To save money, you can stand in the ticket line at the bullring. Except for important bullfights—or during the San Isidro festival—there are generally plenty of seats available. About a thousand tickets are held back to be sold in the five days leading up to and on the day of a fight. Scalpers hang out before the popular fights at the Calle Victoria booking office. Beware: Those buying scalped tickets are breaking the law and can lose the ticket with no recourse.

For a dose of the experience, you can buy a cheap ticket and just stay to see a couple of bullfights. Each fight takes about 20 minutes, and the event consists of six bulls over two hours. Or, to keep your distance but get a sense of the ritual and gore, tour the bull bar on Plaza Mayor.

**Bullfighting Museum** (Museo Taurino): This museum, located at the back of the bullring, is not as good as the ones in Sevilla or Ronda (free, daily 10:00-18:00, +34 917 251 857).

### "Football" and Bernabéu Stadium

Madrid, like most of Europe, is enthusiastic about soccer (which they call *fútbol*). The Real ("Royal") Madrid team plays to a spirited crowd Saturdays and Sundays from September through May (tickets from €50—sold at bullfight box offices listed earlier). One of the most popular sightseeing activities among European visitors to Madrid is touring the 80,000-seat stadium. The €25 unguided visit includes the box seats, dressing rooms, technical zone, playing field, trophy room, and a big panoramic stadium view (Mon-Sat 10:00-19:00, Sun 10:30-18:30, shorter hours on game days, bus #27—see self-guided bus tour on page 84—or Metro: Santiago Bernabéu, +34 913 984 300, www.realmadrid.com). Even if you can't catch a game, you'll see plenty of Real Madrid's all-white jerseys and paraphernalia around town.

# Shopping in Madrid

Madrileños have a passion for shopping. It's a social event, often incorporated into the afternoon paseo, which eventually turns into drinks and dinner. Most shoppers focus on the colorful pedestrian area between and around Gran Vía and Puerta del Sol. Here you'll find H&M and Zara clothing, Imaginarium toys, FNAC books and music, and a handful of small local shops. The fanciest big-name shops (Gucci, Prada, and the like) tempt strollers along Calle Serrano, northwest of Retiro Park. For trendier chains and local fashion, head to pedestrian Calle Fuencarral, Calle Augusto Figueroa, and the streets surrounding Plaza de Chueca (north of Gran Vía, Metro: Chueca). Here are some other places to check out:

### El Corte Inglés Department Store

The giant El Corte Inglés, with several buildings strung between Puerta del Sol and Plaza del Callou, is a handy place to pick up just about anything you need. **Building 3,** full of sports equipment, books, and home furnishings, is closest to Puerta del Sol. **Building 2,** a block up from Puerta del Sol on Calle Preciados, has a handy info desk at the door (with Madrid maps), a travel agency/box office for local events, souvenirs, toiletries, a post office, men's and women's fashions, a boring cafeteria, and a vast basement supermarket with a fancy "Club del Gourmet" section for edible souvenirs. Farther north on Calle del Carmen toward Plaza del Callao is **Building 1,** with electronics, another travel agency/box office, and the "Gourmet Experience"—a floor filled with fun eateries and a rooftop terrace for diners (described on page 112).

The **travel agencies** in buildings 1 and 2 are fast and easy places to buy AVE and other train tickets (plus airline tickets) with a €6 service fee, but they don't sell reservations for rail-pass holders. (Another El Corte Inglés travel agency is in the Atocha train station.)

All El Corte Inglés department stores are open daily (Mon-Sat 10:00-22:00, Sun 11:00-21:00, +34 913 798 000, www.elcorteingles.es). Salespeople wear flag pins indicating which languages they speak. If doing serious shopping here, ask about their discounts (10 percent for tourists) and VAT refund policy (21 percent but with a minimum purchase requirement that you can accumulate over multiple shopping trips.

## ▲El Rastro Flea Market

Europe's biggest flea market is a field day for shoppers, people-watchers, and pickpockets (Sun only, 9:00-15:00). It's best before

11:00, though bargain shoppers like to go around 14:00, when vendors are more willing to strike end-of-day deals. Thousands of stalls titillate more than a million browsers with mostly new junk. Locals have lamented the tackiness of El Rastro lately—on the main drag, you'll find cheap underwear and bootleg CDs, but no real treasures.

For an interesting market day (Sun only), start at Plaza Mayor, where Europe's biggest stamp and coin market thrives. Enjoy this genteel delight as you watch old-timers paging lovingly through each other's albums, looking for win-win trades. When you're done, head south or take the Metro to Tirso de Molina. Walk downhill, wandering off on the side streets to browse antiques, old furniture, and garage sale-style sellers who often simply throw everything out on a sheet. Find a fantastic scene on Plaza del Campillo del Mundo Nuevo where kids and adults leaf through each other's albums of soccer cards and negotiate over trades.

A typical Madrileño's Sunday could involve a meander through the Rastro streets with several stops for *cañas* (small beers) at the gritty bars along the way, then a walk to the Cava Baja area for more beer and tapas (see page 104). El Rastro offers a fascinating chance to see gangs of young thieves overwhelming and ripping off naive tourists while plainclothes police officers circulate and do their best. Don't even bring a wallet. The pickpocket action is brutal.

### Specialty Shops

These places are fun to browse for Spanish specialties and locally made goods.

**Ceramics: Antigua Casa Talavera** has sold hand-made ceramics from Spain's family craftsmen since 1904. They can explain the various regional styles and colors of pottery and tiles, based on traditional designs from the 11th to 19th century (Mon-Fri 10:00-13:30 & 17:00-20:00, Sat 10:00-13:30, closed Sun, Calle Isabel La Católica 2, +34 915 473 417, www.antiguacasatalavera.com).

**Leather: Taller Puntera** is a workshop and store where the new generation carries on a longtime family tradition of Madrileño leather artisans. They design and create all of their products on-site, from bags to shoes and more (Mon-Sat 10:00-14:30 & 16:00-20:30, closed Sun, Plaza Conde de Barajas 4, +34 913 642 926, www.puntera.com).

**Shoes:** For *the* shoe street in Madrid head up Calle Fuencarral and take a right onto Calle Augusto Figueroa. Walk a couple of blocks down to find one local *zapatería* after another. On Gran Vía, Calle Arenal, or Calle Preciados, you'll also find **Camper** shoes, launched in 1975 on the Spanish island of Mallorca. This popular brand is now relatively easy to find around the world, though here in Madrid you may see more styles (daily, Calle Preciados 23, +34 915 317 897, www.camper.com).

**Souvenirs: Casa de Diego** sells *abanicos* (fans), *mantones* (typical Spanish shawls), *castañuelas* (castanets), *peinetas* (hair combs), and umbrellas. Even if you're not in the market, it's fun to watch the women flip open their final fan choices before buying—for them it is not a souvenir, but an important piece of their wardrobe (Mon-Sat 9:30-20:00, closed Sun, Puerta del Sol 12, +34 915 226 643).

**Guitars:** Spain makes some of the world's finest classical guitars. Several of the top workshops, within an easy walk of Puerta del Sol, offer inviting little showrooms that give a peek at their craft and an opportunity to strum the final product. Consider the workshops of **José Romero** (Calle de Espoz y Mina 30, +34 915 214 218) and **José Ramírez** (Calle de la Paz 8, +34 915 314 229). **Union Musical** is a popular guitar shop off Puerta del Sol (Calle de Cedaceros 3, +34 914 293 877). If you're looking to buy, be prepared to spend €1,000.

# Nightlife in Madrid

Those into clubbing may have to wait until after midnight for the most popular places to even open, much less start hopping. Spain has a reputation for partying very late and not stopping until offices open in the morning. (Spaniards, who are often awake into the wee hours of the morning, have a special word for this time of day: *la madrugada*.) If you're out early in the morning, it's hard to tell who is finishing their day and who's just starting it. Even if you're not a party animal after midnight, make a point to be out with the happy masses, luxuriating in the cool evening air between 22:00 and midnight. The scene is absolutely unforgettable.

### ▲▲▲Paseo

Just walking the streets of Madrid seems to be the way the Madrileños spend their evenings. Even past midnight on a hot summer night, entire families with little kids are strolling, enjoying tiny beers and tapas in a series of bars, licking ice cream, and greeting their neighbors. Good areas to wander include from Puerta del Sol to Plaza Mayor and down Calle del Arenal until you hit Plaza de Isabel II; the pedestrianized Calle de las Huertas from Plaza Mayor to the Prado; along Gran Vía from about Plaza del Callao to Plaza de España, following the last section of my "Gran Vía Walk"; and, to window shop with the young and trendy, up Calle de Fuencarral (keep going until you hit traffic).

### ▲Zarzuela

For a delightful look at Spanish light opera that even English speakers can enjoy, try zarzuela. Guitar-strumming Napoleons in red capes; buxom women with masks, fans, and castanets; Spanish-speaking pharaohs; melodramatic spotlights; and aficionados clapping and singing along from the cheap seats, where the acoustics are best—this is zarzuela...the people's opera. Originating in Madrid, zarzuela is known for its satiric humor and surprisingly good music. Performances occur evenings at Teatro de la Zarzuela, which alternates between zarzuela, ballet, and opera throughout the year. The TI's monthly guide has a special zarzuela section. Be aware that not all shows at the Teatro de la Zarzuela are zarzuelas.

**Tickets:** Prices range from €18-50, less for restricted-view seats, 50 percent off for those over 65, Teatro de la Zarzuela box office open Mon-Fri 12:00-20:00 and Sat-Sun 14:30-18:00 for advance tickets or until showtime for same-day tickets, near the Prado at Jovellanos 4, Metro: Sevilla or Banco de España, +34 915 245 400, http://teatrodelazarzuela.mcu.es. To purchase tickets online, go to www.entradasinaem.es and select *"Espacios"* ("Spaces") to find Teatro de la Zarzuela; you'll receive an email with your tickets, which you need to print before you arrive at the theater.

MADRID

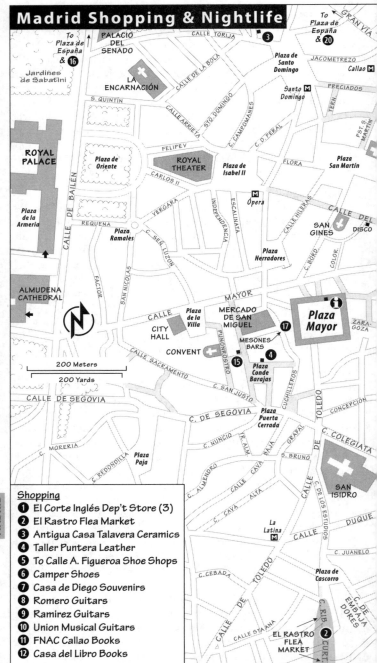

# Madrid Shopping & Nightlife

Shopping
1. El Corte Inglés Dep't Store (3)
2. El Rastro Flea Market
3. Antigua Casa Talavera Ceramics
4. Taller Puntera Leather
5. To Calle A. Figueroa Shoe Shops
6. Camper Shoes
7. Casa de Diego Souvenirs
8. Romero Guitars
9. Ramirez Guitars
10. Union Musical Guitars
11. FNAC Callao Books
12. Casa del Libro Books

MADRID

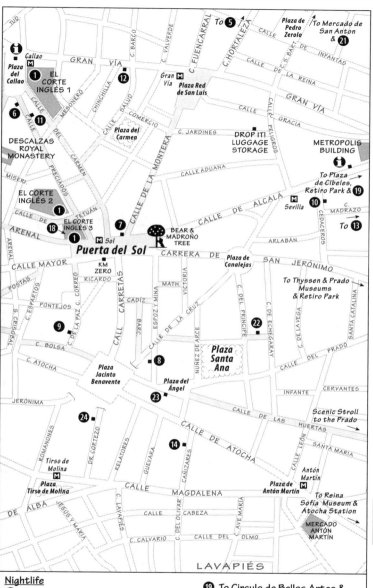

## Nightlife

13 To Teatro de la Zarzuela
14 Taberna Casa Patas (Flamenco)
15 Las Carboneras (Flamenco)
16 To Las Tablas (Flamenco)
17 Mesones ("Cave Bars")
18 Taberna Puertalsol

19 To Círculo de Bellas Artes & Terrace Cibeles
20 To Dear Madrid Hotel
21 To Mercado de San Antón
22 Bar Viva Madrid
23 Café Central Jazz Bar
24 Cine Ideal (Movies)

## ▲▲Flamenco

Although Sevilla is the capital of flamenco, Madrid has a few easy and affordable options. And on summer evenings, Madrid puts on live flamenco events in the Royal Palace gardens (ask TI for details). Among the listings below, Casa Patas is grumpy, while Carboneras is friendlier—but Casa Patas has better-quality artists and a riveting seriousness.

**Taberna Casa Patas** attracts big-name flamenco artists. You'll quickly understand why this intimate venue (30 tables, 120 seats) is named "House of Feet." Since this is for locals as well as tour groups, the flamenco is contemporary and may be jazzier than your notion—it depends on who's performing (€40 includes cover and first drink, Mon-Thu at 22:30, Fri-Sat at 20:00 and 22:30, closed Sun, 1.25-1.5 hours, reservations smart, Cañizares 10, +34 913 690 496, www.casapatas.com). Its restaurant is a logical spot for dinner before the show (€30 dinners, Mon-Thu from 20:00, Fri-Sat from 18:30).

**Las Carboneras,** more downscale, is an easygoing, folksy little place a few steps from Plaza Mayor with a nightly hour-long flamenco show (€39 includes entry and a drink, €77 gets you a table up front with dinner and unlimited cheap drinks if you reserve ahead, RS%—manager Enrique promises a €5/person discount if you book directly and show this book, daily at 20:30, also Mon-Thu at 22:30 and Fri-Sat at 23:00, reservations recommended, Plaza del Conde de Miranda 1, +34 915 428 677, www.tablaolascarboneras.com). Dinner is served one hour before showtime.

**Las Tablas Flamenco** offers a less-expensive nightly show respecting the traditional art of flamenco. You'll sit in a plain room with a mix of tourists and cool, young Madrileños in a modern, nondescript office block just over the freeway from Plaza de España (€32 with drink, €66-76 dinner and show, reasonable drink prices, shows daily at 19:00 and 21:00, 1.25 hours, corner of Calle de Ferraz and Cuesta de San Vicente at Plaza de España 9, +34 915 420 520, www.lastablasmadrid.com).

**More Flamenco:** Regardless of what your hotel receptionist may tell you, other flamenco places—such as Arco de Cuchilleros (Calle de los Cuchilleros 7), Café de Chinitas (Calle Torija 7, just off Plaza Mayor), Corral de la Morería (Calle de Morería 17), and Torres Bermejas (off Gran Vía)—are filled with tourists and pushy waiters.

### Mesones

These long, skinny, cave-like bars, famous for customers drinking and singing late into the night, line the lane called Cava de San Miguel, just west of Plaza Mayor. If you were to toss lowbrow barflies, Spanish karaoke, electric keyboards, crass tourists, cheap sangria, and greasy calamari into a late-night blender and turn it on, this is what you'd get. They're generally lively only on Friday and Saturday.

## Rooftop Bars

Madrid has several great rooftop bars, offering slightly overpriced drinks with views over the sprawling city center. At most of these, you'll pay €5 for a beer or wine, and €8-10 for a cocktail. This can be fun either by day, or in the cool of the late evening. Here are a few good options: To be right in the heart of the action, **Taberna Puertalsol** sits atop the El Corte Inglés department store right on Puerta del Sol; just head into the store and ride the elevator to Floor 5 (daily 12:30-late, Puerta del Sol 10). The classic **Círculo de Bellas Artes** skyscraper is capped with the Azotea cocktail bar, offering reasonably priced drinks overlooking the start of Gran Vía (€5 to ride the elevator; described on page 37). Near the Plaza de España end of Gran Vía, the **Dear Madrid** hotel has a rooftop bar—called "Nice to Meet You"—on its 14th floor (Gran Vía 80). If you're seeking untouristy ambience rather than views, head to the Chueca district, where the locals-packed **Mercado de San Antón** has a fine rooftop bar (market described on page 113). Just north of the Prado, the Palacio de Cibeles (City Hall) has a sixth-floor **Terrace Cibeles;** it feels a little swankier, with lesser views (see page 103).

## Bars and Jazz

If you're just picking up speed at midnight and looking for a place filled with old tiles and a Gen-X crowd, power into **Bar Viva Madrid** (daily 13:00-late, downhill from Plaza Santa Ana at Calle Manuel Fernández y González 7, +34 914 293 640). The same street has other bars filled with music. Or hike on over to Chocolatería San Ginés (described on page 113) for a dessert of *churros con chocolate.*

For live jazz, **Café Central** is the old town favorite. Since 1982 it's been known as the place where rising stars get their start (€15, nightly at 21:00—reserve online, stop by to reserve your table, or come early to score one of the unreserved seats by the bar, food and drinks available, great scene, Plaza del Ángel 10, +34 913 694 143, www.cafecentralmadrid.com).

## Movies

Movies in Spain remain about the most often dubbed in Europe. To see a movie with its original soundtrack, look for "V.O." (meaning "original version") or *V.O.S.E.* ("original version subtitled in *español*"). **Cine Ideal,** with nine screens, is a good place for the latest films in V.O. (assigned seats during most days and showings, good to get tickets early on weekends, 5-minute walk south of Puerta

**MADRID**

del Sol at Calle del Dr. Cortezo 6, +34 913 692 518 for info, www.yelmocines.es). For extensive listings, see the *Guía del Ocio* entertainment guide (described on page 9) or a local newspaper.

# Sleeping in Madrid

Madrid has plenty of centrally located budget hotels and *pensiones*. Most of the accommodations I've listed are within a few minutes' walk of Puerta del Sol.

You should be able to find a sleepable double for €70, a good double for €100, and a modern, air-conditioned double with all the comforts for €150. Prices vary dramatically throughout the year at bigger hotels, but remain about the same for the smaller hotels and *hostales*. It's almost always easy to find a place. Anticipate full hotels only in May (the San Isidro festival, celebrating Madrid's patron saint with bullfights and zarzuelas—especially around his feast day on May 15), around Easter, during LGBT Pride Week at the end of June, and in September (when conventions can clog the city). During the hot months of July and August, prices can be soft—ask for a discount.

With all of Madrid's street noise, I'd request the highest floor possible. Cheaper places have very thin walls and doors, so you might get noise from inside and outside (pack earplugs). Twin-bedded rooms are generally a bit larger than double-bedded rooms for the same price. During slow times, drop-ins can often score a room in business-class hotels for just a few euros more than the budget hotels. Breakfast is generally not offered—when it is, it's often expensive (about €15; see the sidebar for breakfast options).

## MIDRANGE AND FANCIER PLACES

These mostly business-class hotels are good values for those wanting more comfort and amenities than *hostales* offer. Their formal prices may be inflated, but most offer weekend and summer discounts when it's slow. Drivers pay about €24 a day in garages.

### Near Puerta del Sol and Gran Vía

These hotels are located in and around the pedestrian zone north and west of Puerta del Sol. Use Metro: Sol for these listings unless noted otherwise.

**$$$$ Hotel Liabeny** feels like a grand Old World hotel, with a marble-and-wood lobby, an eager-to-please concierge, and 213 plush, spacious, business-class rooms offering all the comforts (aircon, elevator, sauna, gym, off Plaza del Carmen at Salud 3, +34 915 319 000, www.liabeny.es, reservas@hotelliabeny.com).

**$$$$ Hotel Ópera,** with 79 classy rooms, is located just off Plaza de Isabel II, a four-block walk from Puerta del Sol toward the

Royal Palace (RS%, includes breakfast, air-con, elevator, sauna and gym, ask for a higher floor—there are nine—to avoid street noise, Cuesta de Santo Domingo 2, Metro: Ópera, +34 915 412 800, www.hotelopera.com, reservas@hotelopera.com). Hotel Ópera's cafeteria is deservedly popular. If you're here on a weekend, consider their "musical dinners"—great operetta music with a delightful dinner (around €60, Fri-Sat at 21:30, reservations smart, call +34 915 426 382 or reserve at hotel).

**$$$ Hotel Intur Palacio San Martín** is perfectly tucked away from the hustle of the center next to the Descalzas Royal Monastery. It has a beautiful atrium lounge with a vertical garden and 94 comfortable rooms combining modern flair with respect for tradition (air-con, elevator, Plaza San Martín 5, +34 917 015 000, www.hotel-inturpalaciosanmartin.com, sanmartin@intur.com).

**$$$ Hotel H10 Villa de la Reina,** filling a former bank building right along the pulsing Gran Vía, has an elegant, early-20th-century drawing-room lobby and 74 rooms (air-con, elevator, Gran Vía 22, +34 915 239 101, www.h10hotels.com, H10.villa.delareina@H10hotels.com).

**$$$ Hotel Preciados,** a four-star business hotel, has 100 welcoming, modern rooms as well as elegant lounges. It's well located and reasonably priced for the luxury it provides (free mini-bar, air-con, elevator, pay parking, just off Plaza de Santo Domingo at Calle Preciados 37, Metro: Callao, +34 914 544 400, www.preciadoshotel.com, preciadoshotel@preciadoshotel.com).

**$$$ Hotel Francisco I** is on a lively pedestrian street midway between the Royal Theater and Puerta del Sol. It has a mod lobby and 93 rooms (air-con, elevator, Calle del Arenal 15, +34 915 480 204, www.hotelfrancisco.com, info@hotelfrancisco.com).

**$$ Hotel Europa,** with sleek marble, red carpet runners along the halls, happy Muzak charm, and an attentive staff, is a solid value. It rents 100 squeaky-clean rooms, many with balconies overlooking the pedestrian zone or an inner courtyard. The hotel has an honest ethos and offers a straight price (family rooms, air-con, elevator, Calle del Carmen 4, +34 915 212 900, www.hoteleuropa.eu, info@hoteleuropa.eu, run by Antonio and Fernando Garaban and their helpful and jovial staff, Javi, Jim, and Tomás. The recommended **$$ Restaurante-Cafeteria Europa** is a lively and convivial scene—fun for breakfast.

**$$ Hotel Moderno,** renting 90 rooms, has a quiet, professional, and friendly atmosphere. There's a comfy first-floor lounge and a convenient location close to Puerta del Sol (air-con, elevator, Calle del Arenal 2, +34 915 310 900, www.hotel-moderno.com, info@hotel-moderno.com).

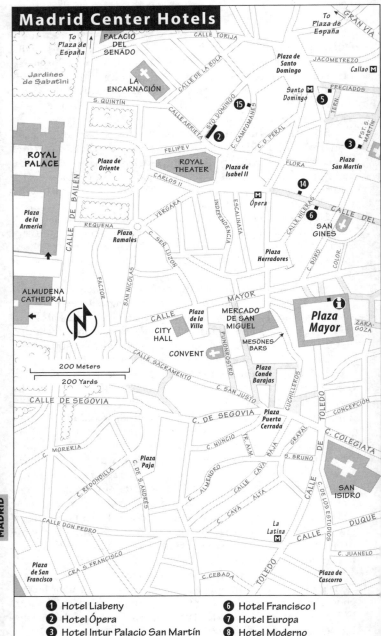

# Madrid Center Hotels

To Plaza de España

To Plaza de España

To GRAN VÍA

PALACIO DEL SENADO

CALLE TORIJA

JACOMETREZO

Callao Ⓜ

PRECIADOS

Plaza de Santo Domingo

Jardines de Sabatini

LA ENCARNACIÓN

S. QUINTÍN

CALLE DE LA BOLA

Santo Domingo Ⓜ

❺

TERN.

PST. S. MARTÍN

❸

CALLE ARRIETA

STO. DOMINGO

❶❺

C. CAMPOMANES

C. D. PERAL

Plaza de Oriente

FELIPE V

ROYAL PALACE

CARLOS II

ROYAL THEATER

Plaza de Isabel II

FLORA

Plaza San Martín

Plaza de la Armería

CALLE DE BAILÉN

REQUENA

Plaza Ramales

C. SER. LUZÓN

VERGARA

INDEPENDENCIA

ESCALINATA

Ópera Ⓜ

❶❹

CALLE VIERAS

❻

SAN GINÉS

CALLE DEL

ALMUDENA CATHEDRAL

FACTOR

SAN NICOLÁS

Plaza Herradores

C. BORD.

COLOR.

Ⓝ

200 Meters

200 Yards

CALLE

CALLE SACRAMENTO

CITY HALL

Plaza de la Villa

CONVENT

MERCADO DE SAN MIGUEL

MESONES BARS

MAYOR

FUNONCOSTRO

Plaza Conde Barajas

Ⓘ Plaza Mayor

ZARAGOZA

CALLE DE SEGOVIA

C. SAN JUSTO

C. DE SEGOVIA

Plaza Puerta Cerrada

CUCHILLEROS

TOLEDO

CONCEPCIÓN

C. MORERÍA

C. NUNCIO

FR. ALM.

GRAFAL

C. COLEGIATA

Plaza Paja

C. REDONDILLA

C. DE S. ANDRÉS

C. ALMENDRO

CALLE CAVA BAJA

S. BRUNO

CALLE CAVA ALTA

C. DE LOS ESTUDIOS

SAN ISIDRO

CALLE DON PEDRO

CRA. S. FRANCISCO

C. CEBADA

La Latina Ⓜ

CALLE

DUQUE

C. JUANELO

Plaza de San Francisco

TOLEDO

Plaza de Cascorro

❶ Hotel Liabeny
❷ Hotel Ópera
❸ Hotel Intur Palacio San Martín
❹ Hotel H10 Villa de la Reina
❺ Hotel Preciados

❻ Hotel Francisco I
❼ Hotel Europa
❽ Hotel Moderno
❾ Petit Palace Posada del Peine

MADRID

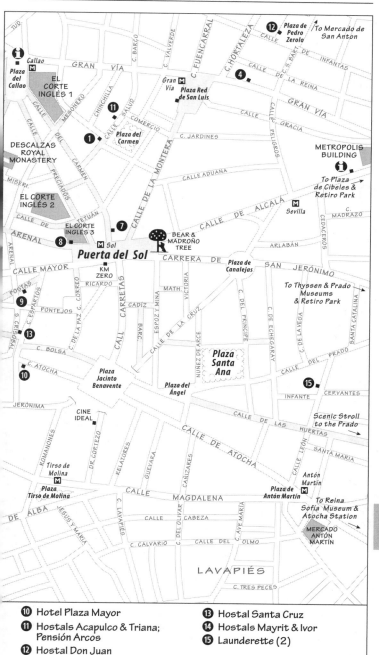

**10** Hotel Plaza Mayor

**11** Hostals Acapulco & Triana; Pensión Arcos

**12** Hostal Don Juan

**13** Hostal Santa Cruz

**14** Hostals Mayrit & Ivor

**15** Launderette (2)

MADRID

## Near Plaza Mayor

Both of these are in a bustling area a block off Plaza Mayor.

**$$$ Petit Palace Posada del Peine** feels like part of a big, modern chain (which it is), but fills its well-located old building with fresh, efficient character. Behind the ornate Old World facade is a comfortable business-class hotel with 67 rooms (air-con, elevator, Calle Postas 17, +34 915 238 151, www.petitpalace.com, posadadelpeine@petitpalace.com).

**$$ Hotel Plaza Mayor,** with 41 solidly outfitted rooms, is tastefully decorated and beautifully situated a block off Plaza Mayor. It occupies an enticing middle ground between pricey business-class hotels and the basic *hostales* (air-con, elevator, Calle de Atocha 2, +34 913 600 606, www.hotel-bb.es, hotel.plazamayor@hotelbb.com).

## Near the Prado

For locations, see the "Madrid's Museum Neighborhood" map on page 54.

**$$$$ DoubleTree by Hilton Prado** has the predictable class of an American chain, but feels more like a European boutique hotel—with 61 rooms, an attentive staff, and a handy location tucked down a quieter side street near the Prado (air-con, elevator, Calle San Agustín 3, +34 913 600 820, www.doubletree3.hilton.com).

**$$$ Mercure Madrid Centro Hotel Lope de Vega** offers good business-class hotel value near the Prado. It is a "cultural-themed" hotel inspired by 17th-century writer Lope de Vega. With 59 rooms, it feels cozy and friendly for a formal hotel (family rooms, air-con, elevator, very limited pay parking—reserve ahead, Calle Lope de Vega 49, +34 913 600 011, www.accor.com, H9618@accor.com).

## CHEAP SLEEPS
## Near Puerta del Sol

The first three listings are in the same building at Calle de la Salud 13, north of Puerta del Sol. The building overlooks Plaza del Carmen—a little square with a sleepy, almost Parisian ambience. The last listing, Hostal Don Juan, is a stone's throw from Gran Vía at the top of Calle de la Montera, which some dislike because of the prostitutes who hang out here, though the zone is otherwise safe and comfortable.

**$ Hostal Acapulco,** a cheery oasis, rents 16 bright rooms with a professional, hotelesque feel. The neighborhood is quiet enough that it's smart to request a room with a balcony (family room, air-con, elevator, fourth floor, reasonable laundry service, overnight luggage storage, parking—reserve ahead, +34 915 311 945, www.

## Breakfast in Madrid

Many hotels don't include (or even offer) breakfast, so you may be out on the streets first thing looking for a place to eat. Nontouristy cafés only offer a hot drink and a pastry, with perhaps a potato omelet and sandwiches (toasted cheese, ham, or both). I like **Restaurante-Cafeteria Europa** just off Puerta del Sol for its classic breakfast scene, with a long bar, plenty of locals, and an easy-access menu (described on page 111). Touristy places will have a *desayuno* menu with various ham-and-eggs deals. Try *churros* at least once (see the listings on page 113 for my favorite places); if you're not in the mood for heavy chocolate in the morning, go local and dip your *churros* in a *café con leche*. If all else fails, a Starbucks is often nearby (just like home). Get advice from your hotel staff for their favorite breakfast place. My typical breakfast, found at any corner bar: *café con leche*, *tortilla española* (a slice of potato omelet), and *zumo de naranja natural* (fresh-squeezed orange juice).

hostalacapulco.com, hostal_acapulco@yahoo.es, Ana, Marco, and Javier).

**$ Hostal Triana,** also a good deal, is bigger—with 40 rooms—and offers a little less charm for a little less money (most rooms have air-con, others have fans; elevator and some stairs, first floor, +34 915 326 812, www.hostaltriana.com, triana@hostaltriana.com, Victor González).

**¢ Pensión Arcos** is tiny, granny-run, and old-fashioned—it's been in the Hernández family since 1936. You must reserve by phone (in Spanish) and pay in cash—but its five rooms are clean, extra quiet, and served by an elevator. You also have access to a tiny roof terrace and a nice little lounge. For cheap beds in a great locale, this place is unbeatable (cheaper rooms with shared bath, air-con, closed Aug, fifth floor, +34 915 324 994, Anuncia and Sabino speak only Spanish).

**$ Hostal Don Juan** sits on a quiet-by-day, busy-by-night square just off the Gran Vía in the beginning of the Chueca neighborhood. Its 44 rooms are sleek and modern, contrasting with the Baroque explosion of varnish and gold in the common areas. It's a charmingly run time warp (air-con, elevator, Plaza Pedro Zerolo 1—former Plaza Vázquez de Mella, second floor, +34 915 223 101, hshostaldonjuan@gmail.com).

### Near Plaza Mayor
**$ Hostal Santa Cruz,** simple and well-located, has 16 rooms at a good price (air-con, elevator, Plaza de Santa Cruz 6, sec-

MADRID

ond floor, +34 915 222 441, www.hostalsantacruz.com, info@ hostalsantacruz.com).

**$ Hostal Mayrit** and **Hostal Ivor** rent 28 rooms with thoughtful touches on pedestrianized Calle del Arenal. It's in a very handy location, so prices are at the higher end of this range (air-con, elevator, near Metro: Ópera at Calle del Arenal 24, reception on third floor, +34 915 480 403, www.hostalivor.com, reservas@hostalivor.com).

### Near the Prado

For locations, see the "Madrid's Museum Neighborhood" map on page 54.

**$$ Urban Sea Hotel Atocha 113** is a basic but contemporary option with 36 minimalist, well-worn rooms between the Prado and the Reina Sofía, near the Atocha train station (small rooftop terrace, self-service snacks, Calle de Atocha 113, +34 913 692 895, www.blueseahotels.com, recepcionatocha@blueseahotels.es).

**$ Hostal Gonzalo** has 15 basic but comfortable rooms. Well-run by friendly and helpful Javier and Antonio, it's popular with European budget travelers (air-con, elevator, Cervantes 34, third floor, Metro: Antón Martín—but not handy to Metro, +34 914 292 714, www.hostalgonzalo.com, hostal@hostalgonzalo.com).

# Eating in Madrid

In Spain, only Barcelona and the Basque Country rival Madrid for taste-bud thrills. You have three dining choices: a memorable, atmospheric sit-down meal in a well-chosen restaurant; a forgettable, basic sit-down meal; or a meal of tapas at a bar or two...or four. Unless otherwise noted, restaurants start serving lunch at 13:00 or 13:30 and dinner around 20:30. Depending on what time you show up, the same place may seem forlorn, touristy, or thriving with local eaters. Many restaurants close in August. Madrid has famously good tap water, and waiters willingly serve it free—just ask for *agua del grifo*. Restaurants and bars in Spain are smoke-free inside, but lighting up is allowed in outdoor seating areas.

I've broken my recommended choices into groups: serious dining establishments, tapas places, and simple, economical venues. For suggestions on where to eat near the Royal Palace, Prado, and Reina Sofía, see their individual sight listings.

### FINE DINING

**$$$$ Restaurante Casa Paco** feels simple, even basic, but it's a Madrid tradition. Check out its old walls plastered with autographed photos of Spanish celebrities who have enjoyed their signature dish—ox grilled over a coal fire. Though popular with tourists, the place is authentic, confident, and uncompromising. It's a worthwhile splurge if you want to dine out well and carnivorously (Tue-Sat 13:00-16:00 & 20:00-24:00, Sun 13:00-16:00, closed Mon, Plaza de la Puerta Cerrada 11, +34 913 663 166).

**$$$$ Sobrino del Botín** is a hit with many Americans because "Hemingway ate here." It's grotesquely touristy, pricey, and the last place "Papa" would go now...but still, people love it and go for the roast suckling pig, their specialty. I'd eat upstairs for a still-traditional but airier atmosphere (daily 13:00-16:00 & 20:00-24:00, a block downhill from Plaza Mayor at Cuchilleros 17, +34 913 664 217, www.botin.es).

**$$$$ Casa Lucio** is a favorite splurge for traditional specialties among power-dressing Madrileños. Juan Carlos and Sofía, the former king and queen of Spain, eat in this formal place, but it's accessible to commoners. This is a good restaurant for a special night out and a full-blown meal, but you pay extra for this place's fame (daily 13:00-16:00 & 20:30-24:00, closed Aug, Calle Cava Baja 35; unless you're the king or queen, reserve several days in advance—and don't even bother on weekends; +34 913 653 252, www.casalucio.es).

**$$$$ Restaurante Palacio de Cibeles,** with a dress-up interior on the sixth floor of the Palacio de Cibeles (City Hall), features an outdoor terrace with spectacular views, an extensive wine list, and a creative, seasonal Spanish menu (daily 13:00-16:00 & 20:00-24:00, Plaza de Cibeles 1—see map on page 54, +34 915 231 454, http://palaciodecibeles.com). The neighboring and swanky **$$$ Terrace Cibeles** serves drinks and pricey light bites on its outdoor terrace late into the night (open only in good weather, daily 13:00-24:00). The second-floor **$$ Colección Cibeles** offers a simplified and less-expensive version of Restaurante Palacio's fare (€15 fixed-price meal, daily 10:00-24:00).

**$$$ El Caldero** ("The Pot") is a romantic spot and a good place for paella and other rice dishes. A classy, in-the-know crowd appreciates its subdued elegance and crisp service. The house specialty, *arroz al caldero* (a variation on paella), is served with panache from a cauldron hanging from a tripod. Most of the formal rice dishes come in pots for two. Wash it all down with the house sangria (Tue-Sat 13:30-16:30 & 20:30-24:00, Sun-Mon 13:30-16:30, Calle de las Huertas 15, +34 914 295 044).

**$$$$ La Bola Taberna,** touristy but friendly, cozy, and tastefully elegant, specializes in *cocido Madrileño*—Madrid stew. The stew, made of various meats, carrots, and garbanzo beans in earthen jugs, is a winter dish, prepared here for the tourists all year. It's served as two courses: First enjoy the broth as a soup, then dig into the meat and veggies. Curious about how it's made? Ask to take a peek in the kitchen. Reservations are smart (cash only, daily lunch seatings at 13:30 and 15:30, Mon-Sat dinner 20:30-23:00, closed Sun for dinner, midway between Royal Palace and Gran Vía at Calle Bola 5, +34 915 476 930, http://labola.es).

**Treating Tapas Bars as Restaurants:** Of the many recommended *tabernas* and tapas bars listed next, several have tables and menus that lend themselves to fine dining. If you don't mind the commotion of the nearby bar action, you can order high on the menu in these places and, I'd say, eat better and more economically than in the more formal restaurants listed earlier.

## TAPAS BAR-HOPPING

For maximum fun, people, and atmosphere, go mobile for dinner: Do the *tapeo*, a local tradition of going from one bar to the next, munching, drinking, and socializing. If done properly, a pub crawl can be a highlight of your trip. Before embarking upon this culinary adventure, study and use the tapas tips in the Practicalities chapter. Try speaking a little Spanish: You'll get a much better (and less expensive) experience. While tiny tapas plates are standard in Andalucía, these days most of Madrid's bars offer bigger plates for around €6 (vegetables) to €15 (fish). Called *raciones*, these are ideal for a small group to share. The real action begins late (around 21:00). While the energy is fun and local later in the evening, you may find it easier to get service and a spot by dining earlier—which is still late by American standards.

You'll occasionally find a bar that gives a free tapa to anyone ordering a drink, but it's a dying tradition in Madrid. If the bartender brings you one, consider it a bonus. To improve your odds, begin by ordering just a drink and see if something comes free. Once you get it (or don't), order additional food as you like.

There are tapas bars almost everywhere, but two areas in the city center are particularly rewarding for a bar-crawl meal: **Calle de Jesús** (near the Prado) is the easiest, with several wonderful and diverse places in a two-block row, while trendy **Calle Cava Baja** has fancier offerings and feels most energetic. A third area, between **Puerta del Sol** and **Plaza Santa Ana,** is more central but overrun with tourists.

## The Great Tapas Row on Calle de Jesús

This two-block stretch of tapas bars across the boulevard from the Prado offers a variety of fun places (for location, see the "Madrid's Museum Neighborhood" map on page 54). While the offerings are pretty similar, each has its own personality. Most have chaotic bars in front and small and inviting sections with tables in back. Make the circuit and eyeball each place to see which appeals—you'll see that there's no reason to spend all your time and appetite at your first stop. Calle de Jesús stretches between Calle de Cervantes and Calle de las Huertas, behind the Palace Hotel. In the middle is the Plaza de Jesús, so named because this is the location of the Basilica of Jesús de Medinaceli (home to a relic that attracts huge crowds of pilgrims on special days). Start near the church at the first recommended bar, Cervecería Cervantes. These places are generally open every day for long hours.

**$$ Cervecería Cervantes** serves hearty *raciones,* specializes in octopus, and has both a fine bar and good restaurant seating (intersection of Plaza de Jesús and Calle de Cervantes, +34 914 296 093).

**$$ Taberna de la Daniela Medinaceli,** part of a local chain, is popular for its specialty *cocido madrileño*—a rich chickpea-based soup. It has a lovely dining area if you want to settle in for a while (Plaza de Jesús 7, +34 913 896 238).

**$$ La Dolores,** with a rustic little dining area, has been a hit since 1908 and is still extremely popular. Its canapés are listed on the wall (Plaza de Jesús 4, +34 914 292 243).

**$$ Cervezas La Fabrica** packs in seafood lovers at the bar; a quieter back room is available for those preferring a table. Prices are the same in both spots. They serve a nice *cava* (Spanish sparkling wine), which goes well with seafood (Calle de Jesús 2, +34 913 690 671).

**$$ Cervecería Los Gatos** is a kaleidoscope of Spanish culture, with chandeliers swinging above wine barrels in the intense bar area and characteristic tables in the more peaceful zone behind (Calle de Jesús 2, +34 914 293 067).

**$$$ Taberna Maceira,** perhaps the best of the bunch, feels like Northern Spain. It's a Galician place with a wonderfully woody and rustic energy. A sit-down restaurant (not a bar), it specializes in octopus, cod, *pimientos de Padrón*, and *caldo gallego* (white bean soup)—all classic Galician specialties of northwest Spain. The *We're out of Coca-Cola (no hay Coca-Cola)* sign is up every single day (Mon-Sat 13:00-16:00 & 20:30-24:00, closed Sun, Calle de Jesús 7, +34 914 291 584).

## Tapas on Calle Cava Baja

A few minutes' walk south of Plaza Mayor, Calle Cava Baja fills each evening with a young, professional crowd prowling for chic tapas and social fun. Come at night only and treat the entire street as a destination. I've listed a few standards, but excellent new eateries are always opening up. For a good, authentic Madrid dinner experience, survey the options, then choose your favorites.

# Madrid Center Restaurants

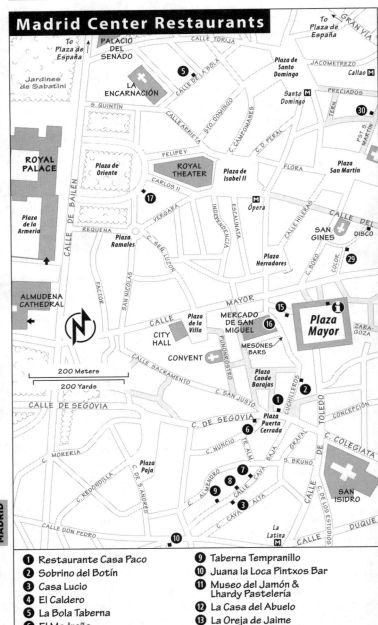

- ❶ Restaurante Casa Paco
- ❷ Sobrino del Botín
- ❸ Casa Lucio
- ❹ El Caldero
- ❺ La Bola Taberna
- ❻ El Madroño
- ❼ Txakolina Pintxoteca Madrileña
- ❽ Taberna Los Huevos de Lucio
- ❾ Taberna Tempranillo
- ❿ Juana la Loca Pintxos Bar
- ⓫ Museo del Jamón & Lhardy Pastelería
- ⓬ La Casa del Abuelo
- ⓭ La Oreja de Jaime
- ⓮ Casa Toni
- ⓯ Casa Rúa
- ⓰ Mercado de San Miguel

MADRID

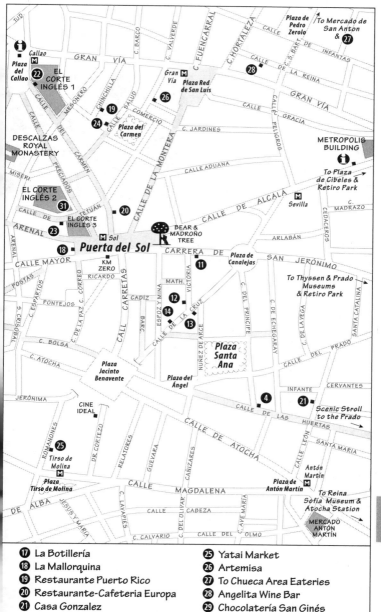

**MADRID**

17  La Botillería
18  La Mallorquina
19  Restaurante Puerto Rico
20  Restaurante-Cafeteria Europa
21  Casa Gonzalez
22  El Corte Inglés Cafeteria
23  Casa Labra Taberna Restaurante
24  Takos Al Pastor

25  Yatai Market
26  Artemisa
27  To Chueca Area Eateries
28  Angelita Wine Bar
29  Chocolatería San Ginés
30  Chocolaterías Valor
31  El Corte Inglés Supermarket

Remember, it's easier and touristy early, and jammed with locals later. (For a formal dining experience on this street, come early and pick a place you like with tables in the back, or see the places recommended under "Fine Dining," earlier. Taberna Tempranillo or Juana la Loca would be my first choices.)

These tapas bars, listed in the order you'll reach them as you walk from Plaza Mayor up Calle Cava Baja, are worth special consideration.

**$$$ El Madroño** ("The Berry Tree," a symbol of Madrid), more of a cowboy bar, serves all the clichés. If Knott's Berry Farm was Spanish, this would be its restaurant. Preserving a bit of old Madrid, a tile copy of Velázquez's famous *Drinkers* grins from its facade. Inside, look above the stairs for photos of 1902 Madrid. Study the coats of arms of Madrid through the centuries as you try a *vermut* (vermouth) on tap. Or ask for a small glass *(chupito)* of the *licor de madroño*. Indoor seating is bright and colorful; the sidewalk tables come with good people-watching. Munch *raciones* at the bar or front tables to be in the fun scene, or have a quieter sit-down meal at the tables in the back (daily 8:00-24:00, a block off the top of Calle Cava Baja at Plaza de la Puerta Cerrada 7, +34 913 645 629).

**$$ Txakolina Pintxoteca Madrileña** is a thriving bar and is one of a handful on this street serving elaborately composed, Basque-style *pinchos* (fancy open-faced sandwiches—*pintxo* in Basque) to a young crowd. If you won't make it to San Sebastián, this place offers a decent approximation (Calle Cava Baja 26, +34 913 664 877).

**$$ Taberna Los Huevos de Lucio,** owned by the same family as the reputable Casa Lucio (described under "Fine Dining," earlier), is a jam-packed bar serving good tapas, salads, *huevos estrellados* (fried eggs over fried potatoes), and wine. For a sit-down meal, head to the tables in the back (avoid the basement, Calle Cava Baja 30, +34 913 662 984).

**$$ Taberna Tempranillo,** ideal for hungry wine lovers, offers fancy tapas and fine wine by the glass (see the board or ask for their English menu). While there are a few tables, the bar is just right for hanging out. With a spirit of adventure, use their fascinating menu to assemble your dream meal. When I order high on their menu, I'm generally very happy (closed Aug, Calle Cava Baja 38, +34 913 641 532).

**$$ Juana la Loca Pintxos Bar** ("Crazy Juana") overlooks a lonely square at the top end of Calle Cava Baja (on the left). It feels more sophisticated and civilized, with elegant *raciones,* refined-yet-tight seating, gorgeously presented dishes from a foodie menu, and reasonable prices considering the quality. Their classic is the runny *tortilla de patatas* with piles of decadently caramelized onions. To settle in for a sit-down meal, arrive early to snare a table (Plaza Puerta de Moros 4, +34 913 665 500).

## Central Pub-Crawl Tapas Route

The little streets between Puerta del Sol, San Jerónimo, and Plaza Santa Ana are submerged in a flood of tourism. But they're also very central...and hold some tasty surprises. If you can get past the touristy trappings, this loop offers a handy, no-brainer intro to Spanish tapa-hopping.

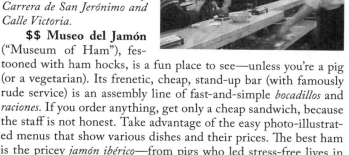

• *Start at the intersection of Carrera de San Jerónimo and Calle Victoria.*

    **$$ Museo del Jamón** ("Museum of Ham"), festooned with ham hocks, is a fun place to see—unless you're a pig (or a vegetarian). Its frenetic, cheap, stand-up bar (with famously rude service) is an assembly line of fast-and-simple *bocadillos* and *raciones.* If you order anything, get only a cheap sandwich, because the staff is not honest. Take advantage of the easy photo-illustrated menus that show various dishes and their prices. The best ham is the pricey *jamón ibérico*—from pigs who led stress-free lives in acorn-strewn valleys. Point clearly to what you want, and be very specific to avoid being served a pricier meal than you intended. For a small sandwich, ask for a *chiquito* (daily 9:00-24:00, air-con).

• *Across the street is the touristy and overpriced bull bar,* **La Taurina.** *(I wouldn't eat here, but you're welcome to ponder the graphic photos that celebrate the gory art of bullfighting.) Next door, take a detour from your pub crawl with something more suited to grandmothers.*

    **$$ Lhardy Pastelería** offers a genteel taste of Old World charm in this district of rowdy pubs. This peaceful time warp has been a fixture since 1839 for Madrileños wanting to duck in for a cup of consommé or a light snack. Step right in, and pretend you're an aristocrat back between the wars. Serve yourself. Pay as you leave (on the honor system). Help yourself to the silver water dispenser (free), a line of elegant bottles (each a different Iberian fortified wine: sherry, port, and so on), a revolving case of meaty little pastries, and a fancy soup dispenser (chicken broth consommé, try it with a splash of sherry...local style—bottles in the corner, help yourself; Mon-Sat 10:00-22:00, Sun until 15:00; Carrera de

San Jerónimo 8, +34 915 222 207). A very classy **$$$$** dinner-only restaurant hides upstairs.

• *Next, forage up Calle Victoria. The bars on this street and nearby lanes offer bloated prices and all the clichés. Near the end of the street, you'll find...*

**$$ La Casa del Abuelo** serves sizzling plates of tasty little *gambas* (shrimp) and *langostinos* (prawns), with bread to sop up the delightful juices. Try *gambas a la plancha* (grilled shrimp) or *gambas al ajillo* (ah-HEE-yoh, a small clay dish of shrimp cooked in oil and garlic that'll burn the roof of your mouth if you're not careful). Wash it down with a glass of sweet red house wine (Calle Victoria 12). The original, characteristic, stand-up bar is on the right side of the street; their sit-down annex is on the left.

• *Just beyond, at the intersection with Calle de la Cruz, is...*

**$$ La Oreja de Jaime** is known for its sautéed pigs' ears *(oreja)*. While pig ears are a Madrid dish (fun to try, hard to swallow), this place is Galician—they serve *pimientos de Padrón* and the distinctive *ribeiro* (ree-BAY-roh) wine, served Galician-style, in characteristic little ceramic bowls to disguise its lack of clarity (Calle de la Cruz 12).

• *A few steps up Calle de la Cruz on the right is...*

**$$ Casa Toni** is good for classic dishes like *patatas bravas* (fried potatoes in a spicy sauce), *berenjena* (deep-fried slices of eggplant), *champiñones* (sautéed mushrooms), and gazpacho—the cold tomato-and-garlic soup that is generally served only during the hot season, but available here year-round just for tourists like you (Calle de la Cruz 14).

## EATING REASONABLY
### On or near Plaza Mayor

Madrileños enjoy a bite to eat on Plaza Mayor (without its high costs) by grabbing food to go from a nearby bar and just planting themselves somewhere on the square to eat (squid sandwiches are popular). But for many tourists, dinner at a sidewalk café right on Plaza Mayor is worth the premium price (consider Cervecería Pulpito, southwest corner of the square at #10).

**Calamari Sandwiches:** Plaza Mayor is famous for its *bocadillos de calamares*. For a tasty squid-ring sandwich, line up at **$ Casa Rúa** at Plaza Mayor's northwest corner, a few steps up Calle Ciudad Rodrigo. Hanging up behind the bar is a photo-advertisement of Plaza Mayor from the 1950s, when the square contained a park (daily 11:00-23:00).

**$$ Mercado de San Miguel:** This early-20th-century market sparkles after a recent renovation and bustles with a trendy food circus of eateries (daily 10:00-24:00). While it's expensive, touristy, and often crowded, it's also fun and accessible. You can stroll while you munch, hang out at bars, or try to find a seat at one of the market's food-court-style tables. For tips on grazing here, see page 113.

**Facing the Royal Palace: $$$ La Botillería** is recommended mostly for its location next to the National Theater and overlooking Plaza de Oriente. It's a venerable and elegant (and expensive) opera-type café with fine tables on the square. The menu is quite expensive, but they have a decent €19 weekday lunch special (Plaza de Oriente 2, +34 915 484 620, www.botilleria.es, more interesting menu after 20:00).

## Near Puerta del Sol and Plaza Mayor

**$$ La Mallorquina** ("The Girl from Mallorca"), on the downhill end of Puerta del Sol, is a venerable pastry shop serving the masses at the bar (cheap *Napolitana* pastries and *rosquillas*—doughnuts) and takeout on the ground floor. But upstairs is a refined little 19th-century café—popular for generations. It offers an accessible menu and a relative oasis of quiet (daily 9:00-21:00, closed mid-July-Aug).

**$$ Restaurante Puerto Rico,** a simple, no-nonsense place, serves good meals for great prices to smart Madrileños in a long, congested hall (daily 13:00-24:00, Chinchilla 2, between Puerta del Sol and Gran Vía, +34 915 219 834).

**$$$ Restaurante-Cafeteria Europa** is a fun, high-energy scene with a mile-long bar, old-school waiters, local cuisine, and a fine €12 fixed-price lunch special (inside only). The menu lists three price levels: **bar** (inexpensive), **table** (pricey), or **terrace** (sky-high but with good people-watching). Your best value is to stick to the lunch menu if you're sitting inside, or order off the plastic *barra* menu if you sit at the bar—the ham-and-egg toast or the homemade *churros* make a nice breakfast (daily 7:00-24:00, next to Hotel Europa, 50 yards off Puerta del Sol at Calle del Carmen 4, +34 915 212 900).

**$$$ Casa Gonzalez** is a revered gourmet cheese-and-wine shop with a circa-1930s interior and friendly service. Away from the tourist scene, it offers a genteel opportunity to enjoy a first-class cheese plate and and glass of wine in a fun setting recalling the happy days of the Republic of Spain—after the monarchy but before Franco. Their €20 assortment of five Spanish cheeses—more than enough for two—is a cheese lover's treat (40 wines by the glass, Mon-Sat 9:30-24:00, Sun 11:30-17:00, Calle de León 12, +34 914 295 618, Francisco and Luciano).

**$$$ El Corte Inglés'** "**Gourmet Experience,**" a ninth-floor cafeteria, houses a specialty grocery mart and 10 mini restaurants with a wide range of cuisines—from burgers and Basque tapas to Mexican to Japanese. This snazzy and wildly popular complex is fresh, modern, and not particularly cheap. Take a seat at any of the indoor tables, or out on the open terrace—and ideally grab a table (inside or out) with a grand view over all of Madrid, from Gran Vía and Plaza de España to the Royal Palace (daily 10:00-24:00, in Building 1 at the top of Calle del Carmen, half a block below Plaza del Callao).

**$ Casa Labra Taberna Restaurante** is famous as the birthplace of the Spanish Socialist Party in 1879...and as a spot for great cod. Their tasty little *tajada de bacalao* dishes put them on the map. Packed with Madrileños, it manages to be both dainty and rustic. It's a wonderful scene with three distinct sections: the inexpensive stand-up **bar** (line up for cod and croquettes, power up to the bar for drinks); a peaceful little **sit-down area** in back (still cheap), and a fancy, more expensive **restaurant.** Consider the outdoor tables self-serve. The waiters are fun to joke around with (daily 11:00-15:30 & 18:00-23:00, a block off Puerta del Sol at Calle Tetuán 12, +34 915 310 081).

**$ Takos Al Pastor** is a hip, cheap, authentic taquería, which often has a long line out front (Tue-Sun 13:30-24:00, closed Mon, Calle de la Abada 2, mobile +34 680 247 217).

**Asian:** The trendy **$$ Yatai Market** food court gathers a variety of Asian street food counters under one roof—pad thai, sushi, ramen, bao steamed-bun sandwiches, and so on—with neon signs and shared tables (daily 12:00-24:00, just off Plaza de Tirso de Molina at Calle del Doctor Cortezo 10).

**Vegetarian: $$ Artemisa** is a hit with vegetarians and vegans who like good, healthy food without any hippie ambience (weekday lunch specials, open daily 13:30-16:00 & 20:30-23:30, north of Puerta del Sol at Tres Cruces 4, a few steps off Plaza del Carmen, +34 915 218 721).

## In the Chueca District

Chueca, just a short walk north of Gran Vía, in the past decade has gone from a sleazy no-go zone to a trendy and inviting neighborhood. Riding the Metro to the Chueca stop, you'll emerge right on Plaza de Chueca. The square feels like today's Madrid...without the tourism. A handful of places offer relaxing tables on the square, the neighborhood's San Antón market hall (Mercado de San Antón, just a block away) is now a fun food circus, and nearby streets hold plenty of hardworking, creative new eateries. Here are some good options:

**$$ Antigua Casa Angel Sierra Vermouth Bar** offers an old-time ambience that almost takes you back to 1917, when it opened. Belly up to the bar in its tight front room facing the square or, for more space, use the side entrance to reach a back room filled with giant barrels of vermouth and more spacious tables. They offer a simple menu of light, basic tapas—come here for the ambience, not the food (on Plaza de Chueca, Calle Gravina 11, +34 915 310 126).

**$$ Mercado de San Antón,** with three bustling floors of edible temptations, is flat-out fun for anyone who likes food (daily 10:00-late). There's a supermarket in the basement, and a produce-and-fish market on the ground floor. The first floor is a circle of tapas joints—ranging from Canary Islands to Japanese to veggie—with shared tables looking down on the market action and sample dishes on display for easy ordering. The top floor is a more formal restaurant—**$$$ La Cocina de San Antón** ("Kitchen of San Antón"). It's part of a modern chain whose forte is ham, and it has a nice rooftop terrace (Augusto Figueroa 24, +34 913 300 294).

**$$ Vinoteca Vides** is passionately run by Vicente, who offers a simple one-page list of small plates (finger food, ham, cheese) to go with a long list of quality wines sold by the €3-or-so glass (Mon-Thu 17:00-24:00, Fri-Sat 13:00-24:00, Sun 13:00-17:00, Calle Libertad 12, +34 915 318 444). If you're looking for a convivial bar, this is a great bet. And there are many enticing alternatives nearby.

**$$$ Angelita Wine Bar** is a dressy little restaurant with spacious seating, a short food menu designed to go with the wines, and a long list of wines by the glass. An elegant place for a fine meal, it draws a smart local crowd (Tue-Sat 13:30-17:00 & 20:30-24:00, Mon 20:30-24:00, closed Sun, 100 yards from Gran Vía Metro station at Calle de la Reina 4, +34 915 216 678).

### Churros con Chocolate

Those not watching their calories will want to try the deep-fried doughy treats called *churros* (or the thicker *porras*), best enjoyed by dipping them in pudding-like hot chocolate. Though many *choco-laterías* offer the dunkable fritters, *churros* are most delicious when consumed fresh out of the greasy cauldron at a place that actually fries them. Two Madrid favorites are near Puerta del Sol.

**Chocolatería San Ginés** is a classy institu-

MADRID

tion, beloved for a century by Madrileños for its *churros con choco-late*. While busy all day, it's packed after midnight; the popular dance club Joy Eslava is next door. Order at the counter, get a tick-et, find a seat, and give your ticket to the server who delivers your order (open 24 hours; from Puerta del Sol, take Calle del Arenal 2 blocks west and turn left on bookstore-lined Pasadizo de San Ginés—you'll see the café at #5, behind the big brick church; +34 913 656 546).

**Chocolaterías Valor,** a modern chain and Spanish chocolate maker, does *churros* with pride and gusto. A few minutes' walk from nearly all my hotel recommendations, it's a fine place for breakfast (daily 8:00-22:30, Fri-Sat until 24:00, a half-block below Plaza del Callao and Gran Vía at Postigo de San Martín 7, +34 915 229 288). You can also buy powdered Valor chocolate at **supermarkets** (like the one at El Corte Inglés Building 2) to make the drink at home.

# Madrid Connections

## BY TRAIN

Madrid has two main train stations: Chamartín and Atocha. Both stations offer long-distance trains *(largo recorridos)* as well as small-er local trains (*regionales* and *cercanías*) to nearby destinations.

**Buying Train Tickets:** Train station ticket counters can have long lines, especially during high season or holidays. Consider buy-ing tickets online or at travel agency. There's an El Corte Inglés travel agency at Atocha station (Mon-Fri 8:00-22:00, Sat 10:00-14:00, closed Sun, small fee, on ground floor of AVE side at the far end); you'll also find travel agencies at the El Corte Inglés depart-ment store (see the listing in the "Shopping in Madrid" section, earlier) and at the airport.

**Train Information:** +34 912 320 320, www.renfe.com.

## Chamartín Station

The TI is near track 20. The impressively large information, tick-ets, and customer-service office is at track 11. You can relax in the Sala VIP Club if you have a first-class rail pass and first-class seat or sleeper reservations (between tracks 13 and 14, cooler of free drinks). Baggage storage *(consigna)* is across the street, opposite track 17. The station's Metro stop is also called Chamartín (not "Pinar de Chamartín"). Train connections from here are listed later.

## Atocha Station

The station is split in two: the AVE side (mostly long-distance trains) and the *cercanías* side (mostly local trains to the suburbs—called *cercanías*—and the Metro for connecting into downtown). The two parts are connected by a corridor of shops and eateries.

Each side has separate schedules and customer-service offices. The station's Metro stop is called Atocha Renfe.

**Ticket Offices:** The *cercanías* side has two offices—a small one for local trains and a big one for major trains (such as AVE).

The AVE side has a pleasant, airy office that sells tickets for AVE and other long-distance trains. In the ticket hall, there are three types of sales points: *venta anticipada* (tickets in advance), *salida inmediata* (immediate departures—only tickets for certain designated trains, leaving soon, can be purchased here), and *salidas hoy* (departures today,

but only for certain destinations—for example, Toledo). When you enter the ticket office, grab a number from a machine. If the line at one office is long, check the other offices. Ticket machines in the ticket office and scattered around the station usually don't work with American credit cards.

**AVE Side:** Located in the cavernous old brick station building, the AVE area boasts a lush, tropical garden filling its grand hall. It's used by AVE trains and other fast trains (Grandes Líneas). Here you'll find a customer service and information office (under the escalators), a spacious ticket office (facing the garden, on the right side), a long-hours pharmacy (just past the ticket office), a handful of cafés and restaurants, and a pay WC. Baggage storage *(consignas)* is at the far end of the garden. Be clear on which level to catch your train: Some departures leave from the lower level (*planta baja* on departure boards); others leave from the "first floor" (*plta. primera,* ride up the escalators or elevators). Within the first-floor departure zone (past security) is the Club AVE/Sala VIP lounge for AVE business-class travelers and for first-class ticket holders or Eurailers with a first-class reservation (free drinks, newspapers, showers, and info service).

**Cercanías Side:** This is where you'll find the local *cercanías* trains, *regionales* trains, some eastbound faster trains, and the Atocha Renfe Metro stop. The *Atención al Cliente* office in the *cercanías* section has information only on trains to destinations near Madrid. Clearly marked signs lead you to a direct route to the *cercanías* train that goes to the airport, or to the Metro, taxi stand, or back to the AVE side.

**Terrorism Memorial:** The terrorist bombings of March 11, 2004, took place in Atocha and on local lines going into and out of the station. Security is understandably tight here. A moving memorial is in the *cercanías* part of the station (on the upper level, above the Atocha Renfe Metro stop). Walk inside and under the cylinder to read the thousands of condolence messages in many languages. The 36-foot-tall cylindrical glass memorial towers are visible from outside on the street.

## AVE Trains

Spain's bullet trains open up good itinerary options. You can get from Madrid's Atocha station to **Barcelona** nonstop in 2.5 hours (at nearly 200 mph), with trains running almost hourly. The AVE train is faster and easier than flying, but not necessarily cheaper. Second-class tickets are about €110-130 one-way; first-class tickets are €180. Advance purchase and online discounts are available through the national rail company (Renfe), but sell out quickly. Save by not traveling on holidays. Your ticket includes one commuter-train transfer in Madrid or Barcelona. Avlo, a low-cost bullet train run by Renfe, may also be an option for the Madrid-Barcelona route (check www.renfe.com for status).

The AVE is also handy for visiting **Sevilla** (and, on the way, **Córdoba**). Consider this exciting, exhausting day trip: 7:00-depart Madrid, 8:45-12:40-in Córdoba, 13:30-20:45-in Sevilla, 23:15-back in Madrid.

Other AVE destinations include **Granada, Toledo, Segovia, Valencia, Alicante,** and **Malaga.** Prices vary with times, class, and date of purchase—they're usually cheapest up to two months ahead. Eurail Pass holders pay a seat reservation fee (for example, Madrid to Sevilla is €13 second class, and Madrid to Toledo is €4; must purchase at Renfe ticket windows—not available at ticket machines). Reserve each AVE segment ahead.

## Train Connections

Below I've listed both non-AVE and (where available) AVE trains.

**From Madrid by Train to: Toledo** (AVE or cheaper Avant: nearly hourly, 30 minutes, from Atocha), **El Escorial** (*cercanías*, 2/hour, from Atocha and Chamartín, but bus is better—see next chapter), **Segovia** (best on AVE, up to 4/hour, 30 minutes plus 20-minute city bus to Segovia center, from Chamartín, take train going toward Valladolid), **Ávila** (nearly hourly, 1.5-2 hours, from Madrid's Príncipe Pío station; also 2/day, 1.5-2 hours, from Chamartín), **Salamanca** (4/day on speedy Alvia, 1.5 hours; or 7/day on much slower regional Media Distancia train, 3 hours; both from Chamartín), **Valencia** (AVE: nearly hourly, 2 hours, from Atocha; in Valencia, AVE passengers arrive at Joaquín Sorolla station), **Santiago de Compostela** (6/day, 5-5.5 hours, longer trips transfer in Ourense), **Barcelona** (AVE: at least hourly, 2.5-3 hours, from Atocha), **San Sebastián** (6/day, 5-8 hours, from Chamartín),

**Bilbao** (2-4/day, 5-7 hours, some transfer in Zaragoza, from Chamartín), **Pamplona** (6/day direct, 3.5 hours, more with transfer in Zaragoza, from Atocha), **Burgos** (6/day, 2.5-4.5 hours, from Chamartín), **León** (8/day, 2.5-5 hours, from Chamartín), **Granada** (AVE: 3/day, 3.5 hours, from Atocha, **Sevilla** (AVE: hourly, 2.5 hours, departures from 16:00-19:00 can sell out far in advance, from Atocha), **Córdoba** (AVE: almost hourly, 2 hours; Altaria trains: 4/day, 2 hours; all from Atocha), **Málaga** (AVE: hourly, 2.5-4 hours, from Atocha), **Algeciras** (4/day, half with transfer in Antequera, 5.5-6 hours, from Atocha), **Lisbon,** Portugal (1/night, 10.5 hours, from Chamartín; and 1/night, 11.5 hours, from Atocha), **Marseille,** France (1/day direct, 8 hours, from Atocha; also stops at Montpellier, Nîmes, Avignon, and Aix-en-Provence).

## BY BUS

Madrid has several major bus stations with good Metro connections. There are also several routes serving Barajas Airport's Terminal 4. Multiple bus companies operate from these stations, including Alsa (www.alsa.es), Avanza (www.avanzabus.com), and La Sepulvedana (www.lasepulvedana.es). If you take a taxi from any bus station, you'll be charged a legitimate €3 supplement (not levied for trips to the station).

**Plaza Elíptica Station:** Served by Alsa. Buses to Toledo leave from here (2/hour, 1-1.5 hours, *directo* faster than *ruta,* Metro: Plaza Elíptica).

**Estación Sur de Autobuses** (South Station): Served by Alsa, Socibus, and Avanza. From here, buses go to **Ávila** (nearly hourly, 6/day on weekends, 1.5 hours, Avanza), **Burgos** (2/day, 3.5 hours, Alsa), **Salamanca** (hourly express, 2.5-3 hours, Avanza), **León** (10/day, 4 hours, Alsa), **Santiago de Compostela** (4/day, 9 hours, includes 1 night bus, Alsa), **Granada** (nearly hourly, 5-6 hours, Alsa), and **Lisbon** (2/day, 9 hours, Alsa). The station sits squarely on top of the Méndez Álvaro Metro (has TI, +34 914 684 200, www.estacionautobusesmadrid.com).

**Moncloa Station:** This station, in the Moncloa Metro station, serves **León** (6/day, 3.5-4.5 hours, Alsa), **Santiago de Compostela** (3/day, 9 hours, Alsa), **El Escorial** (4/hour, fewer on weekends, 1 hour, see next chapter), and **Segovia** (about 2/hour, La Sepulvedana). To reach the **Valley of the Fallen,** it's best to connect via El Escorial.

**Avenida de América Station:** Served by Alsa. Located at the Avenida de América Metro, buses go to **Lisbon** (4/day, 9 hours), **Burgos** (hourly, 3 hours), **Granada** (3/day, 6 hours), and **Pamplona** (nearly hourly, 6 hours).

MADRID

## BY PLANE
## Adolfo Suárez Barajas Airport

Ten miles east of downtown, Madrid's massive airport (code: MAD, www.aena.es) has four terminals. Terminals 1, 2, and 3 are connected by long indoor walkways (about a 10-minute walk apart); the newer Terminal 4 is farther away, and also has a separate satellite terminal called T4S. Be clear on which terminal your flight uses before heading to the airport. To transfer between Terminals 1-3 and Terminal 4, you can take a 10-minute shuttle bus (free, leaves every 10 minutes from departures level), or ride the Metro (stops at Terminals 2 and 4). Make sure to allow enough time if you need to travel between terminals (and then for the long walk within Terminal 4 to the gates).

**Services:** At the Terminal 1 arrivals area, you'll find the helpful Turismo Madrid TI (Mon-Sat 8:00-20:00, Sun 9:00-14:00, +34 913 058 656), ATMs, a flight info office, a post office window, a pharmacy, eateries, and car-rental agencies. Upstairs at the check-in level, Terminal 1 has an El Corte Inglés travel agency. The super-modern Terminal 4 offers essentially the same services, as well as a Renfe office (where you can get train info and buy long-distance train tickets, long hours daily). You'll find baggage storage *(consigna)* in Terminals 1, 2, and 4.

**Handy Domestic Flights:** Consider flying between Madrid and other cities in Spain (see the Practicalities chapter). Domestic airline Vueling (www.vueling.com) is popular for its discounts (e.g., Madrid-Barcelona flight as cheap as €30 if booked in advance).

### Getting Between the Airport and Downtown

**By Public Bus:** The yellow **Exprés Aeropuerto** runs between all terminals of the airport and downtown, making three stops: O'Donnell, Plaza de Cibeles, and Atocha train station (€5, pay driver in cash, departs from arrivals level every 15-20 minutes, ride takes about 40 minutes, runs 24 hours a day). Once at Atocha, you can take a taxi or the Metro to your hotel. The bus back to the airport leaves Atocha from near the taxi stand on the *cercanías* side. From 23:30 to 6:00, the bus only goes to Plaza de Cibeles, not all the way to Atocha.

**Bus #200** (from all terminals) is less handy than the express bus because it leaves you farther from downtown (at the Metro stop at Avenida de América, northeast of the historical center). This bus departs from the arrivals level about every 10 minutes and takes about 20 minutes to reach Avenida de América (runs 6:00-24:00, buy €1.50 ticket from driver, or get a Multi Card with 10 shareable rides—see page 15).

**By *Cercanías* Train:** From Terminal 4, passengers can ride a *cercanías* train to either of Madrid's stations (€2.60, 2/hour, 25 minutes to Atocha, 12 minutes to Chamartín). Those returning to Madrid's airport by AVE train from elsewhere in Spain can transfer for free to the *cercanías* at Atocha: Scan your AVE ticket at the *cercanías* ticket machine to receive a ticket for the airport train. Be sure to board a train labeled T-4. For terminals 1, 2, or 3, the bus is a more convenient choice.

**By Metro:** Considering the ease of riding the Exprés Aeropuerto bus in from the airport, I wouldn't recommend taking the Metro. The subway involves two transfers to reach the city; it's not difficult, but usually involves climbing some stairs (for Metro tips, see page 14).

**By Minibus Shuttle:** The AeroCity shuttle bus provides door-to-door transport in a seven-seat minibus with up to three hotel stops en route. It's promoted by hotels, but if you want door-to-door service, simply taking a taxi generally offers a better value (www.aerocity.com).

**By Taxi:** With cheap and easy alternatives available, there's not much reason to take a taxi unless you have lots of luggage or just want to go straight to your hotel. If you do take a taxi between the airport and downtown, the flat rate is €30 (no charge for luggage). Uber also serves the airport, and the fare is usually about the same (but can go higher with demand). Plan on getting stalled in traffic.

### Getting Between the Airport and Other Towns

Some buses leave from the airport to far-flung destinations, such as Pamplona (see www.alsa.es; buy ticket online or from driver).

## BY CAR

Avoid driving in Madrid. If you're planning to rent a car, pick it up as you depart the city.

### Route Tips for Drivers

To leave Madrid, follow signs for *A-6* (direction *Villalba* or *A Coruña*) for Segovia, El Escorial, or the Valley of the Fallen (see next chapter for details). For Madrid-Toledo routes, see page 210.

**From Madrid to Segovia** (60 miles/97 km): After leaving Madrid on A-6, exit 39 gets you to Segovia via a slow, winding route over the scenic mountain. Exit at 60 (after a long toll tunnel), or get there more quickly by staying on the toll road all the way to Segovia. At the Segovia aqueduct, follow *casco histórico* signs to the old town (on the side where the aqueduct adjoins the crenellated fortress walls).

# NORTHWEST OF MADRID

*El Escorial • Valley of the Fallen • Segovia • Ávila*

Spain's lavish, brutal, and complicated history is revealed throughout Old Castile. This region, northwest of Spain's capital city, is where the dominant Spanish language *(castellano)* originated and is named for its many castles—battle scars from the long-fought Reconquista. Before slipping out of Madrid, consider several fine side-trips here, all conveniently reached by car, bus, or train.

An hour from Madrid, tour the imposing palace at El Escorial, headquarters of the Spanish Inquisition. Nearby, at the awe-inspiring Valley of the Fallen, pay tribute to the countless victims of Spain's bloody civil war. Segovia, an altogether lovely burg with a remarkable Roman aqueduct, fine cathedral, and romantic castle, is another worthwhile destination. And Ávila warrants a quick stop to walk its perfectly preserved medieval walls.

All of these sights are located in the rugged, mountainous part of Castile in and near the Sierra de Guadarrama range. Be prepared for hilly terrain, cooler temperatures (thanks to the altitude), and often-snowcapped mountains on the horizon...giving this area an almost alpine flavor.

## PLANNING YOUR TIME

History buffs can see **El Escorial** and the **Valley of the Fallen** in less than a day—but don't go on a Monday, when both sights are closed. By bus, see them as a day trip from Madrid; by car, see them en route to Segovia.

If you just like nice towns,

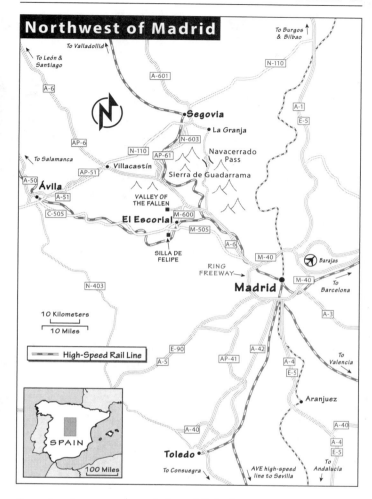

**Segovia,** also easy to reach from Madrid, is worth a half-day of sightseeing (and potentially more for lingering). If you have time, spend the night—the city is a joy in the evenings. **Ávila,** while charming, merits only a quick stop to marvel at its medieval walls and, perhaps, St. Teresa's finger.

Thanks to speedy train connections, it's possible to see Segovia on the way from Madrid to Salamanca. It's trickier but doable to also squeeze in Ávila: Take the fast train (or bus) to Segovia, then bus from Segovia to Ávila, and finally continue to Salamanca by bus or train.

Note that **Toledo** and **Salamanca**—are also popular and doable side-trips from Madrid.

# El Escorial

The Monasterio de San Lorenzo de El Escorial, worth ▲▲, is a
symbol of power rather than el-
egance. This 16th-century palace, 30 miles northwest of Madrid, was built at a time when
Catholic Spain felt threatened
by Protestant "heretics," and
its construction dominated the
Spanish economy for a generation (1562-1584). Because of
this bully in the national budget,
Spain has almost nothing else to show from this most powerful
period of her history.

To its builder, King Philip II, El Escorial embodied the wonders of Catholic learning, spirituality, and arts. To 16th-century
followers of Martin Luther, it epitomized the evil of closed-mind-
ed Catholicism. To architects, the building—built on the cusp
between styles—exudes both Counter-Reformation grandeur and
understated Renaissance simplicity. Today it's a time capsule of
Spain's Golden Age, giving us a better feel for the Counter-Reformation and the Inquisition than any other building. It's packed
with history, art, and Inquisition ghosts. (And at an elevation of
nearly 3,500 feet, it can be very cold.)

## GETTING THERE

Most people visit El Escorial from Madrid. By public transportation, the bus gets you closer to the palace than the train. Remember
that it makes sense to combine El Escorial with a visit to the nearby
Valley of the Fallen.

**By Bus:** Buses to El Escorial leave from Madrid's Moncloa
bus station. At the station, follow signs to Terminal 1 (blue), go up
to the platforms in the blue hallway, and find platform 11 (#664
and #661, 4/hour, fewer on weekends, 1 hour, €4.20 one-way, buy
ticket from driver, Alsa, +34 911 779 951).

Either bus drops you downtown in San Lorenzo de El Escorial, a pleasant 10-minute stroll from the palace (see map): Exit the
bus station from the back ramp that leads over the parked buses
(note that return buses to Madrid leave from platform 3 or 4 below;
schedule posted by info counter inside station). Once outside, turn
left and follow the cobbled pedestrian lane, Calle San Juan, as it
veers right and becomes Calle Juan de Leyva. A few short blocks
later, it dead-ends at Duque de Medinaceli, where you'll turn left
and see the palace. Stairs lead past several decent eateries, through

a delightful square, past the TI (Mon-Sat 9:30-14:00 & 15:00-18:00, Sun 10:00-14:00, free mini museum in back, +34 918 905 313), and directly to the tourist entry of the immense palace/monastery.

**By Train:** Local trains run to El Escorial from Madrid's Atocha and Chamartín stations (*cercanías* line C-3A, 1-2/hour). From the El Escorial station, the palace is a 20-minute walk straight uphill through Casita del Príncipe park. Or you can take a shuttle bus (L1) from the station (2/hour, usually timed with train arrival, €1.30) or a taxi (€7.50) to the town center and the palace.

**By Car:** It's quite simple and takes just under an hour. Head out of Madrid on highway A-6 (watch for signs to *A Coruña*). At kilometer 18, stay on A-6, skipping an exit for El Escorial. Later, around kilometer 37, you'll see the cross marking the Valley of the Fallen ahead on the left. Keep going and exit at kilometer 47 to M-600 (following signs toward *El Escorial/Guadarrama*). The road goes right past the entrance to the Valley of the Fallen (after a half-mile, see a granite gate on right, marked *Valle de los Caídos*), then continues to El Escorial (follow signs to *San Lorenzo de El Escorial*, and then *centro histórico*).

*Parking:* After driving through the drab town of El Escorial, you have several options for parking near the monastery. To park in the convenient garage beneath Plaza de Constitución, watch for the very sharp turnoff on the right immediately before the monastery, then follow blue *P* signs on a loop through town to the garage entrance. Walking out of the garage, the monastery is just across the street and down the stairs (or turn left out of the garage to reach the TI in two short blocks). To park on the street alongside the monastery, bypass the garage turnoff, then turn right when you hit the monastery. Loop around it, watching for pay-and-display parking on your right. In a pinch, another underground garage (Parking Monasterio) is a few blocks east, under Parque Felipe II.

*Leaving El Escorial:* To return to Madrid (or continue to Segovia/Ávila, Toledo, or other points), follow signs to *A-6 Guadarrama.* After about six miles you pass the Valley of the Fallen and hit the freeway.

## ORIENTATION TO EL ESCORIAL

**Cost and Hours:** €12, Tue-Sun 10:00-20:00, Oct-March until 18:00, closed Mon year-round, last entry one hour before closing.

**Free Entry:** The palace is free to enter Wed-Thu beginning at 17:00 (Oct-March from 15:00).

**Information:** +34 918 905 904, www.patrimonionacional.es.

**Tours:** For an extra €4, a 1.5-hour **guided tour** takes you through the complex and other buildings on the grounds, including the House of the Infante and House of the Prince. There are few tours in English; if nothing's running soon, go on your own: Follow the self-guided tour in this chapter, rent the €3 **audioguide,** or download the Monastery of El Escorial **app** ($2).

**Visitor Information:** English descriptions are scattered within the palace. For more information, get the *Guide: Monastery of San Lorenzo El Real de El Escorial,* which follows the general route you'll take (€9, available at shops in the palace).

**Eating:** True to its austere orientation, El Escorial doesn't even have a simple café; for food or drinks, you must venture across the street, into town. The **Mercado San Lorenzo,** a four-minute walk from the palace, is a good place to shop for a picnic (Mon-Fri 9:30-13:30 & 18:00-20:30—17:00-20:00 off-season, Sat 9:30-14:00, closed Sun, Calle del Rey 9). **Plaza Jacinto Benavente** and **Plaza de la Constitución,** just two blocks north of the palace complex, host a handful of nondescript but decent restaurants serving fixed-price lunches or tapas, often at shady outdoor tables.

## ● SELF-GUIDED TOUR

The giant, gloomy building made of gray-black stone looks more like a prison than a palace. About 650 feet long and 500 feet wide, it has 2,600 windows, 1,200 doors, more than 100 miles of passages, and 1,600 overwhelmed tourists. For even a quick visit, allow two hours.

The *monasterio* appears confusing at first—mostly because of the pure magnitude of this stone structure—but the *visita* arrows and signs help guide you through one continuous path.

• *Pass through security, buy your ticket, and follow the signs to the beginning of the tour. You'll go through a series of courtyards and stone halls that lead you into the big courtyard at the very center of the complex. Walk out into the middle of this courtyard and look back.*

### The Courtyard of the Kings (El Patio de los Reyes)

This is the main entrance to El Escorial. It feels less like a monastery or a palace, and more like a fortress—a fortress for God.

Four hundred years ago, the enigmatic, introverted, and extremely Catholic King Philip II (1527-1598) ruled his bulky empire from here, including giving direction to the Inquisition.

Imagine you're Philip in the mid-1500s. Your power is derived from the Roman Catholic Church. Up north, in the German lands, a feisty monk named Martin Luther has been spreading dangerous ideas about how worshippers should create their own, unmediated relationships with God, cutting out the intermediary of priests and popes. You feel that your faith—*the* faith—is under fire. And so, with this bunker mentality, you devise the construction of a new national palace.

Philip II conceived the building to serve several purposes: a grand mausoleum for Spain's royal family, starting with his father, Holy Roman Emperor Charles V; a monastery to pray (a lot) for the royal souls; a small palace to use as a Camp David of sorts for Spain's royalty; and a school to embrace humanism in a way that promoted the Catholic faith.

Spanish architect Juan Bautista de Toledo, who had studied in Italy, was called by Philip II to carry out the El Escorial project, but he died before it was finished. His successor, Juan de Herrera, made extensive changes to Toledo's original design and completed the palace in 1584. The style of architecture, *herreriana*, is known for its use of stone and slate, and is composed of straight lines and little decoration—austere to the extreme.

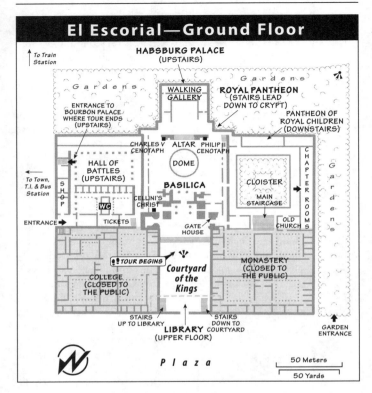

## El Escorial—Ground Floor

To Train Station ↑

HABSBURG PALACE
(UPSTAIRS)

Gardens

Gardens

WALKING GALLERY

ROYAL PANTHEON
(STAIRS LEAD DOWN TO CRYPT)

ENTRANCE TO BOURBON PALACE, WHERE TOUR ENDS (UPSTAIRS)

PANTHEON OF ROYAL CHILDREN
(DOWNSTAIRS)

CHARLES V CENOTAPH

ALTAR

PHILIP II CENOTAPH

HALL OF BATTLES
(UPSTAIRS)

DOME

← To Town, T.I. & Bus Station

SHOP

BASILICA

CLOISTER

CHAPTER ROOMS

Gardens

MAIN STAIRCASE

CELLINI'S CHRIST

WC

OLD CHURCH

ENTRANCE →

TICKETS

GATE HOUSE

→

● TOUR BEGINS

↓

Courtyard of the Kings

MONASTERY
(CLOSED TO THE PUBLIC)

COLLEGE
(CLOSED TO THE PUBLIC)

STAIRS UP TO LIBRARY

STAIRS DOWN TO COURTYARD

GARDEN ENTRANCE

LIBRARY
(UPPER FLOOR)

Plaza

50 Meters
50 Yards

Look up to see the shiny crowns of the six Kings of the Tribe of Judah reigning over the immensity of this courtyard—invoking great biblical rulers to demonstrating the legitimacy of King Philip's (and the Church's) power.

• *Now turn around and face the exit. Find the stairs in the corner (near the exit) and head upstairs to the...*

### Royal Library (Biblioteca Real)

Before you enter the library, pause and look at the top of the fancy wooden doorframe outside. The plaque warns "*Excomunión...*"—you'll be excommunicated if you take a book without checking it out, or if you don't show the guard your ticket. Who needs late fees when you hold the keys to hell? It's clear that education was a priority for the Spanish royalty.

Step inside and savor this room. El Escorial was a place

of learning—*Catholic* learning, of course, which meant that books held a special place. The armillary sphere in front of you—an elaborate model of the solar system—looks like a giant gyroscope, revolving unmistakably around Earth, with a misshapen, under-explored North America. (Galileo Galilei—another troublemaker who dared to defy the word of the Church—was formulating his dangerous heliocentric theories over in Italy even as El Escorial was being completed.) As you walk to the other end of the room, look up at the burst-of-color ceiling fresco. By Pellegrino Tibaldi, this depicts various disciplines labeled in Latin, the lingua franca of the multinational Habsburg Empire.

• Once at the far end of the hall, head downstairs. You'll pass a WC, then go through a souvenir shop, before walking back across the Courtyard of the Kings. Go through the central arch under the six kings into the...

## Basilica (Basílica)

This basilica is the spiritual centerpiece and beating heart of this entire faith-driven enterprise. Walk through the vast, cavernous, dimly lit space until you're positioned just in front of the high altar (at the base of the marble steps).

The basilica, the monastery, and the town adjoining El Escorial are named for San Lorenzo (St. Lawrence), who was martyred by being burned. Find the flame-engulfed grill in the center of the altar wall that features a reclining San Lorenzo taking "turn the other cheek" to new extremes. Lorenzo was so cool, he reportedly told his Roman executioners, "You can turn me over now—I'm done on this side."

Flanking the altar are two sets of golden statues. These are cenotaphs (symbolic tombs) honoring two great Spanish kings who were instrumental in creating this place: on the left, Charles V (the first Habsburg ruler, who joined the mighty empires of Spain and Austria); and on the right, his son, Philip II, who built El Escorial. (Both monarchs are buried in the royal tomb below your feet, which we'll visit later.) From here, you can't see the faces of Charles or Philip...but you're not the target audience. Later on, we'll tour the royal apartments, upstairs. You'll see how several bedchambers were strategically situated in a U-shape overlooking this altar area and these two great kings. The monarchs of Spain and their families could sit up in bed, peek through a window, and be reminded that all they did was in service to God and in honor of their divine ancestors.

The nave is ringed by 36 altars, each adorned with a Baroque canvas. Take a moment to view some of these. Then, on your way back up the nave toward the main door where you entered, detour to the right corner for the artistic highlight of the basilica: Benvenuto Cellini's marble sculpture, *The Crucifixion*. Jesus' features are supposedly modeled after the Shroud of Turin. Cellini carved this

# The Spanish Inquisition

Throughout Spain, you'll encounter palaces, plazas, and historic sites associated with the Spanish Inquisition—a court system run by the Catholic Church to ferret out unorthodoxy and arrest, try, and punish suspected sinners and heretics. Religious inquisitions had existed in Europe since medieval times, but in Spain the Inquisition took on an intensity and violence that seared itself into the European consciousness.

Ironically, it arose in what was once Europe's most diverse country—Spain—where Jews, Muslims, and Christians had for centuries lived side by side. But in the 1300s, Christians began to conquer Muslim lands and confine Jews behind ghetto walls. In 1478, Ferdinand and Isabel, "the Catholic Monarchs," founded the Spanish branch of the Inquisition as part of their campaign to unify the country under Christian rule. In 1492, when Moorish Granada was conquered and Judaism was banned, all remaining Muslims and Jews were forced to convert. It became the Inquisition's job to ensure that these *conversos* really meant it.

Things got ugly.

There were mass rallies, where suspected backsliders were tried and punished. In Sevilla, thousands were burned at the stake in front of the cathedral. Other atrocities took place on Madrid's Plaza Mayor, Toledo's Plaza de Zocodover, and Granada's Plaza de Bib-Rambla.

By the 1500s, the Inquisition had a new enemy—Protestants. Spain's ultra-Catholic kings made it their mission to fight heresy throughout Europe and the New World. Their palace at El Escorial became the movement's de facto global headquarters. In its heyday, the Inquisition prosecuted (or should I say persecuted?) Protestants, Jews, Muslims, unorthodox Catholics, political enemies, scientists, and free-thinkers—anyone who dared question the establishment.

The Spanish Inquisition became notorious for its cruelty and kangaroo courts. The accused were not allowed lawyers. They were tortured to extract bogus confessions. Those found guilty were whipped, hanged, sliced up, or burned at the stake. Some executions were held in banquet halls for nobles' amusement. How many victims were there? Probably many thousands, but it's hard to know, because the atrocities were likely exaggerated by later anti-Catholic propaganda.

By the 1700s, the Inquisition was dying down—except in Spain. Legends grew of dank dungeons, cruel Grand Inquisitors, and daring Don Juans who fought against it. Even the unconventional artist Goya was questioned. Though the Inquisition was officially abolished in 1821, its ominous presence lingered on in Spain for decades. The modern saying, "I didn't expect the Spanish Inquisition!" when questioned  (and the hilarious *Monty Python* sketch) are witty reminders of Spain's painful past.

from Carrara marble for his own tomb in 1562 (according to the letters under Christ's feet).

• *Exit to your left and continue to the Gate House (Portería), which served as a waiting room for people visiting the monks. From here, you'll enter the...*

## Cloister (Claustro)

Turn right and work your way around the cloister, which glows with bright paintings by Pellegrino Tibaldi. Detour briefly up the main staircase, and marvel at the frescos. Luca Giordano depicted *The Glory of the Spanish Monarch* here, as well as painting 12 other frescoes in the monastery in 22 months—speedy Luca!

• *At the end of the cloister's first corridor, on the right, step into the...*

## Old Church (Iglesia Vieja)

This space was used from 1571 to 1586 while the basilica was being finished. During that time, the bodies of several kings, including Charles V, were interred here, and Philip II also had a temporary bedroom here. Among the many paintings, look for the powerful *Martyrdom of St. Lawrence* (by Titian) above the main altar.

• *Continue circling the cloister. Along the next corridor, on the right, are the...*

## Chapter Rooms (Salas Capitulares)

These rooms are where the monks met to do church business. They were (and continue to be) a small, disorganized art gallery lined with a few big names alongside many paintings with no labels—all under gloriously frescoed ceilings.

As you enter, you're face-to-face with **El Greco's *Martyrdom of St. Maurice and the Theban Legion*** (1580-82). Obsessed with saintly sacrifice, Philip II commissioned this from one of the most talented artists of the day. It was supposed to hang inside the basilica. But Philip was so disappointed, he commissioned a different artist to paint the same scene again...and the painting wound up here. Why? Because El Greco—in his drive to depict real human connection—made the beheading of the saint an afterthought of his composition (see the upside-down, headless body on the left edge of the frame). Instead, he focused on a moment he personally found more moving—when St. Maurice convinces his comrades not to give up on their Christian faith. Disappointed as Philip was, artistry wins out: Today, this is the most significant painting at El Escorial.

In the room on the left, look for Titian's *Last Supper*.
• *Head into the room on the right and go down the stairs at the far end. You'll pass a wall of wooden archive boxes, then go through a shop, then continue into the...*

## Pantheon of the Princes (Panteón de los Principes)

El Escorial's middle level (which we just left) is for the church. The upper level is for royal residences. And the lower level—where we are now—is for the dead. These corridors are filled with the tombs of lesser royals. Each bears that person's name (in Latin), relationship to the king, and slogan or epitaph.

Partway through the pantheon is the evocative, wedding-cake **Pantheon of Royal Children** (Panteón de los Infantes), which holds the remains of various royal children who died before the age of seven (and their first Communion). This is a poignant reminder of the scourge of child mortality back in those days, even among super-wealthy royals.

• *Continue down another hall of the Pantheon, with more tombs of lesser royals. You'll walk up a flight of stairs, then down a long stairway to reach the...*

## Royal Pantheon (Panteón Real)

This is the gilded resting place of 26 kings and queens...four centuries' worth of Spanish monarchy in uniform gray-marble coffins, labeled with bronze plaques. All the kings are here—but the only queens allowed are mothers of kings.

A postmortem filing system is at work in the Pantheon. From the entrance, kings are on the left, queens on the right. (The only exception is Isabel II, since she was a ruling queen and her husband was a consort.)

The first and greatest, Charles V and his Queen Isabel (labeled in German, *Elisabeth*), flank the altar on the top shelf. Their son and the builder of El Escorial, Philip II, rests below Charles and opposite (only) one of Philip's four wives. And so on. Spanish monarchy buffs can find all their favorites.

This prime real estate comes with a waiting process. Before a royal corpse can rest here, it needs to decompose in a nearby room for at least 25 years. The bones of the current king's (Felipe VI) great-grandmother, Victoria Eugenia (who died in 1969), were transferred into the crypt in late 2011 (bottom left, as you face the door). And the last two empty niches are already booked: Felipe's grandfather Don Juan (who died in 1993) has been penciled in for the top coffin above the door (see it faintly: *Johannes III*). Technically, he was never crowned king of Spain—Generalísimo Francisco Franco took control of Spain before Don Juan could ascend to the throne, and he was passed over for the job when Franco reinstituted the monarchy. Felipe's grandmother who died in 2000 is the most recent guest in the rotting room (under Juan's tomb—*Maria de Mercedibus*). So where does that leave Felipe's parents, Juan Carlos and Sofía, and monarchs still to come (and go)? This hotel is *completo*.

• *Head back up the stairs, and continue up to the...*

## Habsburg Palace (Palacio de los Austrias)

This wing is named for the Habsburg monarchs who built El Escorial. Remember that Philip II's father, Charles V, united the realms of Spain and Austria under the Habsburg crown, kicking off Spain's Golden Age and funding El Escorial. We'll meet the clan a few rooms from now. (At the end of this tour, we'll also see the apartments of Spain's next—and current—dynasty, the French-born Bourbons.)

You'll begin in **Philip II's apartment.** Look at the king's humble bed...barely queen-size. Remember how Philip wanted to view Mass at the basilica's high altar without leaving his bed? Peek through the window. The red box next to his pillow holds the royal bedpan. But don't laugh—the king's looking down from the wall to your left. At age 71, Philip II, the gout-ridden king of a dying empire, died in this bed (1598).

As you enter the **King's Antechamber,** study the fine inlaid-wood door, one of a set of five (a gift from the German emperor that celebrates the exciting humanism of the age). The slate strip angling across the room on the floor is a sundial from 1755. It lined up with a (now plugged) hole in the wall so that at noon a tiny beam hit the middle of the three lines. Palace clocks were set by this. Where the ray crossed the strip indicated the date and sign of the zodiac.

A second sundial is in the **Walking Gallery** that follows. Here the royals got their exercise privately, with no risk of darkening their high-class skins with a tan. Study the 16th-century maps along the walls and look for Charles V's 16th-century portable altar at the end of the room.

The **Audience Chamber** is now a gallery filled with portraits of the—let's be honest—quite unattractive Habsburg royals. These portraits provide an instructive peek at the consequences of mixing blue blood with more of the same blue blood (inbreeding among royals was a common problem throughout Europe in those days). Holy Roman Emperor **Charles V** (1500-1558, who is known as King Charles I in Spain) is over the fireplace mantel. Charles, Philip II's dad, was the most powerful man in Europe, having inherited not only the Spanish crown, but also control over Germany, Austria, the Low Countries (Belgium and the Netherlands), and much of Italy. When he announced his abdication in

1555, his son Philip II inherited much of this territory...plus the responsibility of managing it. Philip's draining wars with France, Portugal, Holland, and England—including the disastrous defeat of Spain's navy, the Spanish Armada, by England's Queen Elizabeth I (1588)—knocked Spain from its peak of power and began centuries of decline.

The guy with the red tights to the right of Charles is his illegitimate son, **Don Juan de Austria**—famous for his handsome looks, thanks to a little fresh blood. Other royal offspring weren't so lucky: When one king married his niece, the result was **Charles II** (1665-1700, to the right of the door you came in). His severe underbite (an inbred royal family trait) was the least of his problems. An epileptic before that disease was understood, poor "Charles the Mad" would be the last of the Spanish Habsburgs. He died without an heir in 1700, ushering in the continent-wide War of the Spanish Succession and the dismantling of Spain's empire.

Continuing through the palace, notice the adjustable **sedan chair** that Philip II, thick with gout, was carried in (for seven days) on his last trip from Madrid to El Escorial. He wanted to be here when he died.

Go through the **Guards' Room** to the **King's Apartments** and find the small portrait of Philip II flanked by two large paintings of his daughters. The palace was like Philip: austere. Notice the simple floors, plain white walls, and bare-bones chandelier. Peek into the bedroom of one of his daughters, Isabel Clara Eugenia. The sheet warmer beside her bed was often necessary during the winter. If the bed curtains are drawn, bend down to see the view from her bed...of the high altar in the basilica next door. The entire complex of palace and monastery buildings was built around that altar.

• *Go up several stairs to the...*

### Hall of Battles (Sala de Batallas)

Its paintings celebrate Spain's great military victories—including the Battle of San Quentin over France (1557) on St. Lawrence's feast day, which inspired the construction of El Escorial. The sprawling series, painted in 1590, helped teach the new king all the elements of warfare. Stroll the length for a primer on army tactics and formations.

• *Head back down the same stairs, and then down again to the level where you entered. Follow* exit *signs through a series of courtyards; you'll pass a hall on the right that houses good temporary exhibits. Step in and check out what's on.*

*From there, carry on toward the exit. Just before you leave, notice the sign on the right, directing you up the stairs to the...*

## Bourbon Palace (Palacio de los Borbones)

These royal apartments—the frilly yin to the Habsburgs' austere yang—offer a delightful change of pace and an antidote to the otherwise oppressively somber palace.

Remember Charles II, the inbred, epileptic Habsburg king who never bore an heir? His death kicked off the War of Spanish Succession (1701-1714). The result was that the French grandson of Louis XIV became King Philip V of Spain. And Philip V's son, Charles III, modified this part of the palace to have a French-style layout. It was occupied by royalty in the fall, so they kept warm by covering the walls with tapestries, mostly with scenes of hunting, the main activity when they retreated here. Most of the tapestries were made in the Royal Tapestry Factory in Madrid (which you can still visit today).

As you wander through several rooms, look for tapestries made from Goya cartoons, including—in the first room, the Banqueting Hall—*Dance on the Banks of the Manzanares Canal* (the cartoon is in Madrid's Municipal Museum). Continuing through the collection, savor several more playful, colorful Goya tapestries depicting cheery slices of life. Take a quick spin through room after vivid room of sumptuous apartments, listening for the ticking of the clock collection, a contribution of Charles IV. Wandering these grand halls, think of the through-line of Spanish history...today's King Felipe VI is also a Bourbon, the great-great-great-great-great-great-great-great-great grandson of France's "Sun King," Louis XIV.

• *Our tour is done. From here, you can head on outside. To get a nice view of El Escorial from its fine gardens—rather than the stark plaza that surrounds it on two sides, you can head to...*

## El Escorial Gardens

To reach the gardens (free to enter), circle all the way around the right side of the building as you face it. Going beneath the arcade running over the road, look left for the garden entrance. While the gardens are as stark and geometrical as the building itself (with sharply manicured hedges rather than flowers and trees), this is where you'll enjoy the best views of El Escorial—especially in the afternoon light. Listen for a nagging peacock and enjoy the views over the wooded hillsides to the distant skyscrapers of Madrid.

## NEAR EL ESCORIAL: PHILIP'S SEAT

Drivers can visit the nearby Silla de Felipe II (Philip's Seat), a rocky viewpoint where the king would come to admire his palace as it was being built. It's well-marked from M-505, which runs between Madrid and Ávila. If you leave El Escorial by first heading back toward Madrid and then turning off for Ávila, you'll see the turnoff to Philip's Seat on your left after about a mile. It's a couple minutes' drive up a twisty road to a hill adjacent to the monastery.

# Valley of the Fallen

Six miles from El Escorial, high in the Sierra de Guadarrama Mountains, is the Valley of the Fallen (Valle de los Caídos). A 500-foot-tall granite cross marks this immense and powerful underground monument to the victims of Spain's 20th-century nightmare—the Spanish Civil War (1936-1939). That conflict is still extremely controversial in Spain today—rarely commemorated by monuments or even discussed in museums. Considering that, the Valley of the Fallen is a must for those interested in 20th-century history (or fascist architecture).

Until recently, the Valley of the Fallen was also the final resting place of Generalísimo Francisco Franco, Spain's dictator from 1939 until his death in 1975. But in late 2019, after years of debate, Franco's remains were exhumed and moved to his wife's mausoleum in the Mingorrubio Cemetery in El Pardo, a suburb of Madrid.

## GETTING THERE

Most visitors side-trip to the Valley of the Fallen from El Escorial. If you don't have your own wheels, the easiest way to get between these two sights is to negotiate a deal with a **taxi** (to take you from El Escorial to Valley of the Fallen, wait 30-60 minutes, and then bring you back to El Escorial—figure €45 total). There's also a **bus** service, but the timing isn't the most convenient (€11.20 includes entrance fee, 1/day Tue-Sun at 15:15, 15 minutes, return bus to El Escorial leaves at 17:30—a long time to spend here).

**Drivers** can find tips under El Escorial's "Getting There—By Car," earlier. Pay at the booth as you enter from the main road, then drive about three miles through a pine forest to the site itself. A big parking lot is next to the café, a short walk from the basilica.

## ORIENTATION TO THE VALLEY OF THE FALLEN

**Cost and Hours:** €9, Tue-Sun 10:00-19:00, Oct-March until 18:00, closed Mon year-round, +34 918 905 411, www. valledeloscaidos.es.

**Mass:** You can enter the basilica during Mass, but you can't sightsee the central area or linger afterward. One-hour services run Tue-Sat at 11:00 and Sun at 11:00, 13:00, and 17:30 (17:00 in winter). During services, the entire front of the basilica (altar and tombs) is closed. Mass is usually accompanied by the resident boys' choir, the "White Voices" (Spain's answer to the Vienna Boys' Choir).

**Visitor Services:** There's a **$$** café with WCs at the site's main parking lot.

## VISITING THE VALLEY OF THE FALLEN

The main thing to see at the Valley of the Fallen is the basilica interior. While the cross at the top of the monument is undergoing a lengthy restoration, there is no access to it by funicular or by foot along the trail (marked *Sendero de la Cruz*). Given that, an hour is enough for a quick visit.

Approaching by car or bus, you enter the sprawling park through a granite gate. The best views of the cross are from the bridge (but note that it's illegal for drivers to stop anywhere along this road). On the right, tiny chapels along the ridge mark the stations of the cross, where pilgrims stop on their hike to this memorial.

In 1940, prison workers dug 220,000 tons of granite out of the hill to form an underground basilica, then used the stones to erect the cross (built like a chimney, from the inside). Since it's built directly over the dome of the subterranean basilica, a seismologist keeps a careful eye on things.

The stairs that lead to the imposing **monument** are grouped in sets of tens, meant to symbolize the Ten Commandments (including "Thou shalt not kill"—hmm). The emotional pietà draped over the basilica's entrance is huge—you could sit in the palm of Christ's hand. The statue was sculpted by Juan de Ávalos, the same artist who created the dramatic figures of the four Evangelists at the base

of the cross. It must have had a powerful impact on mothers who came here to remember their fallen sons.

A solemn silence and a stony chill fill the **basilica.** At 300 yards long, it was built to be longer than St. Peter's...but the Vatican had the final say when it blessed only 262 of those yards. It's nearly empty inside, making it feel much larger.

After walking through the two long vestibules, stop at the iron gates of the actual basilica. The line of torch-like lamps adds to the shrine-like ambience. Franco's prisoners, the enemies of the right, spent a decade dig-

**NORTHWEST OF MADRID**

# The Spanish Civil War (1936-1939)

Thirty-three months of warfare killed roughly 500,000 Spaniards. Unlike America's Civil War, which split the US north and south, Spain's war was between classes and ideologies, dividing every city and village, and many families. It was especially cruel, with atrocities and reprisals on both sides.

The war began as a military coup to overthrow the democratically elected Republic, a government that the army and other conservative powers considered too liberal and disorganized. The rebel forces, called the Nationalists (Nacionalistas), consisted of the army, monarchy, Catholic Church, big business, and rural estates, with aid from Germany, Italy, and Portugal. Trying to preserve the government were the Republicans (Republicanos), also called Loyalists: the government, urban areas, secularists, small business, and labor unions, with aid from the United States (minimal help) and the "International Brigades" of communists, socialists, and labor organizers.

In the summer of 1936, the army rebelled and took control of its own garrisons, rejecting the Republic and pledging allegiance to Generalísimo Francisco Franco. These Nationalists launched a three-year military offensive to take Spain region by region, town by town. The Republican government cobbled together an army of volunteers, local militias, and international fighters. The war pitted conservative Catholic priests against socialist factory workers, rich businessmen against radical students, farmers loyal to the old king against small businessmen.

Spain's civil war attracted international attention. Adolf Hitler and Benito Mussolini sent troops and supplies to their fellow fascist Franco. It was Hitler's Luftwaffe that helped Franco bomb the town of Guernica (April 1937), an event famously captured on canvas by Pablo Picasso (to read about the painting, see page 75). On the Republican side, hundreds of Americans (including Ernest Hemingway) steamed over to Spain, some to fight for democracy as part of the "Abraham Lincoln Brigade."

By 1938, only Barcelona and Madrid held out. But they were no match for Franco's army. On April 1, 1939, Madrid fell and the war ended, beginning 36 years of iron-fisted rule by Franco.

ging this memorial out of solid rock. (Though it looks like bare rock still shows on the ceiling, it's just a clever design.) The sides of the monument are lined with copies of 16th-century Brussels tapestries of the Apocalypse, and alabaster statues of the Virgin Mary perch above the arches of the side chapels. Notice the hooded figures peering out at you all over the space.

Take the long walk down the nave, then up 10 steps into the

main part of the church, populated with rough wooden pews. Under a glittering mosaic dome is the high altar. At the base of the dome, four gigantic bronze angels look down over you.

Interred behind the high altar and side chapels (marked "RIP, 1936-1939, died for God and country") are the remains of approximately 34,000 people, including both Franco's Nationalists and the 12,000 or so anti-Franco Republicans who lost their lives in the war (the urns are not visible). This is also where Franco was interred until his body was moved to Madrid in 2019—you might still see flowers strewn on the site of Franco's original grave.

In front of the altar is the grave of José Antonio Primo de Rivera (1903-1936), the founder of Spanish fascism, who was killed by Republicans during the civil war; as one of the fallen, he remains buried in the basilica. Next to the fascist's grave, the statue of a crucified Christ is lashed to a timber Franco himself is said to have felled. The seeping stones seem to weep for the victims.

Today, families of the buried Republicans and Nationalists, along with many Spaniards, remain conflicted about the Valley of the Fallen. The war is still a deep wound in Spanish society, and the sight inspires heavy emotions and controversy about what the future of the monument should really be.

As you leave, stare into the eyes of those angels with swords and think about all the "heroes" who keep dying "for God and country," at the request of the latter.

The expansive **view** from the monument's terrace includes the peaceful, forested valley and sometimes snow-streaked mountains.

# Segovia

A beautiful city built along a ridge, Segovia is one of Madrid's most tempting day trips...and even better overnight. Fifty miles from Madrid, this town of 55,000 boasts a thrilling Roman aqueduct, a grand cathedral, and a historic castle. Historically, Segovia was a Roman town that limped along through the centuries, finally becoming a medieval stronghold of the kings and queens of Castile.

While merely a footnote in the annals of Spanish history, Segovia enjoyed a certain prosperity (thanks to its lucrative textile industry) and remains one of Spain's most pleasant towns. Since the city is more than 3,000 feet above sea level and just northwest of a mountain range, it's exposed to cool northern breezes, and people come here from Madrid for a break from the summer heat. It's a fun place to simply hang out and enjoy some low-impact sightseeing.

**Day-Tripping from Madrid:** Considering the easy train and bus connections, Segovia makes a fine day trip from Madrid (30 minutes one-way by AVE train, 1.5 hours by bus; see "Segovia Connections" for details). The disadvantages of this plan are that you spend the coolest hours of the day (early and late) en route, you miss the charming evening scene in Segovia, and you'll pay more for a hotel in Madrid than in Segovia. If you have time, spend the night. But even if you just stay the day, Segovia offers a rewarding and convenient break from the big-city intensity of Madrid.

# Orientation to Segovia

Segovia is a medieval "ship" ready for your inspection. Start at the stern—the aqueduct—and stroll up Calle de Cervantes and Calle Juan Bravo to the prickly Gothic masts of the cathedral. Explore the tangle of narrow streets around playful Plaza Mayor, then descend to the Alcázar at the bow.

**Tourist Information:** The TI at Plaza del Azoguejo, at the base of the **aqueduct,** specializes in Segovia and has friendly staff, two wooden models of Segovia helpful for orientation, pay WCs, and a gift shop (Mon-Sat 10:00-18:30, Sun until 17:00, +34 921 466 720, www.turismodesegovia. com). A different TI, on **Plaza Mayor,** covers both Segovia and the surrounding region (at #10; daily Mon-Sat 9:30-14:00 & 16:00-19:00, Sun 9:30-17:00, shorter hours mid-Sept-June, +34 921 460 334, www.turismocastillayleon.com). A smaller TI at the **AVE train station** opens for weekend day-trippers (Sat-Sun 10:00-13:30 only, +34 921 447 262).

## ARRIVAL IN SEGOVIA

If day-tripping from Madrid, confirm the return schedule when you arrive here.

**By Train:** There's no luggage storage at the AVE train station (called Guiomar). From the station, ride bus #11 for 20 minutes to the base of the aqueduct. Bus #12 also takes you into town, but it drops you off at the bus station, a 10-minute walk to the aqueduct.

**By Bus:** You'll find luggage storage near the exit from the bus station (tokens sold daily 9:00-14:00 & 16:00-19:00, gives you access to locker until end of day). It's a 10-minute walk from the bus station to the town center: Exit left out of the station, continue straight across the street, and follow Avenida Fernández Ladreda, passing San Millán church on the left, then San Clemente church on the right, before coming to the aqueduct.

**By Car:** It's best not to drive into the heart of town, which requires maneuvering your car uphill through tight bends. Instead, park in the free lot northwest of the bus station by the statue of Cándido, along the street called Paseo de Ezequiel González. If the walk up the hill from this lot to the Alcázar is too much—or if the lot is full (which happens often), there's a central but pricey option—the Acueducto Parking underground garage. Enter this garage kitty-corner from the bus station, or—at its opposite end—from near the base of the aqueduct. If you must park in the old town, look for spots marked with blue stripes, pay the nearby meter, and place the ticket on your dashboard (pay meter every 2 hours; free parking 20:00-9:00, Sat afternoon, and all day Sun).

## HELPFUL HINTS

**Free Churches:** Segovia has plenty of little Romanesque churches that are free to enter shortly before or after Mass (see TI for a list of times). Many have architecturally interesting exteriors that are worth a look. Keep your eyes peeled for these hidden treasures: Church of Santos Justo y Pastor, above the aqueduct; San Millán church on Avenida Fernández Ladreda; San Martín church, on a square of the same name; and San Andrés church on the way to the Alcázar on Plaza de la Merced.

**Shopping:** A flea market is held on Plaza Mayor on Thursdays (roughly 8:00-15:00, food also available).

**Group Tours:** The TI on Plaza del Azoguejo, at the base of the aqueduct, offers a two-hour "World Heritage" tour in English (€14, includes entrance to the Alcázar and sometimes the cathedral, 3/week in English at 11:00, check schedule and reserve at TI, +34 921 466 720).

**Walk with a View:** With its trio of visually striking landmarks (aqueduct, cathedral, Alcázar) perched atop a ridge, Segovia boasts more than its share of fine views. If you're up for a longish walk, consider following the valley road all the way around the base of Segovia's promontory. Much of the route is labeled *Ruta Turística Panorámica*. From the bus-station area, follow Cuesta de los Hoyos west, loping around under the Alcázar (with striking views of its Disney-like towers). Then, when you cross the river, turn right and hook back around the north side of town—detouring to the Vera Cruz Church. From there, you can take the steep trail back up to the Alcázar, or continue all the way along the river, then cut back up to the aqueduct.

**NORTHWEST OF MADRID**

# Segovia Walk

This 30-minute self-guided walk starts at the Roman aqueduct and goes uphill along the pedestrian-only street to the main square. It's most enjoyable just before dinner, when it's cool and filled with strolling Segovians.

• *Start at...*

## Plaza del Azogüejo and the Roman Aqueduct

This lively square, often enlivened by a cheery carousel, is named "small market" (compared to the big market—Plaza Mayor—at the end of this walk).

The square is dominated by Segovia's defining feature: its 2,000-year-old, hundred-foot-high *acueducto romano*—worth ▲▲. Ancient Segóbriga was approximately the same size as today's Segovia—with some 50,000 inhabitants, including soldiers at a military base, all of whom needed a reliable water supply. Emperor Trajan's engineers built a nine-mile aqueduct to channel water from the Río Frío to the city, culminating at the Roman castle (today's Alcázar). The exposed section of the aqueduct that you see here is 2,500 feet long and 100 feet high, has 118 arches, was made from 20,000 granite blocks without any mortar, and can still carry a stream of water.

The aqueduct was damaged in the Reconquista warfare of the 11th century and was later rebuilt by Queen Isabel. It functioned until the late 19th century. Notice the cross at the base and the statue in the high niche of the Virgen de la Fuencisla—Segovia's patron saint. (In Roman days this held a statue of Hercules.)

From the square, a grand stairway leads from the base of the aqueduct to the top—offering close-up looks at the imposing work and a sweeping water's-eye-view panorama over the length of the aqueduct. Back at ground level, as you walk through Segovia's streets, keep an eye out for small plaques depicting the arches of the aqueduct, which tell you where the subterranean channel runs through the city.

Facing the square is the flashy **Mesón de Cándido**—the most famous of many Segovia restaurants serving the famous local specialty, roast suckling pig *(cochinillo asado).* (For recommendations of places to try this specialty, see "Eating in Segovia," later.) On the other side of the aqueduct is a practical little roundabout where buses zip to and from the train station.

• *Now head up...*

## Segovia's Main Street

With the aqueduct at your back, head uphill on **Calle de Cervantes,** appreciating the workaday nature of the town and some of its more imaginative architecture. This street is known as the Calle Real—the "Royal Street"—because it leads, eventually, to the Alcázar.

Pause after about a block, at the gap in the buildings on the left, and enjoy the **viewpoint** (Mirador de la Canaleja). Survey the rooftops of Segovia's lower neighborhood, San Millán, and notice how the city is carved out of a very hilly terrain. On the horizon are the often-snowcapped Sierra de Guadarrama mountains that separate Segovia and Madrid.

Continue up the street. Just uphill on the right, you can't miss the unmistakably prickly facade of the so-called **"house of a thousand beaks"** (Casa de los Picos). This building's original Moorish design is still easy to see, despite the wall just past the door that blocks your view from the street. This wall, the architectural equivalent of a veil, hid this home's fine courtyard—Moors didn't flaunt their wealth. You can step inside to see art students at work and perhaps an exhibit on display, but it's most interesting from the exterior.

Notice the house's truncated **tower**—one of many fortified towers that marked the homes of feuding local noble families. In medieval Spain, clashing loyalties led to mini civil wars. In the 15th century, as Ferdinand and Isabel centralized authority in Spain, nobles were required to lop their towers. You'll see the once-tall, now-stubby towers of 15th-century noble mansions all over Segovia.

Continue up the main drag (which has now become Calle de Juan Bravo). Another example of a once-fortified, now-softened house with a cropped tower is about 50 yards farther up, on the left, at tiny Plaza del Platero Oquendo.

Continue uphill until you come to the complicated **Plaza de San Martín,** a commotion of history surrounding a striking statue of Juan Bravo. When Spain's King Charles V, a Habsburg who didn't even speak Spanish, took power, he imposed his rule over Castile. This threatened the local nobles, who, inspired and led by Juan Bravo, revolted in 1521. Although Juan Bravo lost the battle—and his head—he's still a symbol of Castilian pride. This statue was erected in 1921, on the 400th anniversary of his death.

**NORTHWEST OF MADRID**

Accommodations
1 Hotel Palacio San Facundo
2 Hotel Real Segovia
3 Hotel Infanta Isabel
4 La Hostería Natura
5 Hotel Eurostars Plaza Acueducto
6 Hotel Apartments Aralso
7 Hostal Don Jaime

Eateries
8 José María
9 Mesón de Candido
10 Café Jeyma
11 La Concepción Restaurante
12 Restaurante Bar José
13 Narizotas
14 La Almuzara
15 Calle de Infanta Isabel Tapas
16 Café La Colonial
17 Limón y Menta Pastries

100 Meters
100 Yards

NORTHWEST OF MADRID

In front of the Juan Bravo statue stands the bold and bulky **House of Siglo XV.** Its fortified *Isabelino* style was typical of 15th-century Segovian houses. Later, in a more peaceful age, the boldness of these houses was softened with the decorative stucco work called *esgrafiado*—Arabic-style floral and geometrical patterns—that you see today (for example, in the big house behind Juan Bravo). The 14th-century Tower of Lozoya, behind the statue, is another example of the lopped-off towers.

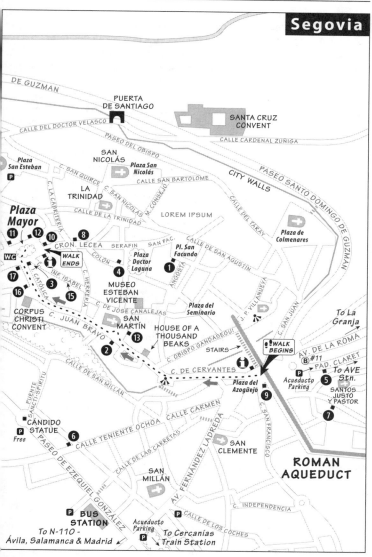

**Segovia**

On the same square, the 12th-century **Church of St. Martín** is Segovian Romanesque in style: a mix of Christian Romanesque (clustered columns with narrative capitals) and Moorish styles (minaret-like towers built with bricks).

Continue up the street another 100 yards, until you reach a triangular square. The Gothic arch on the left is the entrance to the **Corpus Christi Convent.** For €1, you can pop in to see the Franciscan church, which was once a synagogue, which was once a mosque (closed Tue and Fri). It is sweet and peaceful, with lots of art featuring St. Francis, and allows you to see the layers of religious history here. Also in the building's entryway, look for the little window where cloistered nuns sell the treats they make on the premises.

Back out on the little square, notice the narrow street forking off to the left, which leads to Segovia's **former Jewish quarter.** As throughout Europe, Jews were relegated to the less-desirable land (lower on the hill, and therefore more vulnerable to attackers). While there's not much to see from this time, those with a special interest can follow this street a couple of blocks down. The columned building on the left (at #12) was once the house of Abraham Seneor, who was a rabbi and an accountant for Spain's royal family. This building now holds municipal offices, as well as an information center about the Jewish story of Segovia.

• *To stick with the main part of this walk, back at the Corpus Christi Convent take the right fork up to pop out in Segovia's inviting...*

## Plaza Mayor

This was once the scene of executions, religious theater, and bullfights with spectators jamming the balconies. The bullfights ended in the 19th century. When Segovians complained, they were given a gentler form of entertainment—bands in the gazebo. Today the very best entertainment here is simply enjoying a light meal, snack, or drink in your choice of the many restaurants and cafés lining the square.

The Renaissance church opposite the twin-spired City Hall and behind the TI was built to replace the church where Isabel was proclaimed Queen of Castile in 1474. The symbol of Segovia is the aqueduct where you started—find it in the seals on the Theater Juan Bravo and atop the City Hall. Finally, treat yourself to the town's specialty pastry, *ponche segoviano* (marzipan cake), at the recommended Limón y Menta, the bakery on the corner where you entered Plaza Mayor.

# Sights in Segovia

The three big sights in Segovia are its cathedral, Alcázar, and aqueduct. The aqueduct is covered on the "Segovia Walk," earlier; the cathedral and Alcázar are described next.

### ▲▲Segovia Cathedral (Catedral de Segovia)

Segovia's cathedral, built from 1525 through 1768 (the third on this site), was Spain's last major Gothic building. Embellished to the hilt with pinnacles and flying buttresses, the exterior is a great example of the final, overripe stage of Gothic, called Flamboyant.

Yet the Renaissance arrived before it was finished—as evidenced by the fact that the cathedral is crowned not by a spire, but by a dome. The spacious and elegantly simple interior provides a delightful contrast to the frilly exterior.

**Cost and Hours:** €7 combo-ticket includes cathedral and tower, individual tickets available; cathedral—€3, free Sun 9:00-10:00, Nov-March 9:30-10:30 (cathedral access only—no cloisters), open daily 9:30-21:30, Nov-March until 18:30; tower—€7, visits by guided tour only, tours depart every 90 minutes 10:30-19:30 (fewer in winter), English tour at 15:00; +34 921-462-205, https://catedralsegovia.es/.

**Visiting the Cathedral:** As you enter, angle right to the **choir,** which features finely carved wooden stalls from the previous church (1400s). The *cátedra* (bishop's chair) is in the center rear of the choir.

The many side chapels are mostly 16th-century and come with big locking gates—a reminder that they were the private sacred domain of the rich families and guilds that "owned" them. They could enjoy private Masses here with their names actually spoken in the blessings and a fine burial spot close to the altar.

Find the **Capilla La Concepción** (as you face the choir, it's the last chapel ahead on the right, just inside the door to the terrace). Its many 17th-century paintings hang behind a mahogany wood gate imported from colonial America. The painting, *Tree of Life,* by Ignacio Ries (left of the altar), shows hedonistic mortals dancing atop the Tree of Life. As a skeletal Grim Reaper prepares to receive them into hell (by literally chopping down the tree...timberrrr), Jesus rings a bell imploring them to wake up before

it's too late. The chapel's center statue is Mary of the Apocalypse (as described in Revelations, standing on a devil and half-moon, which looks like bull's horns). Mary's pregnant, and the devil licks his evil chops, waiting to devour the baby Messiah.

Opposite from where you entered, a fine **portal** (which leads into the cloister) is crowned by a painted Flamboyant Gothic pietà in its tympanum.

Step through that portal into the **cloister,** turn right, and circle counterclockwise. The first room you'll come to is a nice little museum containing paintings and silver reliquaries. Continuing around the cloister, the next door leads into the sumptuous, gilded chapter room—draped with precious Flemish tapestries. Out in the bottom of the stairwell, notice the gilded wagon. The Holy Communion wafer is placed in the top of this temple-like cart and paraded through town each year during the Corpus Christi festival. At the top of the stairs is a collection of tapestries and vestments under delicate fan vaulting. Back out in the cloister, hanging on the wall between rooms, a glass case displays keys to the 17th-century private chapel gates. Circle the rest of the way around the cloister, enjoying the peace. From the cloister courtyard, you can see the Renaissance dome rising above the otherwise Gothic rooftop.

The 290-foot tower offers stunning views of the city and the surrounding area. You can climb 190 steps to the top on a guided tour several times a day (enter directly opposite the Capilla La Concepción).

### ▲▲Alcázar

Segovia has one of the most fanciful, striking castles in all of Spain, thanks to a Romantic Age remodel job. It's the closest thing Spain has to its own Neuschwanstein. In the Middle Ages, this fortified palace was one of the favorite residences of the monarchs of Castile, and a key fortress for controlling the region. The Alcázar grew through the ages, and its function changed many times: After its stint as a palace, it was a prison for 200 years, and  then a royal artillery school. It burned in 1862, after which it was remodeled in the eye-pleasing style you see today. First ogle the exterior. Then visit the finely decorated interior and view terrace. And finally—if you don't mind the steps—you can climb to the top of the tower for the only 360-degree city view in town. This description quickly covers the highlights, but the audioguide is a good investment if you'd like the full story.

**Cost and Hours:** Palace—€5.50, daily 10:00-20:00, Nov-March until 18:00, €3 audioguide describes each room (45 minutes, €5 deposit); tower—€2.50, same hours as palace except closed in windy or rainy weather; +34 921 460 759, www.alcazardesegovia. com.

**Visiting the Alcázar:** Buy your ticket in the building on the left as you face the Alcázar (and ask for a map near the ticket desk). Then head over the **drawbridge.** Peer down into the deep, deep "moat," and appreciate the strategic smarts of building a castle on a promontory at the tip of Segovia's ridge.

Once inside, follow signs to the start of the tour. You'll enjoy a one-way route through 11 **royal rooms.** What you see today inside the Alcázar is rebuilt, like the outside—a Disney-esque exaggeration of the original. Still, its fine Moorish decor and historic furnishings are fascinating. The sumptuous ceilings are accurately restored in Mudejar style.

Entering the exhibit, you'll be greeted by knights on horseback, then find your way to the Throne Room, whose ceiling is the artistic highlight of the palace. Facing the throne are portraits of Ferdinand and Isabel, whose union made Spain a medieval powerhouse.

Next, in the Gallery Room—with another fine ceiling—is a big mural of Queen Isabel the Catholic being proclaimed Queen of Castile and León in Segovia's main square in 1474. Enjoying the views of the countryside from the huge windows, it's clear the current building was designed in the "just for show" late 19th century, rather than the original "danger lurks around every corner" Middle Ages.

Carry on through more rooms, including the Pine Cone Room, where 392 pinecone-shaped adornments hang from the Mudejar ceiling. The Royal Bedroom is made cozy by hanging tapestries on the stony walls.

Pause to savor the striking Hall of the Monarchs. The upper walls feature statues of the 52 rulers of Castile and León who presided during the long and ultimately successful Reconquista (711-1492): from Pelayo (the first, over the room's exit door and a bit to the left), clockwise to Juana VII (the last). There were only seven queens during the period (the numbered ones).

From here, head through the small, window-lined Cord Room (decorated with the cord-like belts of the Franciscan order) to reach the chapel. As you face the main altar, notice the painting in the center of the altar on your left: A scene of St. James the Moor-Slayer—with Muslim heads literally rolling at his feet. James is the patron saint of Spain. His name was the rallying cry in the centuries-long Christian crusade to push the Muslim Moors back into Africa.

Exiting the royal rooms, step into the modest **armory.** The finest item is the 16th-century, ornately carved ivory crossbow, with a hunting scene shown in the accompanying painting.

From the armory, step out onto the **terrace** (the site of the original Roman military camp, circa AD 100; may be closed in winter and in bad weather). Taking in its vast views, marvel at the natural fortification provided by this promontory cut by the confluence of two rivers. The Alcázar marks the end (and physical low point) of the gradual downhill course of the nine-mile-long Roman aqueduct. Can you find the mountain nicknamed *Mujer Muerta* ("dead woman")?

On your way back out, you can cut through the Museum of Artillery, recalling the period (1764-1862) when this was the royal artillery school. It shows the evolution of explosive weaponry, with old photos and prints of the Alcázar.

Finally, back at the drawbridge, you can choose to climb the **tower.** Hiking 152 steps up a tight spiral staircase rewards you with sweeping views over town and the countryside.

### Museo de Arte Contemporáneo Esteban Vicente

A collection of abstract art by local artist Esteban Vicente (1903-2001) is housed in two rooms of the remodeled remains of Henry IV's 1455 palace. Wilder than Rothko but more restrained than Pollock, Vicente's vibrant work influenced post-WWII American art. For contemporary art aficionados, the temporary exhibits can be more interesting than the permanent collection.

**Cost and Hours:** Free; open Tue-Fri 11:00-14:00 & 16:00-19:00 (July -Sept 17:00-20:00), Sat 11:00-20:00, Sun 11:00-15:00, closed Mon; +34 921 426 010, www.museoestebanvicente.es.

## JUST OUTSIDE THE OLD CENTER

### ▲Vera Cruz Church

Perched on a ridge below the Alcázar is this unusual, historic church. Built in the 13th century by an order of chivalric knights (possibly the Knights Templar), this 12-sided Romanesque church once supposedly housed a piece of the "true cross." Pick up an English flier at the entrance and step into the simple, nearly unadorned interior, where you'll find a unique floor plan: a circular nave ringing a giant central column called an edicule. The inner chamber was used for chivalrous ceremonies. (While this architecture was typical of churches built by knights' orders, few survive today.) You'll see the red Maltese cross, signifying that the church is still linked with the Knights Hospitaller, who still use it from time to time. With its unique shape and history, the space carries a mystical feeling. And the views back up to the Alcázar from here are excellent as well.

**Cost and Hours:** €2, Wed-Sun 10:30-13:30 & 16:00-19:00, Tue 16:00-19:00 only, until 18:00 in winter, closed Mon and when caretaker takes his autumn holiday; outside town beyond the castle, 25-minute walk from main square; +34 921 431 475.

## NEAR SEGOVIA
### ▲La Granja de San Ildefonso Palace

This "little Versailles," six miles south of Segovia, is much smaller and happier than nearby El Escorial. The palace and gardens were

built by the homesick French-born King Philip V, grandson of Louis XIV. Today it's restored to its original 18th-century splendor, with its royal collection of tapestries, clocks, and crystal (actually made at the palace's royal crystal factory). Plumbers and gardeners imported from France and Italy made Philip a garden that rivaled Versailles'. The Bourbon Philip chose to be buried here (in the adjacent church) rather than with his Habsburg predecessors at El Escorial.

**Cost and Hours:** Palace—€9, Tue-Sun 10:00-20:00, Oct-March until 18:00, closed Mon year-round, last entry one hour before closing, audioguide-€3, guided tour-€4 (ask for one in English—you might need to wait); park—free except when fountains are running (when you may need a palace ticket or €4 fountains-only ticket to enter), daily 8:00-20:30, until 21:30 in summer, shorter hours off-season; +34 921 470 019, www.patrimonionacional.es.

**Getting There:** Linecar buses make the 25-minute trip from Segovia (catch at the bus station) to San Ildefonso-La Granja (check schedule online, +34 921 427 705, www.linecar.es). Drivers find the palace at the top of town, facing a peaceful park; there's no official parking lot, but plenty of free street parking nearby.

**Visiting the Palace and Gardens:** The **palace** interior ranks low on a European scale (nearby, Madrid's Royal Palace and El Escorial's Bourbon Palace are better). And it's hard to appreciate without the audioguide. After touring three large rooms of tapestries, you'll circulate through the typical lineup of royal apartments—ceiling frescoes, glittering chandeliers, gilded furniture, marble floors, and lots of paintings by little-known artists. The ground-floor halls are lined with Neoclassical states and garden views.

You'll exit the palace into the real draw: the **gardens.** (You can also enter the gardens directly—for free—by circling all the way around the right side of the palace.) The sprawling grounds radiate out from the palace in a Versailles-like grid-and-axis layout, with a more rugged section just beyond. The pine trees and snowcapped peaks on the horizon help give it an almost alpine feel. The gardens are decorated with fanciful fountains, most featuring mythological stories. However, the fountains run only on certain days (check the website for the schedule and entry details; when they're running, you may need a ticket to enter the gardens).

# Sleeping in Segovia

The best places are on or near the central Plaza Mayor. This is where the city action is—the best bars, most tourist-friendly and *típico* eateries, and the TI. During busy times—on weekends and in July and August—reserve in advance.

## NEAR PLAZA MAYOR

**$$$ Hotel Palacio San Facundo,** on a quiet square a few blocks off Plaza Mayor, is luxuriously modern in its amenities but has preserved its Old World charm. This palace-turned-monastery has 29 colorful, business-class rooms surrounding a skylit central patio (air-con, elevator, pay parking, +34 921 463 061, Plaza San Facundo 4, www.hotelpalaciosanfacundo.com, info@hotelpalaciosanfacundo.com, Isabel).

**$$ Hotel Real Segovia** is a classic hotel (quick to brag about the many old-time movie stars who stayed here). They rent 37 beautifully updated rooms with all the modern amenities right along the main drag, between the aqueduct and Plaza Mayor. In spite of its central location, many of its rooms face the quiet countryside, and its top-floor terrace has some of Segovia's best views (air-con, elevator, pay parking, Juan Bravo 30, +34 921 462 663, www.hotelrealsegovia.com).

**$$ Hotel Infanta Isabel,** right on Plaza Mayor, has 38 elegant rooms—some with plaza views—and a welcoming staff. It faces both the main square and a popular tapas bar-lined street—it's smart to request a quiet room (air-con, elevator, pay parking, Plaza Mayor 12, +34 921 461 300, www.hotelinfantaisabel.com, admin@hotelinfantaisabel.com).

**$ La Hostería Natura** is a *hostal* with more personality. Their 18 colorful, tiled rooms—accessed by an old wooden staircase—are a few short blocks away from Plaza Mayor (air-con, Calle Colón 5, +34 921 466 710, www.naturadesegovia.com, info@naturadesegovia.com).

## NEAR THE AQUEDUCT

**$$$ Hotel Eurostars Plaza Acueducto** has little character but provides the comforts of a business-class hotel. It's right at the foot of the aqueduct and next to the bus stops for the AVE train station. Some of its 72 rooms have full or partial views of the aqueduct (air-con, elevator, gym, pay parking; Avenida Padre

Claret 2, +34 921 413 403, www.eurostarshotels.com, reservas@eurostarsplazaacueducto.com).

**$ Hotel Apartments Aralso** is a practical choice—a 10-minute hike below the aqueduct, near the bus station. This solidly built guesthouse in a workaday residential area rents 12 well-appointed, functional rooms with fully equipped kitchens. Sweetly run by André and María, it's a good choice for those who don't mind being a bit outside the creaky old center (family rooms, air-con, elevator, nearby pay parking, Calle Teniente Ochoa 8, +34 921 444 816, www.apartamentosaralso.com, reservas@apartamentosaralso.com).

**$ Hostal Don Jaime,** on a gentle hill just above the aqueduct, is a friendly, family-run place with 38 basic, older yet well-maintained rooms in two buildings (a few single rooms with shared bath, family rooms, breakfast included for Rick Steves readers, pay parking, Ochoa Ondategui 8, +34 921 444 787, www.hostaldonjaime.com, hostaldonjaime@hotmail.com).

# Eating in Segovia

Look for Segovia's culinary claim to fame, roast suckling pig (*cochinillo asado:* 21 days of mother's milk, into the oven, and onto your plate—oh, Babe). It's salty and tender, wrapped in crispy skin that's the stuff of pork-lovers' dreams—and worth a splurge here, or in Toledo or Salamanca.

For slightly lighter fare, try *sopa castellana*—soup mixed with eggs, ham, garlic, and bread—or warm yourself up with the *judiones de La Granja,* a popular soup made with flat white beans from the region. Segovia also has a busy tapas bar scene, featuring small bites served up with every drink you order.

*Ponche segoviano,* a dessert made with an almond-and-honey *mazapán* base, is heavenly after an earthy dinner or with a coffee in the afternoon (at the recommended Limón y Menta).

## PLACES TO EAT ROAST SUCKLING PIG

While some of the places listed later also serve this classic local dish, these two are the most renowned options for those who really want to pig out in the old town.

**$$$$ José María** doesn't have the history or fanfare of Cándido (see next), but Segovians claim this high-energy place serves the best roast suckling pig in town. It thrives with a hungry mix of tourists and locals. The bar leading into the restaurant is a scene in itself. Muscle up to the bar and get your drink and tapa before going into the dining room. It's smart to reserve ahead (daily 12:30-24:00, air-con, a block off Plaza Mayor at Cronista Lecea 11, +34 921 466 017, www.restaurantejosemaria. com).

**$$$$ Mesón de Cándido,** one of the top restaurants in Castile, is famous for its memorable dinners. Even though it looks like a ye-olde tourist trap at the base of the aqueduct, it's a grand experience. Take time to wander around and survey the photos of celebs—from Juan Carlos I to Antonio Banderas and Melanie Griffith—who've dined here. Try to get a table in a room with an aqueduct view (daily 13:00-16:30 & 20:00-23:00, reservations recommended, Plaza del Azoguejo 5, air-con, under aqueduct, +34 921 428 103, www.mesondecandido.es). Three gracious generations of the Cándido family still run the show.

## MOSTLY PIG-FREE PLACES IN THE OLD CENTER

**Plaza Mayor,** the main square, provides a great backdrop for a light lunch, dinner, or drink. Compare menus and views and choose your best. Things here are fairly interchangeable, and you'll pay a premium for the location, but café prices are generally reasonable, and many offer a good selection of tapas and *raciones*. Grab a table at the place of your choice and savor the scene. Good options include **$$$ Café Jeyma,** with a great cathedral view (but the worst reputation for food); **$$$ La Concepción Restaurante,** closer to the cathedral; and **$$$ Restaurante Bar José.**

**$$$ Narizotas** mixes traditional Segovian fare with a few imaginative and non-Castilian alternatives. Dine outside on a delightful square or inside with modern art under medieval timbers. For a wonderful dining experience, try their chef's-choice mystery samplers, either the "Right Hand" (€36, about nine courses) or the "Left Hand" (€31, about six courses). They offer less elaborate three-course meals for €14-25 and an enticing à la carte menu (daily 9:00-17:00 & 20:00-23:00, Fri-Sat until 24:00, midway down Calle Juan Bravo at Plaza de Medina del Campo 2, +34 921 462 679, www.narizotas.net).

**$$ La Almuzara** is a garden of veggie and organic delights: whole-wheat pizzas, pastas, tofu, seitan, and even a few dishes with meat (Tue 20:30-24:00, Wed-Sun 12:30-16:00 & 20:00-24:00, closed Mon, between cathedral and Alcázar at Marques del Arco 3, +34 921 460 622).

**Segovia's Trendy Tapas Strip:** Many of the eateries described above have good tapas bars up front. But to sample several bars in one go, stroll down **Calle de Infanta Isabel** (angling off the Plaza Mayor). The places here skew young and trendy, but inside you'll find a mixed-ages crowd. **Divinos** (at #12) has creative tapas in a cut-rate industrial-mod plywood atmosphere (sit in the dining room in back, rather than the less appealing bar up front). Farther along, **El Sitio** (#9) feels more traditional. This street also has several music and dance clubs that don't get going until late.

**Breakfast:** In the morning, I like to eat on Plaza Mayor (many choices) while enjoying the cool air and the people scene. Or, 100 yards down the main drag toward the aqueduct, **$$ Café La Colonial** serves good breakfasts (with seating on a tiny square or inside, Plaza del Corpus).

**Nightlife:** After hours, the bars on Plaza Mayor, Calle de Infanta Isabel, and Calle de Isabel la Católica are packed. There are a number of late-night dance clubs along the aqueduct.

**Dessert: Limón y Menta** offers a good, rich *ponche segoviano* (marzipan) cake by the slice—or try the lighter, crunchy, honey-and-almond *crocantinos* (Mon-Fri 9:00-20:30, Sat-Sun until 21:00, seating inside, Calle de Isabel la Católica 2, +34 921 462 141).

**Market:** An outdoor produce market thrives on Plaza Mayor on Thursday (roughly 8:00-15:00). Nearby, on Calle del Cronista Ildefonso Rodríguez, a few stalls are open daily except Sunday. **Carrefour Express,** a small supermarket, is across from the Casa de los Picos (daily 9:00-21:00, Calle Juan Bravo 54).

# Segovia Connections

## BY PUBLIC TRANSPORTATION

**From Segovia to Madrid:** Choose between the fast AVE train and the bus. Even though the 30-minute AVE train takes less than half as long as the bus, the train stations in Segovia and Madrid are less convenient, so the total time spent in transit is about the same. (Skip the *cercanías* commuter trains, as they take two hours and don't save you much money.)

The **AVE train** goes between Segovia's Guiomar station (labeled "Segovia AV" on booking sites) and **Madrid's Chamartín station** (up to 4/hour, 30 minutes). An Alvia train goes from the same station to **Salamanca** (4/day, 1.5 hours). To get to Guiomar station, take city bus #11 from the base of the aqueduct (20 minutes, buses usually timed to match arrivals).

**Buses** run from Madrid's Moncloa station to Segovia. If arriving at Moncloa station in Madrid, follow the signs for the color-coded terminals to Terminal 1 (blue). From there, signs marked *Taquillas Segovia* lead you to the ticket office, or look for the ticket machines, which accept cash or chip-and-PIN credit cards (2/hour, 1.5 hours, www.avanzabus.com).

When riding the bus from Madrid to Segovia, about 30 minutes after leaving Madrid you'll see—breaking the horizon on the left—the dramatic concrete cross of the Valley of the Fallen. Its grand facade marks the entry to the mammoth underground memorial.

**From Segovia by Bus to: Ávila** (4/day, 2/day on weekends, 1 hour, Avanza, www.avanzabus.com). Some Ávila buses continue to **Salamanca** (3.5 hours)—but the train is much faster.

## ROUTE TIPS FOR DRIVERS

**From Segovia to Salamanca** (100 miles/160 km): Leave Segovia by driving around the town's circular road, which offers good views from below the Alcázar. Then follow signs for *Ávila* (road N-110). Notice the fine Segovia view from the three crosses at the crest of the first hill. You could stay on N-110 all the way to Ávila, but it's cheap to hop on the speedy AP-51 tollway at Villacastín, about halfway to Ávila. If time allows, exit at **Ávila** for a look at the town walls and to stretch your legs. Continuing from Ávila to Salamanca, be ready to pull over for the best views

of the Ávila walls: Just after you cross the river at the far end of the town wall, watch for the *Cuatro Postes* pullout on the right (it's just uphill from the river). Soon after, hop on the speedy and free A-50 expressway, which zips you to Salamanca in under an hour.

About 20 miles before Salamanca, you'll spot a huge bull on the left side of the road. As you get closer, it becomes more and more obvious it isn't alive. (It's not realistic to pull over for a photo if you're on the expressway, but it's reachable if you take the slower N-501.) Soon you'll see the massive church towers of **Salamanca** on the horizon and enjoy great panoramic views of the city from across the river as you get closer.

# Ávila

Ávila is famous for its perfectly preserved medieval walls, as the birthplace of St. Teresa, and for its yummy *yema* treats. For more than 300 years, Ávila was on the battlefront between the Muslims and Christians, changing hands several times—hence its heavily fortified appearance. But today, perfectly peaceful Ávila has a charming old town that weathers only occasional incursions of day-trippers from Madrid, Segovia, or Salamanca (each about an hour away by car). Ávila doesn't quite crack the top tier of great walled European cities—it's sort of a wannabe Carcassonne. But it's handy to reach, has several fine churches and monasteries, and makes for an enjoyable quick stop between Segovia and Salamanca.

# Orientation to Ávila

Surrounded by modern sprawl, Ávila's walled old center is shaped like an elongated, backwards "D." The flat side of the "D"—facing east—is where you'll find the TIs, parking, and most of the sights (including two points to access the top of the walls). On a quick visit, most people focus on this busy little zone. Inside the walls, Ávila is sleepy: from the cathedral (which abuts the eastern wall), it's a 10-minute walk on the main drag, Calle de los Reyes Católicos, past the market to the humble main square, Plaza Mercado Chico. A five-minute walk south of there is the only other important sight within the walls, the Convent of St. Teresa.

**Tourist Information:** Ávila's city TI is just outside the northeast corner of the walls, facing the Basilica of San Vicente (daily 9:00-20:00, Nov-March until 18:00, free WCs, well-equipped shop, helpful wooden models of the town and important wall sections, +34 920 350 000 ext. 370, www.avilaturismo.com). A less helpful regional TI is inside the wall ticket office, near the cathedral (Mon-Sat 9:30-14:00 & 17:00-20:00, Sun 9:30-17:00, shorter hours mid-Sept-May, +34 920 211 387).

**Sightseeing Pass:** The **VisitÁvila** pass is €15 and valid for 48 hours. It includes the wall, cathedral, museum of St. Teresa, and a handful of other sights. If you plan on seeing them all you can save a few euros.

## ARRIVAL IN ÁVILA

**By Bus or Train:** Ávila's bus and train stations sit kitty-corner from each other about a mile east of the wall. There are lockers at Ávila's bus station, but not at the train station. To reach the Basilica of San Vicente, you can walk (allow 15-20 minutes) or take city bus #4 or #1. From the bus station, exit to the right, go down through the underpass, and look right for the "Puente de la Estación" stop. To catch these buses from the train station, exit straight ahead to find the "Renfe" stop (to the right of the roundabout).

**By Car:** To get close to the sights, choose between two big, handy pay garages: Most convenient (and well-marked as you approach town) is the **Sta. Teresa garage,** a five-minute walk from the cathedral and main wall entry point, beneath Plaza de Santa Teresa (your license plate will be photographed as you enter; pay at the machine before you leave by punching in your plate number). The **Rastro garage** is just south of the city wall (use this only if you're making a quick stop at the Convent of St. Teresa and nothing else). To save money, you could use the big, free lot behind the sprawling **Lienzo Norte conference center,** north of the city wall and farther from the main sights (20-minute walk to the cathedral). There's also ample pay-and-display **street parking** outside of the walls (marked by blue lines), but there's a two-hour limit—so this works only for a quick visit.

# Sights in Ávila

### ▲Walls of Ávila

Built from around 1100 on even-more-ancient remains, Ávila's fortified wall is the oldest, most complete, and best-preserved in Spain. Walking around the wall, climbing the towers, and peeking between crenellations is a fun stroll. But there's not much to see up top—the views are better from ground level (and best from Cuatro Postes, across the river—see next). If it's blazing hot and you're short on time, the wall walk is skippable. But if you want to play "king of Castile"...it's right there, waiting for you.

**Cost and Hours:** €5, includes audioguide, free Tue 14:00-16:00; open daily 10:00-20:00, July-Aug until 21:00; Nov-March Tue-Sat 10:00-18:00, closed Mon; last entry 45 minutes before closing, ticket includes English audioguide.

**Walking the Wall:** There are two stretches of wall that you can walk along (both covered by the same ticket—but you can't re-enter a section you've already entered). The **main section** (called "Tramo 1")—stretching eight-tenths of a mile, one way—is along the north side. Enter the wall by the gate closest to the cathedral (Puerta del Peso de la Harina). From here, you can head up to the northeast corner, then curve left and go all  the way along the north side. There are two other entrances/exits for this stretch: Puerta del Carmen (about halfway along the north side) and Puerta Puente Adaja (on the far west end, opposite the cathedral). Go as far as you like. Then, either exit at one of those two points and return to ground level, or go back the way you came on top of the wall. The **shorter section** ("Tramo 2"), just about 300 yards one way, can be accessed at the Puerta del Alcázar, just off Plaza de Santa Teresa.

**Viewing the Wall:** The best views of the wall itself are actually from street level. If you're wandering the city and see arched gates leading out of the old center, pop out to the other side and take in the impressive wall from the ground. Drivers can see the especially impressive north side as they circle to the right from Puerta de San Vicente.

**Paseo Outside the Wall:** An interesting paseo scene takes place along the outside of the wall each night—make your way along the southern wall (Paseo del Rastro) to Plaza de Santa Teresa for spectacular vistas across the plains.

## Viewing Ávila from Cuatro Postes

The best overall view of the walled town of Ávila is about a mile away on the Salamanca road (N-501), at a clearly marked turnout for the Cuatro Postes (four posts). Drivers should keep an eye out on the right, after they cross the river and are on their way uphill. If you're without wheels, you have a few options: You could walk or take a public bus to the far west end of the wall (to the bridge called Ponte de Allaja), then hike uphill for about 10-15 minutes to Cuatro Postes. Or you can catch a tourist trolley (€5.50, www. eltranvia.es) or tuk-tuk (€6.50, www.tuktukavila.com) for a little loop tour around town, which includes a sweat-free ride up to the viewpoint. All run infrequently—confirm your options at the TI.

## Ávila Cathedral (Catedral de Ávila)

While it started as Romanesque, Ávila's cathedral, finished in the 16th century, is considered the first Gothic cathedral in Spain. Its position—with its granite apse actually part of the fortified wall—underlines the "medieval alliance between cross and sword." The cathedral interior doesn't rank very high on a Spanish scale (and even just in Ávila, San Vicente's is more interesting). It's heavy, stony, and bottom-heavy, with delicate Gothic windows illuminating a much lighter (and light-filled) top half. The focal point is the exquisitely carved outer stone wall of the choir (or "retrochoir")—with Plateresque carvings of Jesus' life. In the right transept, find your way into the sacristy, cloister, and museum (including a minor painting by El Greco).

**Cost and Hours:** €6, includes audioguide, Mon-Sat 10:00-21:00, Sun from 11:45, generally closes 2-3 hours earlier off-season, Plaza de la Catedral.

**Tower:** You can pay €2 for an assigned time, then climb the 130 spiral stairs of the cathedral tower, earning a great panoramic view over Ávila (1-3/day, more in July-Aug, Sat-Sun only in winter).

## Basilica of San Vicente

Sitting just outside the northeast corner of the wall (facing the TI), this hulking church—with its distinctive Romanesque-arch arcade facing the busy street—is worth a peek. The 12th-century interior oozes history, with rough tombstones embedded in the floor, heavy columns framing round windows, a glittering altarpiece,

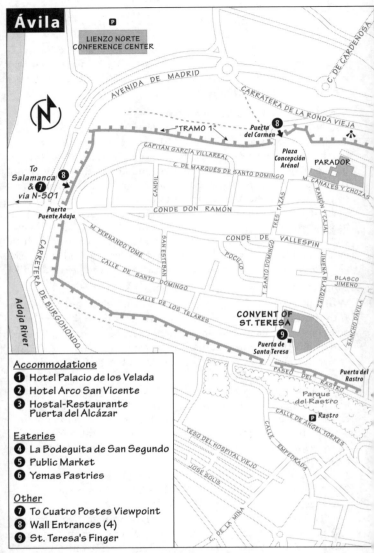

## Ávila

**LIENZO NORTE CONFERENCE CENTER**

AVENIDA DE MADRID

CARRATERA DE LA RONDA VIEJA

C. DE CARDENOSA

"TRAMO 1"

Puerta del Carmen

CAPITÁN GARCÍA VILLAREAL

C. DE MARQUÉS DE SANTO DOMINGO

Plaza Concepción Arénal

PARADOR

M. CANALES Y CHOZAS

To Salamanca & via N-501

Puerta Puente Adaja

CONDE DON RAMÓN

RAMÓN Y CAJAL

TRES TAZAS

CONDE DE VALLESPIN

M. FERNANDO TOME

SAN ESTEBAN

CALLE DE SANTO DOMINGO

POCILO

J. SANTO DOMINGO

JIMENA BLAZQUEZ

BLASCO JIMENO

CARRETERA DE BURGOHONDO

CALLE DE LOS TELARES

CONVENT OF ST. TERESA

SANCHO DAVILA

Adaja River

Puerta de Santa Teresa

Puerta del Rastro

PASEO DEL RASTRO

Parque del Rastro

Rastro

CALLE DE ANGEL TORRES

TESO DEL HOSPITAL VIEJO

CALLE EMPEDRADA

JOSE SOLIS

C. DE LA MINA

### Accommodations
1. Hotel Palacio de los Velada
2. Hotel Arco San Vicente
3. Hostal-Restaurante Puerta del Alcázar

### Eateries
4. La Bodeguita de San Segundo
5. Public Market
6. Yemas Pastries

### Other
7. To Cuatro Postes Viewpoint
8. Wall Entrances (4)
9. St. Teresa's Finger

and a huge, canopied, colorfully painted tomb holding three local fourth-century martyrs.

**Cost and Hours:** €2.50, includes audioguide, Mon-Sat 10:00-18:30, Sun 16:00-18:00, off-season closed for lunch 13:30-16:00.

### Convent of St. Teresa

Built in the 17th century on the spot where the saint was born, this convent is a big hit with pilgrims (10-minute walk from cathedral).

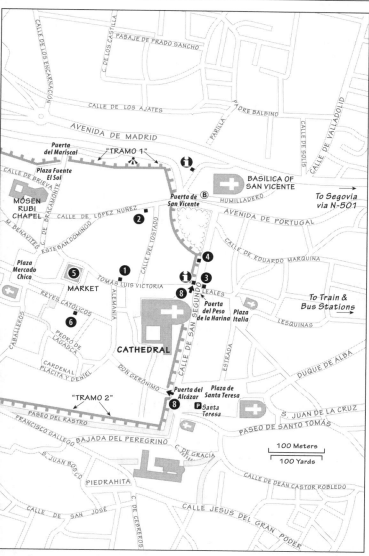

St. Teresa (1515-1582)—reforming nun, mystic, and writer—bought a house in Ávila and converted it into a convent with more stringent rules than the one she belonged to. She faced opposition in her hometown from rival nuns and those convinced her visions of heaven were the work of the devil. However, with her mentor and fellow mystic St. John of the Cross, she established convents of Discalced (shoeless) Carmelites throughout Spain, and her visions and writings led her to sainthood (she was canonized in 1622).

Inside the humble convent **church,** a lavishly gilded side chapel marks the actual place of her birth (left of main altar, door may be closed).

The finger is housed in the little **Sala de Reliquias** at the back of the church shop (as you face the church, it's on your right). You'll see Teresa's finger, complete with a fancy emerald ring, along with one of her sandals and two bones of St. John of the Cross.

A **museum** dedicated to the saint is in the crypt (around the left side as you face the church). Inside under heavy stone vaults, you'll see a wide collection of items relating to Teresa, including replicas of her spartan bedroom and items she might have used. There's also an extensive collection of books, portraits, stamps, and coins of St. Teresa—helping explain why this woman and this convent are so important to so many people around the world.

**Cost and Hours:** Convent—free, daily 10:00-13:30 & 17:00-19:00, no photos of finger allowed; museum—€2, Tue-Sun 10:00-14:00 & 16:00-19:00, shorter hours off-season, closed Mon year-round.

### Yemas

These pastries, made by local nuns, are more or less soft-boiled egg yolks that have been cooled and sugared (*yema* means yolk). They're sold all over town. The shop **Las Delicias del Convento** is a retail outlet for the cooks of the convent (€4 for a small box, Mon-Sat 10:30-20:00, Sun until 18:00, between the TI and convent at Calle de los Reyes Católicos 12, +34 920 220 293).

# Sleeping and Eating in Ávila

**Sleeping:** With Salamanca and Segovia so close, you're unlikely to need a bed in Ávila, but here are a few possibilities. Consider **$$ Hotel Palacio de los Velada** (in a five-centuries-old palace at Plaza de la Catedral 10, +34 920 255 100, www.veladahoteles.com); **$ Hotel Arco San Vicente** (one block from the Basilica of San Vicente at Calle López Núñez 6, +34 920 222 498, www.arcosanvicente.com), or **$ Hostal Puerta del Alcázar** (next to the Puerta del Peso de la Harina, just outside the wall at San Segundo 38, +34 920 211 074, www.puertadelalcazar.com).

**Eating:** Restaurants around Plaza del Mercado Chico, the main square of the old center, are good spots to try Ávila specialties called *chuletón*, a thick steak, and *judías del Barco de Ávila*, big white beans often cooked in a meaty stew. Other good eating options include **$$$ Restaurante Puerta del Alcázar** (filled with more locals than hotel guests, San Segundo 38, +34 920 211 074) and **$$$ La Bodeguita de San Segundo** (good for a light lunch, outside the wall near the cathedral at San Segundo 19, +34

920 257 309). For a coffee or hot chocolate, try the courtyard café of the recommended **$$ Hotel Palacio de los Velada.** For **picnic** supplies, head to the town's market house between Plaza del Mercado Chico and the cathedral, or the Friday-morning farmers market on Plaza del Mercado Chico.

# Ávila Connections

The bus terminal is closed on Sundays, but you can purchase tickets when you board. Bus info: Avanza (www.avanzabus.com), Jiménez Dorado (www.jimenezdorado.com). Train info: +34 912 320 320, www.renfe.com.

**From Ávila to: Segovia** (4 buses/day, 2/day weekends, 1 hour, Avanza), **Madrid Chamartín** (2 trains/day, 1.5-2 hours), **Madrid Príncipe Pío** (nearly hourly trains, 1.5-2 hours), **Madrid Estación Sur** (nearly hourly buses, 6/day on weekends, 1.5 hours, Jiménez Dorado), **Salamanca** (7 trains/day, 1-1.5 hours; 4-5 buses/day, 1.5 hours, Avanza).

# TOLEDO

About an hour south of Madrid, Toledo teems with tourists, souvenirs, and great art by day, and delicious dinners, echoes of El Greco, and medieval magic by night. Incredibly well preserved and full of cultural wonder, the entire city has been declared a national monument. To keep the city's historic appearance intact, the Spanish government has forbidden any modern exteriors.

Toledo was once Spain's capital and packs 2,500 years of tangled history—Roman, Jewish, Visigothic, Moorish, and Christian—onto a rocky perch protected on three sides by the Tajo River. This rich mix of heritages makes Toledo one of Europe's cultural highlights and a great way to sample Spain's cultural layers all in one place.

Today, Toledo thrives as a provincial capital and tourist destination—it's a slick 30-minute train ride from Madrid. And whether you arrive by car, train, or bus, getting into town is easy. You'll find an old city center that's largely traffic-free.

Despite its tremendously kitschy tourist vibe, this stony wonderland remains the historic, artistic, and spiritual center of Spain. Toledo sits enthroned on its history, much as it was when Europe's most powerful monarch, the Holy Roman Emperor Charles V (King Charles I in Spain), and its most famous resident artist, El Greco, called it home. Be sure to get off the main walkways and explore some of the back streets. In just a few steps, you'll find a corner of Toledo all your own.

## PLANNING YOUR TIME

To see Toledo's top sights—including its museums (great El Greco) and cathedral (best in Spain)—and to experience its medieval atmosphere (wonderful after dark), you'll need at least a night and a day. A second day offers a more relaxing visit and lets you see more than the highlights. (Even Toledo's "second-tier" sights rank high on a Spain-wide scale.) Keep in mind that early and late trains tend to sell out to commuters and other day-trippers. After dark, Toledo is the rare Spanish city that feels downright sleepy.

Here's a good one-day plan: Upon arrival, head to the main square, Plaza de Zocodover, and get oriented by following my self-guided walk. Then visit the cathedral interior and the finest El Greco, inside Santo Tomé church. With any remaining time, consider the Army Museum (for history aficionados), the Santa Cruz Museum (for art lovers), the El Greco Museum (the artist's life and times), two remarkably well-preserved historic Mudejar synagogues (Tránsito and Santa María Blanca), or the royal burial church at San Juan de los Reyes. Thorough visits to all of these would take two days, but selective sightseers can mix and match to fill one memorable day.

Plan around lunchtime closures at a few sights, and take a break during Toledo's notorious midday heat in summer. In the evening—or before returning to Madrid—wander the back lanes, sample sweet *mazapán*, people-watch at Plaza de Zocodover, and dine well—*carcamusas* (pork stew), anyone?

## Orientation to Toledo

Toledo sits atop a circular hill, with the cathedral roughly dead-center. Lassoed into a tight tangle of streets by the sharp bend of

the Tajo River (called the "Tejo" in Portugal, where it hits the Atlantic at Lisbon), Toledo has Spain's most confusing medieval street plan. But it's a small town within its walls, with only 10,000 inhabitants (84,000 live in greater Toledo, including its modern suburbs). The major sights are well signed, and locals will politely point you in the right direction. (You are, after all, the town's bread and butter.)

The top sights stretch from the main square, Plaza de Zocodover (zoh-koh-doh-VEHR), southwest along Calle del Comercio (nicknamed Calle Ancha, "Wide Street") to the cathedral, and beyond that to Santo Tomé and more. Most tourists never stray from this axis. Make a point to get lost. The town is compact. When it's time to return to someplace familiar, pull out your map or ask, "*¿Para Plaza de Zocodover?*" From the far end of town, handy bus #12 circles back to Plaza de Zocodover.

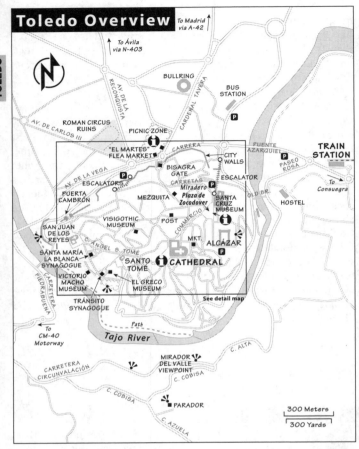

**Toledo Overview**

To Madrid via A-42

To Ávila via N-403

BULLRING

BUS STATION

ROMAN CIRCUS RUINS

AV. DE LA RECONQUISTA

AV. DE CARLOS III

CARDENAL TAVERA

PICNIC ZONE

CARRERA

PUENTE AZARQUIEL

TRAIN STATION

"EL MARTES" FLEA MARKET

CITY WALLS

PASEO ROSA

AV. DE LA VEGA

BISAGRA GATE

CARRETAS

ESCALATOR

To Consuegra

PUERTA CAMBRÓN

ESCALATORS

Miradero

Plaza de Zocodover

SANTA CRUZ MUSEUM

OLD BR.

HOSTEL

MEZQUITA

VISIGOTHIC MUSEUM

POST

COMMERCIO

SAN JUAN DE LOS REYES

C. ANGEL S. TOMÉ

MKT.

ALCÁZAR

SANTA MARÍA LA BLANCA SYNAGOGUE

SANTO TOMÉ

CATHEDRAL

CARRETERA FIERABUENA

VICTORIO MACHO MUSEUM

EL GRECO MUSEUM

See detail map

TRÁNSITO SYNAGOGUE

To CM-40 Motorway

Path

Tajo River

CARRETERA CIRCUNVALACIÓN

C. COBISA

MIRADOR DEL VALLE VIEWPOINT

C. ALTA

C. COBISA

C. COBISA

PARADOR

C. AZUELA

300 Meters

300 Yards

Although the city is very hilly (in Toledo, they say, everything's uphill—it certainly feels that way), nothing is more than a short hike away.

## TOURIST INFORMATION

Toledo has four TIs, which share a website: www.toledo-turismo.com. The TI at the **train station** is handy, but don't confuse it with the private sales agency nearby (the real TI is marked with a purple sign and an *i* in a circle; daily 9:30-15:00, +34 925 239 121). Other TIs are at **Bisagra Gate,** in a freestanding building in the park just across from the gate (Mon-Sat 10:00-18:00, Sun until 14:00, +34 925 251 005); inside **City Hall** on Plaza del Ayuntamiento, facing the cathedral (daily 10:00-18:00, WC, +34 925 254 030); and at the far-left of the orange government building that dominates

**Plaza de Zocodover** (Mon-Sat 9:00-17:00, Sun 10:00-15:00, +34 925 267 666).

**Sightseeing Passes:** Skip the Toledo Pass or Toledo Card—neither save you money over individual tickets.

The **Pulsera Turística** wristband (€10, sold at participating sights) doesn't cover the cathedral, Santa Cruz Museum, or the Army Museum, but it makes sense if you plan to see at least four of the monuments and churches it does cover: Santo Tomé, Santa María la Blanca Synagogue, Monastery of San Juan de los Reyes, Mezquita del Cristo de la Luz, Church of El Salvador, Real Colegio de Doncellas Nobles, and Church of San Ildefonso/Jesuitas (no time limit as long as it stays on your wrist, nontransferable).

## ARRIVAL IN TOLEDO

Since the train and bus stations are below the town center, and parking can be a challenge, "arriving" in Toledo means getting uphill to Plaza de Zocodover. This involves a taxi (affordable), a city bus (cheap), or a walk plus a ride up a series of escalators.

**By Train:** Toledo's early-20th-century train station is Neo-Moorish and a national monument itself for its architecture and art, both of which celebrate the three cultures that coexisted here.

Early and late trains can sell out; reserve ahead. If you haven't yet bought a ticket for your departure from Toledo, get it before you leave the Toledo station. Choose a specific time rather than leave it open-ended. (If you prefer more flexibility, take the bus.)

From the train station to Plaza de Zocodover, a **taxi** is about €5 (the ride to individual hotels might cost a bit more). It's easy to take **city bus** #5, #61, or #62; leaving the station, the bus stop is 30 yards to the right (€1.40, pay on bus, confirm by asking, "*¿Para Plaza de Zocodover?*"). Skip the red-and-purple tourist buses that meet arriving day-trippers at the station—they're a bad value.

It costs very little to take the public bus, or even a taxi, so there's little reason to **walk** (especially in warm weather). But if you feel the need, allow 25 minutes and turn right as you leave the station and follow the fuchsia line on the sidewalk labeled *Up Toledo, Follow the Line*. Track this line (and periodic escalator symbols) past a bus stop, over the bridge, around the roundabout to the left, and into a bus parking area. From here, go up a series of escalators: You'll emerge about a block downhill from Plaza de Zocodover.

**By Bus:** At the bus station, buses park downstairs. Luggage lockers and a small bus-information office—where you can buy locker tokens—are upstairs, opposite the cafeteria. Before leaving the station, confirm your departure time (around 2/hour to Madrid). Buses don't often book up, and you can put off buying a return ticket until just minutes before you leave Toledo.

From the bus station, Plaza de Zocodover is a €4.50 **taxi** ride

# Toledo at a Glance

▲▲▲**Toledo Cathedral** One of Europe's best, with a marvelously vast interior and great art. **Hours:** Mon-Sat 10:00-18:30, Sun from 14:00. See page 184.

▲▲**Santo Tomé** Simple chapel with El Greco's masterpiece, *The Burial of the Count of Orgaz.* **Hours:** Daily 10:00-18:45, mid-Oct-Feb until 17:45. See page 176.

▲**Army Museum** Covers all things military; located in the imposing fortress, the Alcázar. **Hours:** Tue-Sun 10:00-17:00, closed Mon. See page 180.

▲**Santa Cruz Museum** Renaissance building housing wonderful artwork, including eight El Grecos. **Hours:** Mon-Sat 9:30-18:30, Sun 10:00-14:00. See page 178.

▲**El Greco Museum** Small collection of paintings, including the *View and Plan of Toledo,* El Greco's panoramic map of the city. **Hours:** Tue-Sat 9:30-19:30—Nov-Feb until 18:00, Sun 10:00-15:00, closed Mon. See page 195.

▲**Tránsito Synagogue and Sephardic Jewish Museum** Museum of Toledo's Jewish past. **Hours:** Tue-Sat 9:30-19:30—until 18:00 off-season, Sun 10:00-15:00, closed Mon. See page 196.

▲**Victorio Macho Museum** Collection of 20th-century Toledo sculptor's works, with expansive river-gorge view. **Hours:** Mon-Fri 10:00-14:00 & 17:00-19:00, closed Sat-Sun. See page 198.

▲**Monastery of San Juan de los Reyes** Church/monastery intended as final resting place of Isabel and Ferdinand. **Hours:** Daily 10:00-18:45, mid-Oct-March until 17:45. See page 199.

▲**Visigothic Museum** Romanesque church housing the only Visigothic artifacts in town. **Hours:** Tue-Sat 9:45-14:15 & 16:00-18:30, Sun 10:00-14:00, closed Mon. See page 191.

or a short **bus** ride (catch #5 or #12 downstairs; €1.40, pay on bus). It's also possible to **walk:** Exit the bus station, go straight through the roundabout, and continue straight ahead. Look for a tunnel burrowed into the cliff (below the big, blocky convention center), where you can ride a series of escalators into town, letting you off just below Plaza de Zocodover.

**By Car:** Arriving by car, you can enjoy a scenic big-picture orientation by following the *Ronda de Toledo* signs on a circular drive around the city. You'll see the city from many angles along the Circunvalación road across the Tajo Gorge. Stop at a viewpoint or drive to Parador de Toledo, just south of town, for an expansive city view (from the balcony). The best time for this trip is the magic hour before sunset, when the top viewpoints are busy with tired old folks and frisky young lovers.

A car is useless within Toledo's city walls, where the narrow, twisting streets are no fun to navigate (watch your mirrors). Many hotels offer discounted parking rates at nearby garages; ask when making your reservation.

The most convenient place to park is the big underground **Miradero Garage** at the convention center (€16/day; drive through Bisagra Gate, go uphill half a mile, look for sign on the left directing you to *Plaza del Miradero*). From here you can ride an escalator into town. Farther into town, there's parking at the **Alcázar Garage** (just past the Alcázar—€2/hour, €20/day). There are also two big, free, **uncovered parking lots:** the one between the river and the bus station is best if you want to use the escalators to get up to the center; the other lot is between the river and the train station. North of the city walls, you'll find pay parking and another set of escalators going up near the **Glorieta de la Reconquista roundabout,** but at the top you'll still be far from Plaza de Zocodover.

## HELPFUL HINTS

**Sightseeing Tips:** Many of Toledo's sights have **free audioguides** that you can download or listen to while you're at the sight (using free Wi-Fi networks). When buying your ticket, look for signs (or ask) about how this works.

**Taxis:** There are three taxi stands in the old center: Plaza de Zocodover, Bisagra Gate, and Santo Tomé. For around €15, taxis routinely give visitors scenic circles around town with photo stops.

**Nightlife:** Toledo is sleepy after dark. If there's something going on, it's likely at **Circulo del Arte,** a bar and music venue that fills a jaw-dropping 12th-century Mudejar hall—with keyhole brick arches—hiding in back streets near the top of town. It offers a diverse slate of musical events—some free, others with a cover (schedule at www.circuloartetoledo.org, Plaza San Vicente 2, +34 925 256 653).

**Local Guidebook:** *Toledo de la Mano* (*Toledo Hand-in-Hand*, €12) has helpful walking tours and sight descriptions that delve into the city's history and traditions. It's sold at gift shops in the cathedral and at sights such as Santo Tomé church, Santa María la Blanca Synagogue, and the Mezquita del Cristo de la Luz.

TOLEDO

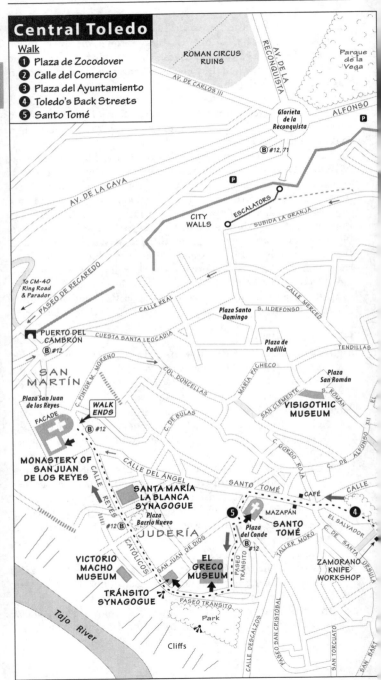

**Central Toledo**

Walk
1. Plaza de Zocodover
2. Calle del Comercio
3. Plaza del Ayuntamiento
4. Toledo's Back Streets
5. Santo Tomé

ROMAN CIRCUS RUINS

Parque de la Vega

AV. DE LA RECONQUISTA

AV. DE CARLOS III

ALFONSO

Glorieta de la Reconquista

B #12, 71

P

AV. DE LA CAVA

CITY WALLS

ESCALATORS

SUBIDA LA GRANJA

To CM-40 Ring Road & Parador

PASEO DE RECAREDO

CALLE REAL

Plaza Santo Domingo

S. ILDEFONSO

CALLE MERCED

PUERTO DEL CAMBRÓN

B #12

CUESTA SANTA LEOCADIA

Plaza de Padilla

TENDILLAS

SAN MARTÍN

C. PINTOR M. MORENO

COL. DONCELLAS

MARIA PACHECO

Plaza San Román

S. ROMÁN

Plaza San Juan de los Reyes

FACADE

WALK ENDS

B #12

C. DE BULAS

SAN CLEMENTE

VISIGOTHIC MUSEUM

C. DE ALFONSO XII

MONASTERY OF SAN JUAN DE LOS REYES

CALLE DEL ÁNGEL

C. GORDO ROJA

CALLE REYES

SANTO TOMÉ

CAFÉ

CALLE

4

SANTA MARÍA LA BLANCA SYNAGOGUE

#12 B

Plaza Barrio Nuevo

JUDERÍA

5

MAZAPÁN

SANTO TOMÉ

EL SALVADOR

C. DE SANTA URSULA

Plaza del Conde

B #12

VICTORIO MACHO MUSEUM

CATÓLICOS

SAN JUAN DE DIOS

EL GRECO MUSEUM

PASEO TRÁNSITO

TALLER MORO

ZAMORANO KNIFE WORKSHOP

TRÁNSITO SYNAGOGUE

PASEO TRÁNSITO

Park

CALLE DESCALZOS

PASEO SAN CRISTOBAL

SAN TORCUATO

SAN BAR

Tajo River

Cliffs

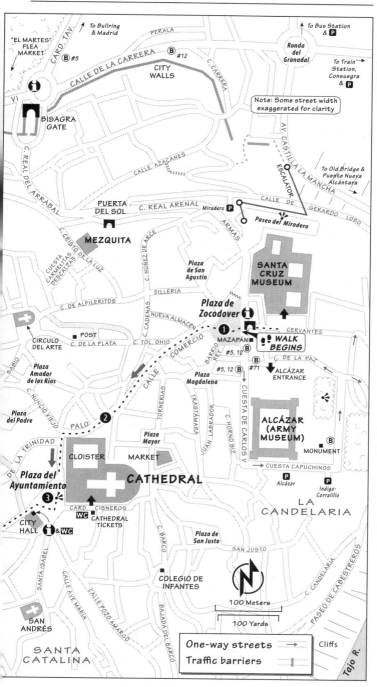

# Tours in Toledo

In this chapter, I've covered all the sightseeing information you'd need for up to two days in Toledo. The main reason to take a tour is to reach the Mirador del Valle viewpoint, on a hilltop across the river. Avoid tourist buses—most sightseeing is in Toledo's walkable old core, where buses can't go, and it's cheaper to pay for a taxi into town and then hop on the tourist train (described next).

## Tourist Train

For a pleasant city overview, take the **TrainVision Tourist Train**— a 45-minute putt-putt through Toledo and around the Tajo River Gorge. It's a cheesy but fine way for nondrivers to enjoy views of the city from across the Tajo Gorge (€6.50, buy ticket from kiosk on Plaza de Zocodover, leaves Plaza de Zocodover daily 1-2/hour 10:00-18:30, later in summer, recorded English/Spanish commentary, +34 625 301 890). For the best views, sit on the right side, not behind the driver. There's a five-minute photo stop at the viewpoint.

## Public Buses

For the cheapest tour, use public transportation. Take my "Bus #12 Self-Guided Tour" through town (see page 201). Or, for a "gorge-ous" loop trip, try bus #71, which leaves from opposite the entrance of the Alcázar (hourly 7:45-21:45) and offers the same classic view across the gorge as the tourist train; its route circles around to the Mirador del Valle viewpoint, where you can get off and snap some photos, then wait about an hour at the same stop for the next bus to take you back.

## Local Guides

**Juan José Espadas** (a.k.a. Juanjo) is a good guide who enjoys sharing his hometown with travelers. He gracefully brings meaning to the complex mix of Toledo's history, art, religion, and culture (€150/3 hours, mobile +34 667 780 475, juanjo@guiadetoledo.es).

Adolfo Ferrero is a personable guide with a background in art history (€150/3 hours, mobile +34 629 177 810, www. toledodelamano.com, adolfo.ferrero@toledodelamano.com).

# Toledo Walk

This walk snakes through the center of town from Plaza de Zocodover to the cathedral and Santo Tomé and then down to the Jewish Quarter, linking all of Toledo's top sights (described in more detail under "Sights in Toledo"). Use this walk to get oriented, and pick and choose which sights appeal to you (prioritize the cathedral interior and Santo Tomé). On a quick day trip from Madrid, stick to the first half of this walk (about an hour if you don't enter any sights); with more time, add the second half, which covers the

Jewish Quarter (an additional half-hour). At the end, you can ride bus #12 back to Plaza de Zocodover. To trace the route, see the "Central Toledo" map, earlier.

## PLAZA DE ZOCODOVER TO THE CATHEDRAL AND SANTO TOMÉ

• *Begin at Toledo's main square, where taxis and buses from the train and bus stations drop off arriving visitors.*

### ❶ Plaza de Zocodover

Position yourself in the middle of the square and survey the scene. Surprisingly modest for the main square of one of Spain's finest

and most historic towns, Plaza de Zocodover is Toledo's transportation hub and your gateway to the old town. The word "Zocodover" derives from the Arabic for "livestock market." This was once the scene of Inquisition judgments and bullfights, but it's now a lot more peaceful. Older people arrive in the morning, and young people come in the evening.

The tourist train to the panoramic Mirador del Valle viewpoint south of town leaves from here, as do city buses #5, #61, and #62 to the train station. Just uphill, near the taxi stand, is the stop for bus #12, which travels around the old town to Santo Tomé (and works as a good self-guided tour—described at the end of this section), and for bus #71, which heads out to the viewpoint.

Toledo is the capital of Castile-La Mancha, and the orange-hued **government building**—sort of the "state capitol"—overlooks Plaza de Zocodover. Look for the three flags: one for Europe, one for Spain, and one for Castile-La Mancha. And speaking of universal symbols, find the low-key McDonald's. A source of controversy, it was finally allowed...with only one small golden arch. Next came the bigger Burger King, which no one blinked at.

Notice the **double-headed eagle** emblem emblazoned on bus windows (you'll find it all over town). It symbolizes the Habsburg monarchs, who briefly made their home here, but has been appropriated as Toledo's city seal.

The "square" has an oddly triangular footprint. In the 16th century, King Philip II—one of those Habsburgs—tried in vain to knock down some buildings and create a more typical square, like the showcase Plaza Mayor in Madrid. But key buildings were owned by the Church, which refused to grant permission. The cathedral in

# Toledo's History

Perched strategically in the center of Iberia, Toledo was for centuries a Roman transportation hub with a thriving Jewish population. After Rome fell, Toledo became a Visigothic capital (AD 554). In 711 the Moors (Muslims) made it a regional center. Because of its importance, Toledo was the first city in the crosshairs of Christian forces. It fell in 1085, marking the beginning of the end of Muslim Spain, which culminated in the fall of Granada in 1492. A local saying goes, "A carpet frays from the edges, but the carpet of al-Andalus (Muslim Spain) frayed from the very center"—Toledo.

Though the city was now dominated by Christians, many Moors remained, tolerated and respected as scholars and craftsmen. During its medieval heyday (c. 1350), Toledo was a city of the humanities, where God was known by many names. People of different faiths lived in harmony. The Jewish community—educated, wealthy, and cosmopolitan—thrived (relatively) from the city's earliest times. Jews of Spanish origin are called Sephardic Jews.

The city reached its peak in the 1500s, when Spain was in its Golden Age, Toledo's bishops wielded vast political power, Emperor Charles V made it his "Imperial City," and artists like El Greco called it home. All of Spain considered Toledo to be the heart of what was becoming a budding nation-state.

Then suddenly, in 1561, Philip II decided to move the capital to a small town north of here—Madrid. Some say that Madrid was the logical place for a capital in the geographic center of newly formed *España*. Others think Philip wanted more room to grow, or to separate politics from religion. Whatever the reason, Toledo—though still Spain's religious capital—began a slow decline. Its medieval structures were never rebuilt, leaving it mothballed. In the 19th century, Romantic travelers rediscovered it and wrote of it as a mystical place, which it remains today.

---

Toledo—Spain's most important—has always exerted an oversized influence on civic life. And that's one of the many reasons Philip II decided to relocate his capital (in 1561) to Madrid, where he could build whatever he liked. The throne's departure left Toledo a forgotten historic backwater...exactly why it's so beloved by visitors today.

Notice the colorful scenes on the tiled **benches** in the square, illustrating events from Cervantes' *Don Quixote*. Cervantes' wife came from near Toledo, and he knew the city well, often mentioning it in his writings. *Don Quixote* even includes a tongue-in-cheek mention that Cervantes didn't write the work—he just translated it from an Arabic manuscript found in Toledo.

Now walk to the edge of the square along the busy street and face the big governmental building. Look uphill to your right to see two of the four corner turrets of the **Alcázar**—the mighty fortress that was for a time (in the 16th century, before Philip left in a huff) Spain's seat of power. During the Spanish Civil War, Franco's Nationalists holed up inside the Alcázar, and the Republicans laid siege to the fortress (see "The History of the Alcázar" sidebar, later in this chapter). Most of the area around the Alcázar was destroyed—this part of town, including much of Plaza de Zocodover, has been rebuilt (notice the *Restaurado 1945* sign on the governmental building). Today the Alcázar houses the Army Museum, a sprawling exhibit on Spain's military history. (I'll point out the entrance in a moment.)

Dodge buses as you cross the street and look right to see an outpost of **Santo Tomé,** one of Toledo's top shops for the delicious almond candy called *mazapán* (the shops are named for the famous chapel). If you're ready for a treat, stop in and buy an assortment to munch. (For more on *mazapán,* and tips on shopping, see "Shopping in Toledo" later.)

Continue down the stairs straight past the *mazapán* shop, head through the arch, and snap a selfie with the statue of **Cervantes** (who's looking down the street named for him).

Looking back above Cervantes' head, notice that the archway you just came through has a distinctive keyhole shape—a classic feature of **Mudejar** architecture, the hybrid Moorish/Christian style of Muslim craftspeople who stayed behind after the Moors were forced out of Spain. Toledo—which was the first major town retaken by the Reconquista, in 1085—is *the* top Mudejar city in Spain. Cities farther south, like Granada, remained Moorish for centuries longer. In many ways, Toledo is a hinge between the Moorish-flavored south and the distinctly Christian north. Throughout the city, keep an eye out for the distinctly Mudejar look.

A few steps beyond Cervantes, look right up the street to the big, blocky building. This is the entrance to the **Army Museum,** inside the Alcázar fortress. Then continue 30 paces straight ahead (downhill on Cervantes Street) and look left to see the frilly Plateresque entrance to the **Santa Cruz Museum,** with a fine collection of art, including some top El Grecos.

• *Retrace your steps past Cervantes, back up through that keyhole arch, and cross the street into Plaza de Zocodover. Continue straight through*

## Toledo's Muslim Legacy

You can see the Moorish influence in these sights:

- Mezquita del Cristo de la Luz, the last of the town's mosques
- Tránsito Synagogue's Mudejar plasterwork
- Santa María la Blanca Synagogue's mosque-like horseshoe arches and pinecone capitals
- Puerta del Sol (Gate of the Sun) and other surviving gates (with horseshoe arches) along the medieval wall
- The city's labyrinthine, medina-like streets

*the middle of the square and carry on (past Hostal Centro) along Toledo's main shopping artery, the aptly named...*

### ❷ Calle del Comercio

This main drag, connecting Plaza de Zocodover with the cathedral, is jammed with day-trippers. But *Toledanos* still shop here, too. As you stroll, notice a mix of local businesses (clothing stores, banks, lotto shops) and tourist-oriented shops (offering knives, leather, *mazapán*, and damascene—fine inlaid work). Many visitors never break free of this gauntlet, but make sure you do—some of Toledo's most appealing back streets lie just above and below here.

After one block, at the Starbucks, look up the intersecting street to the right (above the yogurt shop) for the most-photographed street sign in town: *Calle de Toledo de Ohío*...in honor of "the other Toledo." Elsewhere in Toledo, a similar sign adorns a suburban street called Calle de Corpus Christi—for the Texan town named for Toledo's biggest religious celebration.

Walk a few blocks along Calle de Comercio as it winds through the heart of town. Where the street widens, take the right fork (Calle del Hombre del Palo). Soon you're walking along the bulky wall of the **cathedral** complex, on your left. At the next fork—at the lovely building with the double-headed eagle on top—take a sharp left and continue downhill alongside the cathedral.

As you walk along the cathedral, look about 20 feet up to see metal girders. These support priceless Flemish tapestries—some dating back to the 16th century—during the annual celebration of **Corpus Christi,** 60 days after Easter. On that day, the communion host is paraded around town in a gigantic gold monstrance (you can see it inside the cathedral). For a month leading up to the big day, the 1.5-mile procession route is rigged with a cloth canopy and hung with ceremonial lights.

You'll pass under a skybridge that connects the cathedral to the bishop's palace—the gigantic, hulking building on your right.
• *Just below that, you pop out into the square called...*

## ❸ Plaza del Ayuntamiento

This square is named for Toledo's **City Hall**—the mini Alcázar straight ahead. Notice that this building flies not three flags but four: the EU, Spain, Castile-La Mancha (purple-and-white), and the city flag of Toledo (purple). The low-profile modern fountain in front of the City Hall—designed to resemble the Tajo river-bed—runs every 30 minutes (a TI and a handy WC are inside City Hall). Look around and see how many double-headed eagles you can count on this very proudly *Toledana* square.

Now turn around to appreciate the **view of the cathedral**—it's hard not to be impressed. The tower rocketing up is capped with three crowns—signifying this cathedral's primacy over all other Spanish churches. On the right side, notice the stubby base of what was planned to be a matching second steeple. As work progressed, the foundation began to crumble (you can see the damage). It was being built on the artificially leveled-out square rather than the angled rock at the base of the existing tower. So plans were scaled back and a domed chapel was built instead.

Study the **facade.** The tympanum (over the door) illustrates the founding story of the cathedral: In the seventh century, the local Bishop Ildefonso wrote a book about the Virgin Mary—who rewarded him by miraculously appearing and offering him a holy vestment, legitimizing Toledo as the leading Christian city of Spain. The original carvings in soft, white limestone were later protected by a harder layer of gray granite carvings. Looking up, you can see how workers created a granite canopy over the limestone rose window (which now peeks out a little window of its own). Between the rose window and the tympanum, granite Apostles peer out from the ledge in a Last Supper scene.

The **cathedral interior** is undoubtedly the top sight in town. To enter, head up the lane on the right side of the cathedral. The ticket office is on the right side of the street. (A self-guided tour of the interior is outlined later, under "Sights in Toledo.")

• *When you're ready to move on, we'll take a stroll through…*

## ❹ Toledo's Back Streets

Leave Plaza del Ayuntamiento on the narrow, uphill lane to the right of the City Hall. Continuing straight ahead, you'll go under an arch, then through a little passage and out a door on the other side.

You'll exit to a fine little square. Straight ahead through the square, in the corner, is one of Toledo's most interesting knife shops, **Fabrica Zamorano.** From the storefront shop, you can head to the workshop in back. Why are knives such a big deal in Toledo? In the Middle Ages, Toledo made the very best steel—using know-how imported from the Middle East via Muslim craftsmen. Don

Quixote-type knights of the age considered having a Toledo-cast sword to be *the* top status symbol.

From where you came through the door, turn right, then right again, and curl steeply uphill. You'll be walking along the apse (on your left) of the Mudejar-style Santa Ursula convent from the 13th century (notice the keyhole arches). Until recently, this was home to *mazapán*-making nuns. They've moved out, but there are still several active nunneries in Toledo.

Cresting the hill on Camino el Salvador, notice the wide-open space on your right. In Toledo's medieval cityscape—where streets are tight and buildings are close together—open space like this is a sure sign that something once here is now gone. Sure enough, this was a site of yet another monastery, which collapsed. Now it's a rare park. The modern, bunker-like building behind the park (cleverly lit with skylights) is an archive.

Reaching the end of the park, jog left slightly to continue along Calle Santo Tomé—toward the rectangular steeple. At the start of this street are two more opportunities to sample *mazapán*. On the right is the endearing **El Café de las Monjas,** which sells desserts created by nuns living in Toledo's convents (notice the adorable-slash-creepy window display of nun-dolls hard at work in the kitchen). Across the street, ahead on the left, is the original branch of the **Santo Tomé *mazapán* shop** that we saw on Plaza de Zocodover. The goodies are made at this location.

• *Continue on Calle Santo Tomé. When you reach the tall, rectangular tower, turn left down the narrow lane just past it. You'll emerge at the long square marking...*

## ❺ Santo Tomé

This otherwise unexceptional church is home to the masterpiece of Toledo's great medieval painter, El Greco. *The Burial of the Count of Orgaz* illustrates the attendants of a local bigwig's funeral, both in heaven and here on earth. You'll likely see a line at the ticket office (facing the long square), but the wait is worth it. (For details and a description of the painting, see the "Santo Tomé" listing under "Sights in Toledo.")

The square extending behind Santo Tomé—**Plaza del Conde**—is the terminus for handy bus #12 (bus stop at far end of square). This marks the end of the first half of this walk. If your time in Toledo is short, visit San Tomé, then hightail it back to Plaza Zocodover on the bus (or walk back via the back streets instead of the clogged Calle del Comercio).

• *With more time, continue through...*

## TOLEDO'S JEWISH QUARTER

You've already entered Toledo's former Jewish Quarter, where up until the Middle Ages, Jews were allowed to live, work, and practice their religion. But in 1492, Isabel and Ferdinand expelled the Jews (except for those who converted to Christianity). Most synagogues and other Jewish institutions were destroyed or repurposed as churches, but two very rare synagogue buildings survived.

To reach the heart of the Jewish Quarter—and those synagogues, among other sights (all described in more detail later, under "Sights in Toledo")—continue steeply downhill on the cobbled street past the Santo Tomé ticket office. Stay on this lane as it curves sharply left, descending below the bottom end of Plaza del Conde.

In a few minutes, the lane takes you past the entrance of the **El Greco Museum** (on your right). While the best paintings by El Greco are displayed in three sights we've already passed—the Santa Cruz Museum, the cathedral, and Santo Tomé—this museum offers a more in-depth look at the painter's life and times.

Across the street from the El Greco Museum is a big park (with a giant memorial to the painter). Turn right here, and in 100 yards you'll run right into the entrance to the **Tránsito Synagogue** building, which offers a very rare-in-Spain look inside a historic synagogue and also houses a fine museum.

Continue past the Tránsito Synagogue on Calle de los Reyes Católicos, which links up several more sights.

A block past the synagogue, a side-street on the left leads to the **Victorio Macho Museum,** with works by Spain's most important 20th-century sculptor (watch for signs to *Real Fundación de Toledo*).

Farther along on the right is a little park with a bus stop. Just beyond that is the **Santa María la Blanca Synagogue,** with a more pristine Mudejar-style interior than the Tránsito Synagogue.

Finally, Calle de los Reyes Católicos passes the huge **San Juan de los Reyes monastery** complex,  originally designed to be the final resting place for Isabel and Ferdinand (who wound up being buried in Granada instead). At the very end of the street, the castle-like church exterior displays a variety of chains that were supposedly used by the Moors to shackle Christians in Granada before the Reconquista. The interior of the monastery and its chapel are also worth a look.

• *Our walk is finished. Across the street from the Monastery of San Juan de los Reyes is another stop for bus #12, which you can take on a scenic ride outside Toledo's walls and then back up to Plaza de Zocodover. See the end of the "Sights in Toledo" section for details.*

# Sights in Toledo

I've organized Toledo's sights geographically: near Plaza de Zocodover, the cathedral and nearby, and in the town's southwest end. You can link the major sights using my self-guided "Toledo Walk," earlier.

## NEAR PLAZA DE ZOCODOVER
### ▲Santa Cruz Museum (Museo de Santa Cruz)

This stately Renaissance building, formerly an orphanage and hospital, was funded by money left by the humanist and diplomat Cardinal Mendoza when he died in 1495. The cardinal, confirmed as Chancellor of Castile by Queen Isabel, was so influential that he was called "the third royal." The museum has a good permanent collection (with eight El Grecos) about Spain under Charles V and his offspring, a peaceful cloister with a good ceramics collection, and temporary exhibits.

**Cost and Hours:** €4, more with special exhibits, free on Sun; open Mon-Sat 9:30-18:30, Sun 10:00-14:00; from Plaza de Zocodover, go through arch to Calle Miguel de Cervantes 3; +34 925 221 402, www.patrimoniohistoricoclm.es.

**Visiting the Museum:** The building's **facade** still wears bullet scars from the Spanish Civil War. The frilly decorations around the main entrance (as well as the cloister arches and stairway leading to the upper cloister) are fine examples of the Plateresque style, an ornate strain of Spanish Renaissance named for the detailed work of silversmiths of the 16th century. Note the Renaissance-era mathematics—ideal proportions, round arches, square squares, and classic columns.

Inside, as you make your way down the long hall toward the El Grecos, browse the **exhibits** that set the stage. A century before El Greco's heyday in Toledo, the "Catholic Monarchs"—Ferdinand and Isabel—were turning Spain into a militantly religious country. They were aided by Cardinal Mendoza (see his portrait and blue banner), who drove the Muslims from Granada, founded this Christian charity hospital, and was buried among kings at the high altar of Toledo Cathedral. In Spain's new ultra-religious climate, paintings of saints and altarpieces were artists' main outlet.

The Catholic Monarchs' grandson, Charles V (see his glittering bust in the left "transept"), spread Spanish Catholicism throughout his worldwide empire. His son, Philip II (see exhibits in the apse, near the El Grecos), was especially devout, battling

Protestants in the Counter-Reformation as well as Muslim Turks (see the big blue banner from the Battle of Lepanto, 1571). This was the environment the Greek immigrant El Greco found when he arrived in Spain in 1577 and started working for the introverted ascetic Philip II. It's little wonder that El Greco's main art was designed to express the intense spiritual fervor of 16th-century Spain.

The highlight of the museum is the dozen or so **El Greco** paintings (a rotating display of some permanent, some on loan). El Greco's specialty was capturing ascetic Christian saints in voluminous robes experiencing their moment of epiphany. They tilt their faces heavenward or express their deep feelings with a simple hand gesture. The scenes are rendered in bright, almost florescent colors that give these otherwise ordinary humans a heavenly aura.

Most impressive is *Assumption of Mary,* a spiritual poem on canvas (housed in its own little caged room). This altarpiece, finished one year before El Greco's death in 1614, is the culmination of his unique style. (The *Assumption* more likely depicts the Immaculate Conception, which is how it's labeled.) Bound to earth, the city of Toledo sleeps, but a vision is taking place overhead. An angel in a billowing robe, as if doing the breaststroke with his wings, flies up, supporting Mary, the mother of Christ. She floats up through warped space, to be serenaded by angels and wrapped in the radiant light of the Holy Spirit. Mary flickers and ripples,  charged from within by her spiritual ecstasy, caught up in a vision that takes her breath away. No painter before or since has captured the supernatural world better than El Greco. (For more on El Greco, see page 195.)

Nearby is El Greco's *Holy Family.* The tender, otherworldly scene of Mary and Anne adoring the Baby Jesus is given a down-to-earth touch with a stormy Toledo sky and a balding Joseph—probably modeled after the work's patron. Notice the little scrap of paper in the lower-right corner, signed with El Greco's full name in Greek.

El Greco's *San Ildefonso* celebrates Toledo's hometown saint and early bishop of the cathedral. He meditates on the Bible while wearing the ornate robe marking him as Spain's "Primate," or head bishop.

Next, find the doorway in the right "transept" that leads into the peaceful Renaissance **cloister.** Turn left to find a collection of ancient artifacts—Arabic funerary columns, a third-century

Roman mosaic that depicts the four seasons, and a marble well bearing an Arabic inscription. Note the grooves in the sides of the well made by generations pulling their buckets up by rope. This well was once located in the courtyard of an 11th-century mosque, which stood where the cathedral does today. The cloister is usually ringed with temporary exhibits (look for signs).

Find the frilly (Plateresque) staircase to the upper level of the cloister and enter the beautiful **Carranza Collection** of tiles and ceramics dating from the end of the Reconquista (1492). Stroll through and see how each region (Valencia, Catalunya) had its own style or color scheme, building up to Toledo's distinctive blue pieces in the final room. From the top level of the courtyard, you may be able to go up a short flight of stairs to a temporary exhibit hall with a view down into the atrium that runs through the navel of the museum.

### ▲Army Museum (Museo del Ejército)

One of Europe's top military museums, the Army Museum is worth ▲▲ and at least three hours for military history buffs. (Those bored by weapons and war can skip it.) Much of Spain's history is military, and this museum—housed in the mighty Alcázar fortress that caps Toledo—tells that part of Spain's story from 1492 to the 20th century. You'll see Spanish military collections of armor, uniforms, cannons, guns, paintings, and models. The posted English information is excellent, and the audioguide is a worthwhile supplement. The museum has one major flaw: its skimpy coverage of the Spanish Civil War (1936-1939).

The permanent exhibits fill four floors: thematic exhibits on T1 and T2, and a chronological sweep through Spanish military history on H1 and H2. Read my descriptions before your visit and target what interests you—or follow my once-over-lightly tour of the highlights.

**Cost and Hours:** €5, free on Sun; free to enter temporary exhibits and archeological ruins—ask for pass at ticket office; open Tue-Sun 10:00-17:00, closed Mon; great audioguide-€3, café/restaurant and view terrace, +34 925 238 800, www.museo.ejercito.es.

**❍ Self-Guided Tour:** The floor plan is sprawling and confusing—be sure to pick up the English map to navigate. We'll breeze quickly through, but even at that, this huge collection will test your endurance. So buck up, soldier.

• *From the ticket booth, head up a series of escalators (over the excavated ruins of earlier fortifications) to the...*

## The History of the Alcázar

The Alcázar is the huge former imperial residence that dominates Toledo's skyline. It's built on the site of Roman, Visigothic, Moorish, and early Renaissance fortresses, the ruins of which are a reminder of the city's strategic importance through the centuries. Today the building itself is free to enter to view the archaeological ruins (there's an entry fee for the Army Museum that's housed here).

Today's structure (originally built in the 16th century, then destroyed in the civil war and rebuilt) became a kind of right-wing Alamo. During the civil war, Franco's Nationalists (and hundreds of hostages), commanded by Colonel José Moscardó, were besieged here by Republican troops for two months in 1936. The Republicans kidnapped Moscardó's teenaged son, Luís, and called the colonel, threatening to execute Luís if his father didn't surrender in 10 minutes. Moscardó asked for his son to be put on the line and told him that he would have to be a hero and die for Spain. Moscardó then informed the Republican leader that he didn't need 10 minutes: the choice was made—he would never give up the Alcázar. (While the Nationalists believed Luís was shot immediately, he was actually executed with other prisoners weeks later in a reprisal for an air raid.)

Finally, after many fierce but futile Republican attacks that destroyed much of the Alcázar, Franco sent in an army that took Toledo, a major victory for the Nationalists. After the war, the place was rebuilt and glorified under Franco. Only one room has been left in a tattered ruin since the siege: the office of Nationalist Colonel Moscardó, which you can see if you visit the Army Museum.

**Permanent Collection** (Floor T2): At the top of the escalators, cut through the gift shop to reach the thematic exhibits. We'll skip these for now and head for the far-right corner, where you can take the elevator or stairs to floor H1 to find the "Start of the Historical Tour," a chronological sweep through 500 years of Spanish history.

**1492-1843** (Floor H1): In the first room (labeled *The Catholic Monarchs*), it's 1492, the Muslims have been driven out (see Boabdil the Moor's captured sword and robe), and a united Spain emerges as a major military power. Conquistadors like Cortés (see his *Historia*) were conquering the New World, and Emperor Charles V (portrait) assumed the role of policeman for all of Europe.

• *From here, begin the clockwise loop around level H1 (following "historical round" arrows), sweeping through Spain's military history.*

Browse through the flags *(banderas)*, weapons, and armor of the period. Next, learn about Spain's many wars in the 1500s, including in the New World (with exhibits of Native American weapons).

You'll pass through the open-air **Charles V Courtyard**— Italian-inspired Renaissance in style and adorned with a proud statue of Holy Roman Emperor Charles V (a.k.a. King Charles I of Spain), the ultimate military king and Europe's most powerful 16th-century leader. It's hard to believe that this massive fortress was virtually demolished in the 1930s and later elegantly restored.

• *Continue through floor H1.*

A dozen steps in, find a darkened room with a press-the-button exhibit on the **Battle of Almansa** (1707). Fought by many armies, this battle encapsulates the ultra-confusing War of the Spanish Succession, when all of Europe fought over who should rule Spain. (The Bourbons of France won.) In the next series of rooms, you see how Napoleon overthrew the Bourbons and brought still more turmoil.

• *Cross the stairwell and go into a room labeled* **The Napoleonic War 1808-14.**

On "El Dos de Mayo" (May 2), Napoleon's troops attacked Madrid. You'll see a tattered uniform of a proud Spanish defender; some swords, hats, and portraits of other Spanish patriots; and small works by the artist Goya, who chronicled the events in famous paintings.

A few steps farther (and a century later), you reach the **Moscardó Room.** It's 1936, in the midst of the Spanish Civil War, and Toledo's Alcázar is under siege. This office was the headquarters of Toledo's Fascist forces, led by Nationalist Colonel José Moscardó, holding out against the Republicans. (For more on the siege and the colonel, see the sidebar.) The room is preserved as it was by the end, battered and bullet-ridden. Photos show how the Alcázar was blasted to smithereens.

Complete your tour of this floor by viewing swords, uniforms, and portraits of the Spaniards who fought against Simón Bolívar and other emancipators of Spain's colonies in America.

• *Now take the stairs or elevator up (a half-flight) to floor CI to glimpse the* **Imperial Chapel** *of Philip II, featuring the 16th-century "Charles V tent." Continue up another half-flight to...*

**1843-20th Century** (Floor H2): Pass through a series of rooms on the **"Liberal State,"** when Spain was in decline and her monarchs battled the forces of democracy. Spain also battled the United States (1898) over **Cuba and the Philippines** (see US Army gear, a video on the sinking of the *Maine,* and insignia from Teddy Roosevelt's charge up San Juan Hill).

Continue to "The 20th Century" and the **Spanish Civil War.** Though the war was *the* event of 20th-century Spanish history, the curators chose to dodge the still-controversial issue by going light on it. Displays trace Primo de Rivera's dictatorship of the 1920s and the rise of the Fascist General Francisco Franco in the 1930s. Continue past the displays of 1930s-era weapons and the stairwell to "How the War Unfolded." There you'll find some timelines and maps, a script of Franco's victory speech, and objects rescued from the rubble of the Alcázar—a motorcycle, a telephone, and a daily ration of bread.

Next, it's **World War II.** Though officially neutral, Franco supported Hitler, while many Spaniards became "El Maquis"— guerrillas fighting the fascists. The final exhibits cover the **1970s**, when Franco died (1975) and his powerful military state made a peaceful transition to democracy.

• *Whew. You've finished your 500-year march through history. Now descend (by elevator or stairs) to...*

**Thematic Exhibits** (Floors T2 and T1): Each room is dedicated to a particular collection: uniforms, medieval armor and swords, cannons and early rifles, toy soldiers collection, medals, wartime photography, and non-European weaponry. The "Crypt" (labeled on your map) has the stark tomb of Colonel José Moscardó—who led the Nationalists during the siege of the Alcázar in 1936—and his wife and kids. Room T9 has artifacts from the entire history of the Alcázar—from Roman pottery to Charles V to the disastrous 1936 siege. If you like these exhibits, a few similar ones are one floor lower (T1). These cover the evolution of Spain's flag and display weapons—from battle axes, swords, and pikes to cannons, muskets, pistols, German lugers, and machine guns.

## Mezquita del Cristo de la Luz

Of Muslim Toledo's 20 mosques, this barren little building (dating from about 1000) is the best survivor. Enter through the modern, rust-colored building just below, buy your ticket, and head into the mosque. Looking up, you'll notice the Moorish fascination with geometry—each dome is a unique design. The lovely keyhole arch faces Mecca. In 1185, after the Reconquista, the mosque was changed to a  church and renamed Iglesia de Cristo de la Luz. In 1187 the Christian apse (with its crude Romanesque art) was added and became the city's first example of Mudejar art and the model for all that would come after it. The small garden, with its fountains, is a reminder of the Quranic image of heaven. At the back of the garden, you can enjoy a view of the Mudejar-style Puerta del Sol gateway. And running along the fence in front of the mosque is a Roman road leading to the city wall (discovered when the mosque was undergoing restoration).

**Cost and Hours:** €2.80, Mon-Fri 10:00-18:45, until 17:45 Sat-Sun and in winter, audioguide-€1, west of Plaza de Zocodover at Cuesta de las Carmelitas Descalzas 10, +34 925 254 191.

## THE CATHEDRAL AND NEARBY
### ▲▲▲Toledo Cathedral

Holy Toledo! Spain's leading Catholic city has a magnificent cathedral. For more than 1,500 years, the people of Toledo have worshipped on this spot. The first were Visigoth Christians, in a small church. Around 711, Islamic Moors conquered the city, tore down that church, and built a magnificent mosque. When Toledo was reconquered (in 1085), Christians started using the mosque for their own services. But in 1226, the now-crumbling structure was dismantled, and construction began on the current cathedral. With its long history, Toledo's cathedral is still considered the spiritual heart of Spain.

Over the centuries, the church was decorated with the sights we see today: a five-story Gothic altarpiece, Renaissance-era frescoes, a one-of-a-kind Baroque skylight, a ten-foot-tall golden monstrance, and museum-worthy paintings by El Greco and others. Shoehorned into the old center, the cathedral's exterior is hard to appreciate. But its rich and lofty interior will have you wandering around like a Pez dispenser stuck open, whispering "Wow."

**Cost and Hours:** €10 ticket includes audioguide and Colegio de Infantes; €12.50 ticket adds trip up bell tower at assigned times; cash only, tickets sold in shop opposite church entrance on Calle Cardenal Cisneros (WC inside shop); open Mon-Sat 10:00-18:30, Sun from 14:00, open earlier for prayer only; +34 925 222 241.

### ● Self-Guided Tour

• *Begin in the...*

**Nave:** Wander among the pillars, thick and sturdy as a redwood forest. Sit under one and imagine a time when the lightbulbs were candles and the tourists were pilgrims—when every window provided both physical and spiritual light.

This cathedral is Spain's purest example of the Gothic style. Enjoy the soaring crisscross ceiling, elaborate wrought-iron work,

## Toledo Cathedral

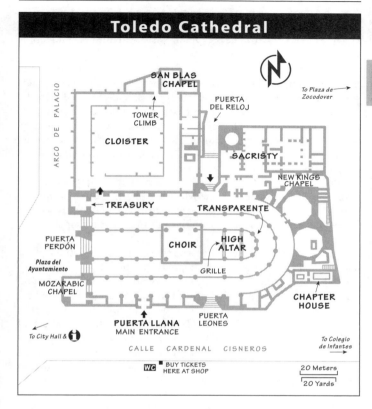

SAN BLAS CHAPEL

PUERTA DEL RELOJ

To Plaza de Zocodover →

ARCO DE PALACIO

TOWER CLIMB

CLOISTER

SACRISTY

NEW KINGS CHAPEL

← TREASURY

TRANSPARENTE

PUERTA PERDÓN

CHOIR

HIGH ALTAR

*Plaza del Ayuntamiento*

GRILLE

MOZARABIC CHAPEL

CHAPTER HOUSE

← To City Hall &

PUERTA LLANA MAIN ENTRANCE

PUERTA LEONES

To Colegio de Infantes →

CALLE CARDENAL CISNEROS

WC  BUY TICKETS HERE AT SHOP

20 Meters
20 Yards

lavish wood carvings, and windows of 500-year-old stained glass. Though Gothic, the church has some unusual features. It's especially wide (200 feet) relative to the length (400 feet) because it follows the footprint of the earlier mosque. (A few red-tinted columns incorporated into the choir wall may have come from that mosque.) The nave is divided into five aisles (not the usual three), clogged with columns, and filled with the choir—the walled enclosure in the middle. Circling the interior are ornate chapels, purchased by the town's most noble families.

• *Head for the space between the choir and the high altar, with its enormous carved altarpiece.*

**High Altar:** Climb two steps and grip the iron grille as you marvel at one of the most stunning altarpieces in Spain. Eighty feet tall and made of real gold on wood, it's one of the country's best pieces of Gothic art. Twenty-seven Flemish, French, and local artists—architects, wood-carvers, painters, and gold-smiths—labored on it for seven years.

Study the wall with the scenes from the **life of Christ,** frame by frame. You can begin in the center with Jesus' birth. On the left side, he's arrested, forced to carry his cross, and crucified. On the right side, he's resurrected and appears to his followers. The images seem to celebrate the colorful Assumption of Mary (upper center), with Mary escorted by six upwardly mobile angels. The crucified Christ on top is nine feet tall—taller than the lower statues—to keep this towering altar approachable.

To the right of the altarpiece is a row of **stone statues** of venerable bishops, saints...and one Muslim. That mellow-looking guy with the cone-shaped hat and beard is the "Wise Moor," who brokered the peaceful handover of the mosque to the Christians in 1085.

To the left of the altarpiece, the two-story **tomb** in the style of a triumphal arch honors the bishop who ushered in the cathedral's Golden Age in the 1500s. Cardinal Mendoza helped Ferdinand and Isabel conquer the Moors in Granada, promoted Columbus, and oversaw completion of this Gothic-style church (its construction took 250 years—1226-1493). He then began a new era of building in a new style—Renaissance. Mendoza and his powerful successors left their imprints, adding the grand altarpiece, the choir, and several of the chapels we'll see later. The wide-ranging decor reflects the church's long history: Gothic, Renaissance, Baroque, and Neoclassical.

Don't miss the finely worked, gold-plated iron **grille** itself—considered to be the best from 16th-century Spain.

• About-face to the...

**Choir:** This intimate space, lined with 120 carved-wood stalls, is where VIPs and hymn-singing musicians (hence the name "choir") can celebrate Mass near the high altar. Stepping inside, you're greeted by a 700-year-old statue of the **Virgin and Child.** Mary smiles sweetly, her body sways seductively, her deeply creased robe is luxuriant, and Jesus playfully tweaks his mother's chin. This "White Virgin" is thought to be a gift from the French king to Spain.

The choir is ringed by **stone statues**—an alabaster genealogy of Christ—starting with Adam and Eve and working counterclockwise to Joseph and "S. M. Virgo Mater" (St. Mary the Virgin

Mother). Compare the stiff, forward-facing statues on the right wall with the more lifelike, twisting, side-posing ones on the left—by Alonso Berruguete, "the Michelangelo of Spain." All this imagery is designed to remind viewers of the legitimacy of the bishop of Toledo's claims to religious power.

The focal point is the archbishop's **throne,** in the center of the far wall. Get close and find the fine alabaster relief just above the throne. It shows the miraculous event that put this cathedral on the map: In the seventh century, Mary came down from heaven to the cathedral to give Toledo's bishop, Saint Ildefonso, a holy robe. This legitimized Toledo as the spiritual capital (and therefore political capital) of the budding nation of Spain. The legend is found in artwork all over the cathedral and the city—including on the music stands nearby and the tympanum outside.

Now turn to the richly carved wooden **stalls,** where worshippers half-sit/half-stand during services. The carvings depict scenes of the Christian Reconquista, specifically the steady one-city-at-a-time finale—the retaking of the towns around Granada. Each castle represents a different town, labeled with its name, besieged by valiant Christian armies. The assault culminates at the archbishop's throne (the two reliefs to either side), with the final victory at Granada in 1492. The soldiers' clothing, armor, and weaponry are so detailed that historians have studied them to learn the evolution of weaponry.

Also check out the **seat backs,** made of carved walnut and featuring New Testament figures—including Peter (key) and Paul (sword) alongside the archbishop himself. Now turn to the stalls' misericords—the tiny seats that allowed tired worshippers to lean while they "stand." These carvings depict various sins and proverbs. They feature folksy, sexy, secular scenes: animals, mermaids, unicorns, and common laborers. Apparently, since you sat on it, it could never be sacred anyway.

The iron **grille** of the choir is notable for the dedication of Domingo de Céspedes, the Toledo ironworker who built it for 6,000 ducats. The project, which lasted from 1541 until 1548, went way over budget. The medieval Church didn't accept cost overruns, so Domingo sold everything he owned to finish it and went into debt. He died a poor but honorable man.

Before leaving the choir, take a moment to absorb the marvelous complexity, harmony, and cohesiveness of the art around you. Look up. There are two fine **pipe organs:** one (frilly, on the left) is early-18th-century Baroque, and the other (austere and pointy, on the right) is late-18th-century Neoclassical. Music has been a big deal here since medieval times. It's part of the tradition that Toledo's bishops trace back to Saint Ildefonso and the days of the Visigoths.

• *As you leave the choir, face the huge altarpiece and go around it to your right to the door in the back-right corner, where you can enter the...*

**Chapter House** (Sala Capitular): Under a lavish ceiling, a **fresco** celebrates the humanism of the Italian Renaissance. There's a Deposition (taking crucified Jesus off the cross), a pietà, and a Resurrection on the front wall; they face a fascinating Last Judgment, where the seven sins are spelled out in the gang going to hell: arrogance (the guy striking a pose), avarice (holding his bag of coins), lust (the easy woman with the lovely hair and fiery crotch), anger (shouting at lust), gluttony (the fat guy), envy, and laziness. Think about how instructive this was in 1600.

Below the fresco, a pictorial review of 1,900 years of Toledo archbishops circles the room. The upper row of **portraits** dates from the 16th century. Except for the last two, these were not painted from life (the same face seems to be recycled over and over). The lower portraits were added one at a time from 1515 on and are of more historic than artistic interest. Imagine sitting down to church business surrounded by all this tradition and theology.

The current cardinal—whose portrait will someday grace the next empty panel—is the top religious official in Spain. When he speaks—especially about controversial topics like divorce, abortion, and contraception—it makes news all over Spain.

As you leave, notice the iron-pumping cupids carved into the pear-tree panels lining the walls.

• *Go behind the high altar to find the...*

**Transparente:** This towering white, red, and gold altarpiece bursting with statues is a unique feature of the cathedral. But that's just half of this multimedia extravaganza.

Look up. In the 1700s, a hole was cut in the ceiling. The opening faces east, and on the morning of the summer solstice, the sun sends a beam into the church to strike the altarpiece, lighten this space for worship, and remind all that God is light. Natural light pours in and down a radiant tunnel of painted angels, which become 3-D angels molded out of stucco—the whole assembly tumbling toward the altar near ground level. On the altar is a marble statue of Mary holding Baby Jesus, who looks up in wonder. Put these elements together, and the result is a Baroque masterpiece.

Now turn to the **altarpiece** itself. Gape up at this riot of angels doing flip-flops, babies breathing thin air, bottoms of feet, and gilded sunbursts. Carved out of marble from Italy, it's bursting with motion and full of energy. Appreciate those tough little cherubs who are supporting the whole thing—they've been waiting for help for about 300 years now.

Step back to appreciate the altar's symbolism: The good news of salvation springs from Baby Jesus, up past the archangels (including one in the middle who knows how to hold a big fish correctly) to the Last Supper high above, and beyond into the light-filled dome. Also notice the two red cardinals' hats hanging on chains from the edge of the hole. A perk that only a cardinal enjoys is to choose a burial place in the cathedral and hang his hat over that spot until the hat rots. I guess the cardinals liked the Transparente, too.

• *Continue around the apse. On the right, enter the...*

**Chapel of the New Kings** (Capilla de Reyes Nuevos): These reclining statues mark the tombs of just some of the monarchs buried in this venerable cathedral. In the 16th century, Emperor Charles V moved these eight tombs of medieval-era kings here. In the short hallway connecting the chapel to the apse, look for a facsimile of an 800-year-old Bible, hand-copied and beautifully illustrated by French monks; it was a gift from St. Louis, the 13th-century king of France. Imagine looking at these lavish illustrations with medieval eyes. (This is a replica; the fragile lambskin original is preserved out of public view.)

• *Back in the apse, the next door on your right takes you into the...*

**Sacristy:** The cathedral's sacristy is a mini Prado, with 19 El Grecos and masterpieces by Francisco de Goya, Titian, Diego Velázquez, Caravaggio, and Giovanni Bellini.

First, notice the fine perspective work on the **ceiling,** painted by Neapolitan artist Luca Giordano around 1690. (You can see the artist himself—with his circa-1690 spectacles—in the far-left corner.) It seems all the angels of heaven are hurrying toward the far end of the room, where Mary (in blue) is descending to earth to give the priestly robe to a kneeling Saint Ildefonso.

The most important painting in the collection—framed by marble columns—is **El Greco's** *The Spoliation* (a.k.a. *Christ Being Stripped of His Garments,* 1579). The great Spanish painter was Greek, and this is the first masterpiece he created after arriving in Toledo. It hangs exactly where he intended it to—in the room where priests donned their sacred robes for Mass.

El Greco shows Jesus surrounded by a sinister mob and suffering the humiliation of being stripped in public before his execution. His scarlet robe is about to be yanked off; the women (lower left) avert their eyes, turning to watch a carpenter at work (lower right) boring the holes for nailing Jesus to the cross. While the carpenter bears down, Jesus—the other carpenter—looks up to heaven. The contrast between the motley crowd gambling for his clothes and Jesus' noble face underscores the quiet dignity with which he endures this ignoble treatment. Jesus' delicate white hand stands out from the flaming red tunic with an odd gesture that's common in El Greco's paintings—with his ring finger and middle finger together (the "Reverse Spock"). Some say this was the way Christians of the day swore they were true believers, not merely Christians-in-name-only, such as former Muslims or Jews who converted to survive.

Other El Grecos adorn the room. His various saints show his trademark style: thin, solemn, weathered men on a neutral background, with simple expressive gestures. Close to the entrance is a scene rarely painted: *St. Joseph and the Christ Child.* Joseph is walking with Jesus, just as El Greco enjoyed walking around the Toledo countryside with his sons. Notice Joseph's gentle expression—and the Toledo views in the background.

To the right of *The Spoliation* is a more down-to-earth depiction of Christ's Passion: Francisco de Goya's *Betrayal of Christ.* It shows Judas preparing to kiss Jesus, thus identifying him to the Roman soldiers.

In an adjoining room are more treasures by master artists, including Titian's probing portrait of Pope Paul III (a friend of Michelangelo) and Cardinal Mendoza's cross.

• *As you step out of the sacristy, walk through an open-air courtyard and make your way back to the nave. Turn right, and head for the far end. As you go, glance high up to your right at a beautiful rose window—the oldest stained glass in the church (14th century). Pass a chapel reserved for worship and head toward the far end. You'll pass a freestanding, fenced-in chapel—supposedly the very spot where the Virgin Mary appeared to Ildefonso.*

*Now locate our final stops: The Treasury is in a chapel straight ahead. Through doors near the Treasury, step outside into the...*

**Cloister:** The cloister is worth a visit for its finely carved colonnade. This area was once the open-air courtyard entrance of the mosque that stood here. Take a peaceful detour around the cloister, passing a subtitled film about the construction of the cathedral, then the funerary San Blas Chapel. The ceiling fresco over the alabaster tomb of a bishop is by a student of the 14th-century Italian Renaissance master Giotto.

• *Returning to the cathedral the way you came, turn right to find the...*

**Treasury:** The star attraction here is a 10-foot-high, 430-pound gold-and-silver **monstrance**—the ceremonial tower designed to hold the Holy Communion wafer (the host) that every year is paraded atop a float through the city during the festival of Corpus Christi ("body of Christ"). Built in 1517 by Enrique de Arfe, it features more than 250 little individual statuettes and details. It's made of 500 pieces held together by 12,500 screws. There are diamonds, emeralds, rubies, and 400 pounds of gold-plated silver. The inner part (which is a century older) is 40 pounds of solid gold. Yeow.

This precious and centuries-old monstrance is still a vital part of civic life, a testament to the Toledo Cathedral's unique position as the religious center of Spain.

• *Your essential cathedral tour is over, but there are several other sights to consider.*

## More Cathedral Sights

**Bell Tower:** If you paid for the bell tower, meet just to the left of the San Blas Chapel at your assigned time. You'll climb several sections of tight spiral staircases (about 200 stairs in all) to reach panoramic views of Toledo and the largest, though cracked, bell in Spain.

**Mozarabic Chapel** (Capilla Mozárabe): Though historic and impressive, this chapel is rarely open to tourists. If you arrive before 10:00 (when the cathedral is open only for prayer; enter from north entrance), you can peek into the otherwise locked chapel. Better yet, attend the 9:00 Mass (daily except Sun) held inside the chapel. This Visigothic Mass (in Spanish) is the oldest surviving Christian ritual in Western Europe. You're welcome to partake in this stirring example of peaceful coexistence of faiths. Toledo's proud Mozarabic community of 1,500 people traces its roots to Visigothic times.

**Cathedral View:** Exiting the cathedral, turn right and walk a half-block to the Plaza del Ayuntamiento, the square presided over by the City. Here you'll find the best exterior view of the cathedral's prickly tower—a fitting end to your tour.

**Colegio de Infantes:** This is where the cathedral displays its fine collection of tapestries and vestments (€2 or included in cathedral ticket, daily 10:00-18:00; from the cathedral go down Calle Barco to Plaza Colegio Infantes, +34 925 258 723). Many of the 17th-century tapestries here are still used to decorate the cathedral during the festival of Corpus Christi. You'll also find the lavish-but-faded *Astrolabe Tapestry* (c. 1480, Belgian). It shows a new view of the cosmos at the dawn of the Age of Discovery: God (far left) oversees all, as Atlas (with the help of two women and a crank handle) spins the universe, containing the circular Earth. The wisdom gang (far right) heralds the wonders of the coming era. Rather than a map of Earth, this is a chart showing the cosmic order of things, as the constellations spin around the stationary North Star (center).

## ▲Visigothic Museum in the Church of San Román (Museo de los Concilios y de la Cultura Visigoda)

Though small, this museum offers a thought-provoking collection of artifacts from Toledo's infancy, displayed in a colorfully decorated church in an untouristed part of Toledo. In the seventh century, Visigoth Christians built a church on this site atop one of Toledo's highest hills. In the 10th century, the church was knocked down and a mosque was built in its place. Three centuries later, the mosque was replaced by the church you see today.

**Cost and Hours:** €2, buy at ticket machine, Tue-Sat 9:45-14:15 & 16:00-18:30, Sun 10:00-14:00, closed Mon, no English information, west of the cathedral at Plaza San Román, +34 925 227 872.

**Visiting the Museum:** Start with the church **interior.** A few Visigoth capitals from the original church were reused and placed atop columns in the nave. The keystone arches, lobed windows, and murals with Christian themes represent the Mudejar mix of Christian and Islamic—each culture both conquering and celebrating their predecessors.

The 13th-century Romanesque **murals** are especially lively. Facing the altar, turn counterclockwise: On the left wall is the ever-popular giant St. Christopher (though this particular fresco is not all that old). In the back corner is an apocalyptic dragon/griffin. The back wall has rows of saints flanking Islamic-style windows. Next, find naked Eve covering herself by the forbidden tree, while God says, "Put some clothes on." On the long wall is a remarkably literal Resurrection: Angels blow trumpets to wake the dead, who lift their coffin lids to climb out. Finally, find three winged angels (one with a bull's head) representing the Evangelists writing their Gospels. Beneath them is St. Eugene ("EVGENII"), the seventh-century bishop who founded Toledo Cathedral in the days of the Visigoths.

Now turn to the **Visigoth artifacts** from the *"Siglo VII"*—the seventh century. (Some are 1,400-year-old originals; some are replicas.) There are column capitals with Roman-style acanthus leaves and stone slabs with Latin inscriptions. To the Romans, the Visigoths were "barbarians" from Germany who conquered and looted the Empire, but in the long run the Visigoths adopted and preserved Roman culture. As Rome fell (AD 500), the Visigoths settled down in Roman Spain, making Toledo their capital and ruling Spain for two centuries.

The Visigoths adopted Christianity and built churches—as is clear from numerous stone fragments here. A carved relief depicts a row of robed saints and naked Adam and Eve. You'll see early Christian symbols: crosses, doves, and olive branches. The

X-shaped symbol flanked by the Greek letters alpha and omega represents how Christ (the X) is the beginning and end of all.

Old coins attest to the Visigoths' thriving Mediterranean trade networks. Manuscripts preserve the Visigoth Law and theological writings that shaped Spanish legal and religious institutions for centuries. (Even Spain's current king traces his lineage—at least, in theory—back to the legendary Visigoth kings.) Pottery, jewelry, and elaborate metal-worked belt buckles give a glimpse into everyday life of these long-ago people.

Most impressive are the **votive crowns** (they look like hanging lanterns). The crowns are made of gold, crusted with gems, dripping with dangling pendants, and filigreed with intricate metalworking. Votive crowns, popular in medieval times, were not designed to be worn. Rather, these ceremonial objects were given to a church or bishop by devoted followers (or nobles needing a favor) to be hung by a chain directly over the altar. Because Toledo was the spiritual center of Spain, the city acquired many. (These crowns are replicas of ones unearthed in a big Visigoth treasure trove 10 miles southwest of Toledo.)

Finally, take in the entire **church.** Imagine it's the year 600, and Toledo is the center of thriving Visigothic Spain. Kings are crowned here in Toledo (including right here in this church). Nobles and bishops from throughout Spain convene here regularly to set policy. They debate whether Jesus was human (as the Arian Visigoths believed) or part of a three-in-one Trinity (as Roman Catholics believed and the Visigoths eventually converted to). During the Visigoth era, Bishop Ildefonso had his vision of the Virgin Mary.

The Visigoths reigned supreme until the year 711, when the Islamic Moors invaded. Because Toledo was the political, cultural, and spiritual head of Spain, by decapitating Toledo, the Moors quickly took the entire peninsula. They built a mosque on top of a Visigoth church, which was, in turn, knocked down to make room for this medieval Mudejar church. Now artifacts from Visigothic times are on display, bringing the story full circle.

If the church **tower** is open, you can climb the steep stairs for a view of Toledo's rooftops.

## SOUTHWEST TOLEDO

These sights cluster at the southwest end of town. For efficient sightseeing, visit them in this order, then return to the center on bus #12 (listed at the end of this section).

### ▲▲Santo Tomé

A simple chapel on Plaza del Conde holds El Greco's most beloved painting—*The Burial of the Count of Orgaz*—which couples heaven and earth in a way only The Greek could. It feels so right to see a painting in the same church where the artist placed it 400 years ago (though moved slightly to accommodate modern crowds). This 15-foot-tall masterpiece, painted at the height of El Greco's powers, is the culmination of his unique style.

**Cost and Hours:** €3, daily 10:00-18:45, mid-Oct-Feb until 17:45, audioguide-€1, +34 925 256 098. There's often a line to get in; try going early or late to avoid tour groups.

**Visiting Santo Tomé:** The year is 1323. Count Don Gonzalo Ruiz of Orgaz, the mayor of Toledo, has died. You're at his burial right here in the chapel that he himself had ordered built. (Count Orgaz's actual granite tombstone is at your feet.) The good count was so holy, even saints Augustine and Stephen have come down from heaven to lower his body into the grave. Meanwhile, above, the saints in heaven wait to receive his blessed soul. (The painting's subtitle is "Such is the reward for those who serve God and his saints.")

More than 250 years later, in 1586, a local priest (depicted on the far right, reading the Bible) hired El Greco to make a painting of the burial to hang over the count's tomb. The funeral is attended by Toledo's most distinguished citizens. (El Greco used local nobles as models.) The two saints, wearing rich robes, bend over to place Count Orgaz, dressed in his knight's armor, into the tomb. The detail work is El Greco at his best. Each nobleman's face is a distinct portrait, capturing a different aspect of sorrow or contemplation. The saints' robes are intricately brocaded and have portraits of saints on them. Orgaz's body is perfectly foreshortened, sticking out toward us. The officiating priest wears a wispy, transparent white robe. Orgaz's armor is so shiny, you can see St. Stephen's reflection on his chest.

The serene line of noble faces divides the painting into two realms—heaven above and earth below. Above the faces, the count's soul, symbolized by a little baby, rises up through a mystical birth canal to be reborn in heaven, where he's greeted by Jesus, Mary, and all the saints. A spiritual wind blows through as colors change and shapes stretch. This is Counter-Reformation propaganda—notice Jesus pointing to St. Peter, the symbol of the pope in Rome, who controls the keys to the pearly gates. With its surreal colors, wavelike clouds, embryonic cherubs, and elongated forms, heaven is as surreal as the earth is sober. But the two realms are united by the cross at right.

## El Greco (1541-1614)

Born on Crete and trained in Venice, Doménikos Theotokópoulos (tongue-tied friends just called him "The Greek") came to

Spain to get a job decorating El Escorial. He failed there, but succeeded in Toledo, where he spent the last 37 years of his life. He mixed all three regional influences into his palette. From his Greek homeland, he absorbed the solemn, abstract style of icons. In Italy, he learned the bold use of color, elongated figures, twisting poses, and dramatic style of the later Renaissance. These elements were then fused in the fires of fanatic Spanish-Catholic devotion.

Not bound by the realism so important to his fellow artists, El Greco painted dramatic visions of striking colors and figures—bodies unnatural and lengthened as though stretched between heaven and earth. He painted souls, not faces. His work is on display at nearly every sight in Toledo. Thoroughly modern in his disregard for realism, he didn't impress the austere Philip II. But his art still seems as fresh as contemporary art does today. El Greco was essentially forgotten through the 18th and most of the 19th centuries. Then, with the Romantic movement (and the discovery of Toledo by Romantic-era travelers, artists, and poets), the paintings of El Greco became the hits they are today.

El Greco considered this to be one of his greatest works. It's a virtual catalog of his lifelong techniques: elongated bodies, elegant hand gestures, realistic faces, surreal colors, voluminous robes, and a mix of heaven and earth. The boy in the foreground—pointing to the two saints as if to say, "One's from the first century, the other's from the fourth...it's a miracle!"—is El Greco's own son. On the handkerchief in the boy's pocket is El Greco's signature, written in Greek. The only guy in this whole scene who doesn't seem to be completely engaged in the burial is the seventh figure from the left, looking directly out at the viewer—El Greco himself.

### ▲El Greco Museum (Museo del Greco)

Housed in a faux 16th-century villa located near the site of El Greco's actual home, this museum offers a look at the genius of his art and Toledo in his day. While you won't find many great works by El Greco here (for those, visit Santo Tomé, the cathedral, and the Santa Cruz Museum), there are a few good ones, along with thoughtful exhibits about his life and work.

**Cost and Hours:** €3, €5 combo-ticket with Tránsito Synagogue, free Sat afternoon from 14:00 and all day Sun; open Tue-Sat 9:30-19:30, Nov-Feb until 18:00, Sun 10:00-15:00, closed Mon; next to Tránsito Synagogue on Calle Samuel Leví, +34 925 223 665.

**Visiting the Museum:** From the ticket office, head through the garden to the museum building. Inside the courtyard, notice the little kitchen, watch the introductory video, and then climb the stairs to begin the one-way route, which shows the evolution of El Greco's art. **Upstairs,** you'll learn about his upbringing in Crete, his training in Venice and Rome, and his arrival in Toledo—each step spurring his style to evolve. One highlight is the long hall lined with portraits of the 12 Apostles, plus Jesus. Compare El Greco's style with Apostles painted by his contemporaries, displayed directly opposite. At the end of the hall is the remarkable *View and Plan of Toledo,* a panoramic map showing the city in 1614—a 400-year-old version of the tourist maps the TI hands out today. It was commissioned to promote the city (suddenly a *former* capital) after the king moved to Madrid. Study the map and list of sights, executed with stunning detail—El Greco must have scratched the writing onto the canvas with a needle dipped in paint.

Continue **downstairs,** where an altar painting of San Bernardine occupies a chapel of its own, under a fine Mudejar ceiling and set inside a simple golden frame El Greco designed himself. The ascetic Italian preacher seems lost in his huge Franciscan robe. At his feet are bishops' hats, representing the prestigious offices he turned down to preach peace to the poor. The painting's lines—the slender cane, the dangling tassel in the robe, the edge of his Bible—all point upward, and Bernadine's robe tapers as it rises, depicting an idealistic saint who clearly had his head in the clouds.

The exhibit wraps up with a description of El Greco's workshop, creative process, and some of his talented students, including his son Jorge Manuel—the kid in the *Burial of Count Orgaz.*

**Nearby:** Across the street is a delightful park, with great views of Toledo's rooftops and river and a giant monument to *Dominico Thetocopvli*—better known as El Greco.

### ▲Tránsito Synagogue and Sephardic Jewish Museum (Sinagoga del Tránsito y Museo Sefardí)

Built in 1361, this is the best surviving slice of Toledo's Jewish past. The austere interior rewards patient visitors with its fine details. Serving as Spain's national Sephardic Jewish museum, the building also displays a modest selection of Jewish artifacts, including traditional costumes, menorahs, and books. Paltry English sheets in each room explain the museum; for more detail, get the audioguide.

**Cost and Hours:** €3, €5 combo-ticket with El Greco Museum, free Sat afternoon from 14:00 and all day Sun; open Tue-Sat 9:30-19:30 (off-season until 18:00), Sun 10:00-15:00, closed Mon; audioguide-€2 (or use free Wi-Fi version); near El Greco Museum on Calle de los Reyes Católicos, +34 925 223 665.

**Background:** This 14th-century synagogue was built at the peak of Toledo's enlightened tolerance—constructed for Jews with Christian approval by Muslim craftsmen. Nowhere else in the city does Toledo's three-culture legacy shine brighter than at this place of worship. But in 1391, just a few decades after the synagogue was built, the Church and the Spanish kings began a violent campaign to unite Spain as a Christian nation, forcing Jews and Muslims to convert or leave. In 1492 Ferdinand and Isabel exiled Spain's remaining Jews, and although a third of them left, others converted to Christianity to remain in the country.

**Visiting the Synagogue:** Your visit comes with three parts: the main hall of the synagogue, a ground floor exhibition space with a history of Spain's Jews, and the women's gallery upstairs, which shows lifestyles and holy rituals among Sephardic Jews.

Pass your bag through an x-ray machine, buy your ticket, and step into the **great hall.** Built as a place for Jews to worship, it still has a few features found in many synagogues today. Men worshipped here on ground level, women in the upper balcony. They all faced the hall's east end (symbolically facing Jerusalem), where a three-arched niche in the wall held the Torah.

But what makes this synagogue unique is that its interior decor looks more Muslim than Jewish. After Christians reconquered the city in 1085, many Moorish workmen stayed on, beautifying the city with the style called Mudejar. The synagogue's intricate, geometrical carving in stucco—nearly all original, from 1360—features leaves, vines, and flowers; there are no human shapes, which are forbidden by the Torah—like the Quran—as being potential objects of idolatry. In the frieze (running along the upper wall, just below the ceiling), the Arabic-looking script is actually Hebrew, quoting psalms (respected by all "people of the book"—Muslims, Jews, and Christians alike).

Move up to the front. Stand close to the holy wall and study the exquisite workmanship (with reminders of all three religions: the coat of arms of the Christian king, Hebrew script, and Muslim decor). Look down. The small rectangular patch of the original floor survived only because the Christian altar table sat there.

The rest of the museum is skippable for most. But if you're interested, head into the **side hall,** with displays about the history of Toledo's Jews and the development of the Jewish Quarter. The Memorial Garden displays Jewish tomb markers from around Spain.

Then head upstairs—through a sunny patio—to reach the

**women's gallery,** which now hosts a small exhibit about Jewish traditions. You'll see candelabras from Hanukah, fancy Torah scrolls, bar mitzvah clothes, wedding regalia, and a circumcision knife, as well as a model of the synagogue itself. There's a display on the Sephardi—Jews who settled in Spain, dispersed across the globe after 1492, but still retain unique customs, language, and heritage. Together, the exhibits help paint a picture of Jewish life in medieval Toledo and today.

### ▲Victorio Macho Museum (Museo Victorio Macho)

Overlooking the gorge and Tajo River, this small and attractive museum—once the home and workshop of the early-20th-century sculptor Victorio Macho—offers a delightful collection of his bold Art Deco-inspired work. The museum's theater hosts a gimmicky multimedia show called the Toledo Time Capsule, which isn't worth the extra fee.

**Cost and Hours:** €3, Mon-Fri 10:00-14:00 & 17:00-19:00, closed Sat-Sun, between the two synagogues at Plaza de Victorio Macho 2, ring doorbell to enter, +34 925 284 225.

**Background:** Victorio Macho (1887-1966) was Spain's first great modern sculptor. When his left-wing Republican (say that three times) politics made it dangerous for him to stay in Franco's Spain, he fled to the USSR, then to Mexico and Peru, where he met his wife, Zoila. They later returned to Toledo, where they lived and worked until he died in 1966. Zoila eventually gave the house and Macho's art to the city.

**Visiting the Museum:** The house and its garden are a cool oasis of calm in the city. Entering the complex, belly up to the terrace for a peaceful and expansive **view** (look for *mirador/balcony* signs for the best viewpoint). From here it's clear how the Tajo River served as a formidable moat protecting the city. Imagine trying to attack. The 14th-century bridge (on the right) connected the town with the region's *cigarrales*—mansions of wealthy families, whose orchards of figs and apricots dot the hillside even today. To the left (in the river), look for the stubs of 15th-century watermills; directly below is a riverside trail that's delightful for a stroll or jog.

The door marked *Crypta* leads to *My Brother Marcelo*—the touching tomb Macho made for his brother. Eventually he featured his entire family in his art.

A dozen steps above the terrace, you'll find a single room, marked *Museo*, filled with Macho's art. A pietà is carved expressively in granite. Next to the pietà, several self-portrait sketches show the artist's genius. The bronze head (from 1904) is a self-portrait at age 17. In the next section, exquisite pencil-on-paper studies illustrate how a sculptor must understand the body (in this case, Zoila's body). The sketch of Zoila from behind is entitled *The*

*Guitar* (Spanish artists traditionally think of a woman's body as a guitar). Other statues show the strength of the people's spirit as leftist Republicans stood up to Franco's fascist forces, and Spain endured its 20th-century bloodbath. The highlight is *La Madre* (from 1935), Macho's life-size sculpture of his mother sitting in a chair. It illustrates the sadness and simple wisdom of Spanish mothers who witnessed so much suffering. Upon a granite backdrop, her white marble hands and face speak volumes.

### Santa María la Blanca Synagogue
### (Sinagoga de Santa María la Blanca)

This synagogue-turned-church has Moorish horseshoe arches and wall carvings. It's a vivid reminder of the religious cultures that

shared (and then didn't share) this city. While it looks like a mosque, it never was one. Built as a Jewish synagogue by Muslim workers around 1200, it became a church in 1391 when Toledo's Jews were first expelled from the city by Christians—hence the mix-and-match name. After being used as horse stables by Napoleonic troops, it was further ruined in the 19th century. Today, fully renovated and sparkling white, it's beautiful in its simplicity. In many ways it's a more evocative and architecturally pleasing sight than the Tránsito Synagogue up the street.

**Cost and Hours:** €3, daily 10:00-18:45, until 17:45 in winter, audioguide-€1, Calle de los Reyes Católicos 4, +34 925 227 257.

### ▲Monastery of San Juan de los Reyes
### (Monasterio de San Juan de los Reyes)

"St. John of the Monarchs" is a grand Franciscan monastery, impressive church, and delightful "Isabeline" cloistered courtyard. The style is late Gothic, contemporaneous with Portugal's Manueline (c. 1500) and Flamboyant Gothic elsewhere in Europe. It was the intended burial site of the Catholic Monarchs, Isabel and Ferdinand. But after the Moors were expelled in 1492 from Granada, their royal bodies were planted there to show Spain's commitment to maintaining a Moor-free peninsula.

**Cost and Hours:** €3, daily 10:00-18:45, mid-Oct-March until 17:45, free Wi-Fi audioguide, San Juan de los Reyes 2, +34 925 223 802.

**Visiting the Monastery:** Before entering and getting your ticket, circle around to take in the **facade** (at the downhill end). It is famously festooned with 500-year-old chains. Moors used these to shackle Christians in Granada until 1492. It's said that the freed

Christians brought these chains to the church, making them a symbol of their Catholic faith and a sign of victory.

Go to the side door to enter the monastery, head down the stairs, and buy your ticket. Then look up. A skinny monk welcomes you (and reminds us of our mortality).

Head into the cloister, then turn right into the glorious **chapel**—made of creamy stone, with clean lines and intricate trim. It's topped with an octagonal dome with interlacing vaults. Even without the royal tombs that would have dominated the space, the chapel gives you a sense of Spain when it was Europe's superpower. The monastery was built to celebrate the 1476 Battle of Toro, which made Isabel the queen of Castile. Since her husband, Ferdinand, was king of Aragon, this effectively created the Spain we know today. (You could say 1476 is to Spain what 1776 is to the US.) Once united, Spain was able to quickly finish the Reconquista, ridding Iberia of its Moors within the next decade and a half.

Sitting in the chapel, you're surrounded by propaganda proclaiming the Catholic Monarchs' greatness. Their coat of arms—

complex because of Iberia's many kingdoms (e.g., a lion for León and a castle for Castile)—is repeated obsessively. Above each one, the eagle with the halo disk represents St. John, protector of the royal family. The yoke and arrows that flank the coat of arms are the symbols of Ferdinand and Isabel. The letters "F" and "Y" intertwined in the designs are for Ferdinand and Ysabel, and the lions underneath remind people of the power of the kingdoms joined together under Ferdinand and Isabel.

As you leave, look up over the door to see the Franciscan coat of arms, with the five wounds of the Crucifixion (the stigmata—which St. Francis earned through his great faith) flanked by angels with dramatic wings.

Enjoy a walk around the **cloister.** Notice details of the fine carvings. At eye level, you'll find (lurking amid the foliage) various animals and fantastic beasts: dragons, lions, eagles, cupids, and naked people. Everything had meaning in the 15th century. In the far corner (kitty-corner across from the entry), just above eye level, find a small monkey—an insulting symbol of Franciscans—on a toilet reading the Bible upside-down. Perhaps

a stone carver snuck in a not-too-subtle comment on Franciscan pseudo-intellectualism, with their big libraries and small brains.

Napoleon's troops are mostly to blame for the destruction of the church, a result of Napoleon's view that monastic power in Europe was a menace. While Napoleon's biggest error was to invade Russia, his second-dumbest move was to alienate the Catholic faithful by destroying monasteries such as this one. This strategic mistake eroded popular support from people who might have seen Napoleon as a welcome alternative to the tyranny of kings and the Church.

The skippable **upper cloister** offers a simple walk around the top level of the courtyard under a finely renovated Moorish-style ceiling.

### ▲Bus #12 Self-Guided Tour (A Sweat-Free Return Trip from Santo Tomé to Plaza de Zocodover)

When you're finished with the sights at the Santo Tomé end of town, you can hike all the way back to Plaza de Zocodover (not fun), or simply catch bus #12 (fun!). The ride offers tired sightseers an interesting 15-minute look at the town walls. You can catch the bus from Plaza del Conde in front of Santo Tomé. This is the end of the line, so buses wait to depart from here twice hourly (at :25 and :55, until 21:25, pay driver €1.40). You can catch the same bus a few stops downhill, at the very bottom of Toledo's sightseeing spine, across the street from the San Juan de los Reyes ticket entrance (a few minutes after it leaves Plaza del Conde). You can do this tour in reverse by riding bus #12 from Plaza de Zocodover to Plaza del Conde (departing at :25 and :55, same price and hours).

If you start at Santo Tomé, here's what you'll see along your way:

Leaving Plaza del Conde, you'll first ride through Toledo's Jewish Quarter. On the right, you'll pass the El Greco Museum, Tránsito Synagogue, and Santa María la Blanca Synagogue, followed by—on your left—the ornate Flamboyant Gothic facade of the Monastery of San Juan de los Reyes. After squeezing through the 16th-century city gate, the bus follows along the outside of the mighty 10th-century wall. (Toledo was never conquered by force...only by siege.)

Just past the big escalator (which brings people up from parking lots into the city) and the Hotel del Cardenal, the wall gets fancier, as demonstrated by the little old Bisagra Gate. Soon after, you see the big new Bisagra Gate, the main entry into the old town. While the city walls date from the 10th century, this gate was built as an arch of triumph in the 16th century. The massive coat of arms of Emperor Charles V, with the double-headed eagle, reminded people that he ruled a unified Habsburg empire (successor of ancient Rome), and they were entering the capital of an empire that, in the 1500s, included most of Western Europe and much of America. (We'll enter the town next to this gate in a couple of minutes.) Just outside the big gate is a well-maintained and shaded park—a picnic-perfect spot and one of Toledo's few green areas.

After a detour to the bus station basement to pick up people arriving from Madrid, you swing back around Bisagra Gate. As recently as 1960, all traffic into the city at this spot passed through this gate's tiny original entrance.

As you climb back into the old town, you'll pass the fine 14th-century Moorish Puerta del Sol (Gate of the Sun) on your right. Then, on your left is the modern Palacio de Congresos Miradero convention center, which is artfully incorporated into the more historic cityscape. Within moments you pull into Plaza de Zocodover.

## Shopping in Toledo

Toledo probably sells more souvenirs than any city in Spain. This is *the* place to buy medieval-looking swords, armor, maces, three-legged stools, lethal-looking letter-openers, and other nouveau antiques. It's also Spain's damascene center, where, for centuries, craftspeople have inlaid black steel with gold, silver, and copper wire. Spain's top bullfighters wouldn't have their swords made anywhere else.

**Knives:** At the workshop of English-speaking **Mariano Zamorano,** you can see swords and knives being made. His family has been putting its seal on handcrafted knives since 1890. Judging by what's left of Mariano's hand, his knives are among the sharpest (Mon-Fri 10:00-14:00 & 16:00-19:00, Sat-Sun 10:30-14:00—although you may not see work done on weekends, 10 percent discount with this book, behind Ayuntamiento/City Hall at Calle Ciudad 19, don't confuse the Zamorano shop—tucked back in the corner—with their bigger neighbor, +34 925 222 634, www.marianozamorano.com).

**Damascene:** You can find artisans all over town pounding gold and silver threads into a steel base to create shiny inlaid plates, decorative wares, and jewelry. The damascene is a real tourist racket, but it's fun to pop into a shop and see the intricate handiwork in action.

**El Martes:** Toledo's colorful outdoor market is a lively scene on Tuesdays at Paseo de Merchan, better known to locals as "La Vega" (9:00-14:00, outside Bisagra Gate near TI).

# Sleeping in Toledo

Day-trippers darken the sunlit cobbles, but few stay to see Toledo's medieval moonrise. Spend the night. Toledo's hotels are modest—it's hard to really splurge here (except for the parador). Most hotels have a two-tiered price system, with prices at least 20 percent higher on Friday and Saturday (I've based my price rankings on weekday rates). Spring and fall are high season; rooms are scarce and prices go up during the Corpus Christi festival as well (usually late May or early June). Most places have an arrangement with parking lots in town that can save you a few euros; ask when you reserve.

## DEEP IN TOLEDO, NEAR THE CATHEDRAL

These places hide out on characteristic lanes near the cathedral; because they're not close to bus stops, it's best to take a taxi on arrival.

**$ Hotel Santa Isabel,** in a 15th-century building two blocks from the cathedral, has 41 clean, modern, and comfortable rooms and squeaky tile hallways (some view rooms, elevator, scenic roof terrace, pay parking—call same day to reserve, drivers enter from Calle Pozo Amargo, Calle Santa Isabel 24, +34 925 253 120, www.hotelsantaisabeltoledo.es, info@hotelsantaisabeltoledo.es).

**$ La Posada de Manolo** rents 14 tight, rustic, cozy rooms across from the downhill corner of the cathedral. Manolo Junior (and wife Almudena) opened this *hostal* according to his father's vision: a place with each of its three floors themed differently— Moorish, Jewish, and Christian. The place has its quirks, and noise carries through its tiled halls, but it has personality and is popular with European tourists (RS%, view terraces, Calle Sixto Ramón Parro 8, +34 925 282 250, www.laposadademanolo.com, toledo@laposadademanolo.com).

**$ Hotel Eurico** cleverly fits 23 dated, simple, but well-priced and well-located rooms into a medieval building buried deep in the old town (air-con, Calle Santa Isabel 3, +34 925 284 178, www.hoteleurico.com, reservas@hoteleurico.com).

## NEAR PLAZA DE ZOCODOVER

**$ Antidoto Rooms'** owner was looking to create an antidote to the epidemic of same-old, same-old, ye olde hotels in Toledo. He succeeded, crafting 10 modern rooms with concrete floors

TOLEDO

# Toledo Hotels & Restaurants

## Accommodations

1. Hotel Santa Isabel
2. La Posada de Manolo
3. Hotel Eurico
4. Antidoto Rooms
5. Hotel Toledo Imperial
6. Hotel La Conquista de Toledo
7. Hotel Pintor El Greco
8. Hotel San Juan de los Reyes
9. Hacienda del Cardenal
10. Hotel Abad
11. El Hostal Puerta Bisagra
12. To Albergue Juvenil San Servando (Hostel)
13. Oh Oasis Hostel
14. To Parador de Toledo

## Eateries & Other

15. Los Cuatro Tiempos Restaurante
16. El Botero Taberna
17. El Trébol
18. Restaurante Ludeña
19. El Nuevo Almacén
20. Madre Tierra Restaurante Vegetariano
21. Restaurante Placido & El Café de las Monjas
22. Mercado Municipal
23. Supermarket
24. Santo Tomé Mazapán Shop (2)

Parque de la Vega

ALFONSO

P

9

To 14
CM-40
Ring Road
& Parador

PASEO DE RECAREDO

CALLE REAL

CALLE MERCED

Plaza Santo Domingo

S. ILDEFONSO

PUERTO DEL CAMBRÓN

(B) #12

CUESTA SANTA LEOCADIA

Plaza de Padilla

TENDILLAS

SAN MARTÍN

C. PINTOR M. MORENO

COL. DONCELLAS

MARÍA PACHECO

Plaza San Román

Plaza San Juan de los Reyes

FACADE

(B) #12

C. DE BULAS

SAN CLEMENTE

S. ROMÁN

VISIGOTHIC MUSEUM

EL

MONASTERY OF SAN JUAN DE LOS REYES

CALLE DEL ÁNGEL

C. GORDO ROJA

C. DE ALFONSO XII

SANTA MARÍA LA BLANCA SYNAGOGUE

CALLE REYES

SANTO TOMÉ

CAFÉ

CALLE

Plaza Barrio Nuevo

#12 (B)

JUDERÍA

MAZAPÁN 24

EL SALVADOR

C. DE SANTA URSULA

8

C. DOCUOS

SAN JUAN DE DIOS

Plaza del Conde

SANTO TOMÉ

(B) #12

VICTORIO MACHO MUSEUM

EL GRECO MUSEUM

PASEO TRÁNSITO

TALLER MORO

ZAMORANO KNIFE WORKSHOP

SAN BART

TRÁNSITO SYNAGOGUE

PASEO TRÁNSITO

7

Tajo River

Park

Cliffs

CALLE DESCALZOS

PASEO SAN CRISTÓBAL

SAN TORCUATO

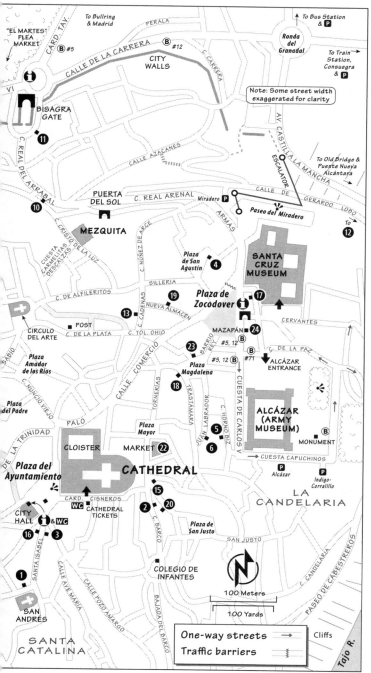

and pops of color, each with a tiny balcony. It's ideally located on a back street just a short stroll from Plaza de Zocodover (elevator, air-con, Calle Recoletos 2, +34 925 228 851, www.antidotorooms.com).

**$ Hotel Toledo Imperial,** sitting efficiently above Plaza de Zocodover, rents 29 nondescript rooms (air-con, elevator, Calle Horno de los Bizcochos 5, +34 925 280 034, www.hoteltoledoimperial.com, reservas@hoteltoledoimperial.com).

**$ Hotel La Conquista de Toledo,** with 35 dated but well-priced rooms, gleams with marble—it almost feels more like a hospital than a hotel (family rooms, air-con, elevator, Juan Labrador 8, +34 925 210 760, www.hotelconquistadetoledo.com, conquistadetoledo@yithoteles.com).

## IN THE JEWISH QUARTER

Most of the hotels I list in Toledo are older and rough around the edges. But the two listed here are slick, more expensive business-class options. They sit lower in the old town—near the Jewish Quarter sights and El Greco Museum—in an area that's less convenient to the central sights or the train and bus stations, but more historic and appealing than the area near Bisagra Gate.

**$$ Hotel Pintor El Greco** is a chain hotel with 56 modern, colorful rooms across the street from the El Greco Museum (elevator, air-con, pay parking, Calle Alamillos del Tránsito 13, +34 925 285 191, www.hotelpintorelgreco.com)

**$$ Hotel San Juan de los Reyes** fills a historic old 19th-century brick factory building with 35 cookie-cutter, characterless, but predictably comfortable rooms, on the road between its namesake monastery and the Tránsito Synagogue (elevator, air-con, pay parking, Calle Reyes Católicos 5, +34 925 283 535, www.hotelsanjuandelosreyes.com).

## NEAR BISAGRA GATE

These places are a bit handier to the train and bus stations and have easier parking for drivers. The trade-off is that they require a steep hike (with the help of escalators) or a bus or taxi ride to reach the core of Toledo's sightseeing. All face busy roads, so expect street noise.

**$$ Hacienda del Cardenal,** a 17th-century cardinal's palace built into Toledo's wall, is quiet and elegant, with 27 rooms, a cool garden, and a stuffy restaurant. This poor man's parador—a pleasant oasis next to the dusty old gate of Toledo—is close to the station, but below all the old-town action (elevator, air-con, enter through town wall 100 yards below Bisagra Gate, Paseo de Recaredo 24, +34 925 224 900, www.haciendadelcardenal.com, hotel@haciendadelcardenal.com).

**$ Hotel Abad,** just a block inside the Bisagra Gate (next to the Puerta del Sol), feels more stylish than the Toledo norm. They rent 28 trendy-rustic rooms with stone walls, wooden rafters, and contemporary furnishings at the higher end of this price range (air-con, elevator, Calle Real del Arrabal 1, +34 925 283 500, www.hotelabadtoledo.com, reservas@hotelabad.com).

**$ El Hostal Puerta Bisagra,** in a sprawling old building, is fresh and modern inside. It's picturesquely located right next to Bisagra Gate, with 38 comfortable rooms at a good value (air-con, elevator, Calle del Potro 5, +34 925 285 277, www.puertabisagra.com, elhostal@puertabisagra.com).

## HOSTELS

**¢ Albergue Juvenil San Servando** youth hostel, located in the 10th-century Moorish castle of San Servando, is lavish but affordable, with 96 beds and small rooms for two or four people (swimming pool, 10-minute walk from train station, 15-minute hike from town center, over Puente de Alcántara outside town, +34 925 224 554, reservations +34 925 221 676, alberguesclm@jccm.es, no English spoken).

**¢ Oh Oasis Hostel** is a fresh, professionally run 21-room hostel right around the corner from Plaza de Zocodover. They have a pleasant rooftop terrace, shared dorms, and private rooms that are even nicer than some more expensive, more traditional *hostales;* however, given the younger clientele, weekends can be noisy (air-con, elevator, Calle Cadenas 5, +34 925 227 650, www.hosteloasis.com, toledo@hostelsoasis.com).

## OUTSIDE TOWN WITH GRAND TOLEDO VIEW

**$$$ Parador de Toledo,** with 79 rooms, is one of Spain's best-known inns. Guests enjoy a sprawling Toledo view across the Tajo Gorge (some view rooms, fixed-price meals sans drinks in their fine restaurant overlooking Toledo, 2 windy miles from town at Cerro del Emperador—it may come up as Carretera de Cobisa on mapping apps, +34 925 221 850, www.parador.es, toledo@parador.es).

# Eating in Toledo

A day full of El Greco and the romance of Toledo after dark puts me in the mood for game (hunted in the hills to the south, along the border with La Mancha) and other traditional cuisine. Typical Toledo dishes include partridge *(perdiz),* venison *(venado),* wild boar *(jabalí),* roast suckling pig *(cochinillo asado),* or baby lamb (*cordero*—similarly roasted after a few weeks of mother's milk). Also popular is the flavorful pork stew called *carcamusas*—everyone seems to have their own recipe. After dinner, find a *mazapán* place for dessert.

Compared to many Spanish cities, Toledo doesn't have a thriving, concentrated tapas scene (its tapas bars are scattered around town). This makes Toledo a good place for a sit-down meal.

## MEMORABLE DINING

**$$$ Los Cuatro Tiempos Restaurante** ("The Four Seasons") specializes in local game and roasts, proficiently served in a tasteful and elegant setting—a mix of traditional and modern. They offer spacious dining with an extensive and inviting Spanish wine list. It's a good choice for a quiet, romantic dinner, and a good value for a filling lunch (Mon-Sat 13:00-16:00 & 20:30-23:00, Sun 13:00-16:00 only, at downhill corner of cathedral, Calle Sixto Ramón Parro 5, +34 925 223 782).

**$$$ El Botero Taberna** is a delightful little hideaway. The barman downstairs serves mojitos, fine wine, and exquisite tapas that are well priced and described. Upstairs is an intimate, seven-table restaurant with romantic, white-tablecloth ambience and modern Mediterranean dishes (Wed-Sun 13:30-16:00 & 21:00-23:30, Mon 13:30-16:00 only, closed Tue, a block from cathedral at Calle de la Ciudad 5, +34 925 229 088).

## SIMPLE RESTAURANTS

Plaza de Zocodover is busy with eateries serving basic food at affordable prices, and its people-watching scene is great. But my recommended eateries are on side streets a bit off the main drag. These places are listed roughly in geographical order from Plaza de Zocodover to Santo Tomé. It's worth a few extra minutes—and the navigating challenge—to find places where you'll be eating with locals as well as with tourists. Toledo also has a lively midday tapas scene, and almost every bar you pop into for a stand-up drink will come with a small plate of something to nibble.

**$$ El Trébol,** tucked peacefully away just a few steps off Plaza de Zocodover, is the place to dine with younger Spaniards. Locals enjoy their *pulgas* (sandwiches), and their mixed grill can feed two. The seating inside is basic, but the outdoor tables are nice (daily 9:00-24:00, Calle de Santa Fe 1, +34 925 281 297).

**$$ Restaurante Ludeña** is a classic eatery with a dive bar up front, a well-worn dining room in back, and a handful of tables on a sunny courtyard. It's very central. Arrive early, as lots of locals duck in here to pretend there's no tourism in Toledo. They serve up big, stick-to-your-ribs portions of traditional comfort food, including a rich, bright-red *carcamusas* pork stew; their filling fixed-price meals are a good value (Mon-Wed 10:30-16:30, Thu-Sun 10:30-16:30 & 20:00-23:00, Plaza de la Magdalena 10, +34 925 223 384).

**$$ El Nuevo Almacén** cooks up classic Spanish ingredients in its tapas, pizzas, sandwiches, and hamburgers. They also serve coffee and Spanish-style breakfasts. It's conveniently located just off Plaza de Zocodover (daily 9:00-24:00, Calle Nueva 7, +34 925 283 937).

**$$ Madre Tierra Restaurante Vegetariano** is Toledo's answer to a vegetarian's prayer. While service is typically slow, the place is bright, spacious, classy, and air-conditioned. Its appetizing vegetarian dishes are based on both international and traditional Spanish cuisine (good tea selection, Wed-Sun 13:00-16:00 & 20:30-23:00, Mon 13:00-16:00 only, closed Tue, 20 yards below La Posada de Manolo just before reaching Plaza de San Justo, Bajada de Tripería 2, +34 925 223 571).

**$$ Restaurante Placido,** run by high-energy Anna and *abuela* (grandma) Sagradio, serves traditional family-style cuisine on a shady terrace or in a wonderful Franciscan monastery courtyard (open daily for lunch and dinner in summer, lunch only in winter, about a block uphill from Santo Tomé at Calle Santo Tomé 2, +34 925 222 603).

**Picnics:** Picnics are best assembled at the humble city market, **Mercado Municipal,** on Plaza Mayor (on the Alcázar side of cathedral, with a supermarket inside open Mon-Sat 9:00-14:30 & 17:00-20:00 and stalls open mostly in the mornings until 14:00, closed Sun). **Supermarket Unide,** on Plaza de la Magdalena, has groceries and lots of other stuff at good prices (daily 9:30-22:00, just below Plaza de Zocodover). For a picnic with people-watching on an atmospheric square, consider Plaza de Zocodover or Plaza del Ayuntamiento.

## AND FOR DESSERT: *MAZAPÁN*

Toledo's famous almond-fruity-sweet *mazapán* is sold all over town. The nuns living in Toledo's convents were once the main providers of this delight—each piece lovingly shaped by hand—but the number of nuns is dwindling. If you can't track down a convent still selling sweets in the labyrinth of Holy Toledo, visit **El Café de las Monjas,** a pastry and coffee shop around the corner from the Santo Tomé church that brings in *mazapán* from local convents (daily 9:00-21:00, Calle Santo Tomé 2).

The big *mazapán* producer is **Santo Tomé** (several outlets, including near Plaza de Zocodover and at Calle Santo Tomé 3, daily 9:00-22:00). Browse their tempting window displays. They sell *mazapán* goodies individually (*sin relleno*—without filling—is for purists, *de piñon* has pine nuts, *imperiales* is with almonds, others have fruit fillings). Boxes are good for gifts, but if you want an assortment, tell them what you want à la carte. Their *Toledana* is a bigger, nutty, crumbly, not-too-sweet cookie with a subtle thread of squash filling.

For a sweet and romantic evening dessert, pick up a few pastries and head down to the cathedral. Sit on the Plaza del Ayuntamiento's benches (or stretch out on the stone wall to the right of the TI). A fountain is on your right, Spain's best-looking City Hall is behind you, and there before you is her top cathedral—built back when Toledo was Spain's capital—shining brightly against the black night sky.

# Toledo Connections

## FROM TOLEDO TO MADRID

Madrid and Toledo are very easily connected. The train makes the trip in 30 minutes to Madrid's fairly central Atocha station; buses depart twice as frequently but take nearly twice as long to reach the more distant Plaza Elíptica. Three or four people traveling together can share a taxi economically. To get elsewhere in Spain from Toledo, assume you'll have to transfer in Madrid; see "Madrid Connections" at the end of that chapter.

**By Train:** Nearly hourly, 30 minutes by AVE or Avant to Madrid's Atocha station (www.renfe.com); early and late trains can sell out—reserve ahead.

**By Bus:** 2/hour, 1-1.5 hours, bus drops you at Madrid's Plaza Elíptica Metro stop, 1/day direct morning bus to Madrid's Barajas Airport Terminal 4, 1.5 hours, Alsa (www.alsa.es); you can almost always just drop in and buy a ticket minutes before departure.

**By Taxi:** While it may seem extravagant, if you have limited time, lots of luggage, and a small group, simply taking a taxi from your Toledo hotel to your Madrid hotel is breathtakingly efficient (€90, one hour door-to-door, +34 925 255 050 or +34 925 227 070). You can ask several cabbies for their best "off the meter" rate. A taxi to the Madrid airport costs €110 (find one who will go "off the meter") and takes an hour.

## ROUTE TIPS FOR DRIVERS

**Toledo to Madrid** (45 miles, 1 hour): It's a speedy, *autovía* north, past one of La Mancha's classic bull billboards, to Madrid (on A-42). The highways converge into M-30, which encircles Madrid. Follow it to the left (*Nor* or *Oeste*) and take the Plaza de España exit to get to the city center. If you're airport-bound, keep heading into Madrid until you see the airplane symbol (N-II).

To drive to Atocha station in Madrid, take the exit off M-30 for Plaza de Legazpi, then take Delicias (second on your right off the square). Parking for rental-car return is on the north side of the train station. The less-convenient toll road AP-42 will also take you from Toledo to Madrid.

**Toledo to Granada** (230 miles; 3.5 hours): Driving between Toledo and Granada, you'll pass through **La Mancha,** which shows a side of Spain that you'll see nowhere else—vast and flat. You feel lost in rough seas of olive-green polka dots. Random buildings look like houses and hotels hurled off some heavenly Monopoly board.

This is the setting of Miguel de Cervantes' *Don Quixote,* published in the early 17th century, after England sank the Armada and the Spanish Empire began

its decline. Cervantes' star character fights doggedly for good, for justice, and against the fall of Spain and its traditional old-regime ideals. Ignoring reality, Don Quixote is a hero fighting a hopeless battle. Stark La Mancha is the perfect stage.

Above Almonacid (8 miles from Toledo), follow the ruined lane past the ruined church up to the ruined castle. The jovial locals hike up with kids and kites.

But the epitome of *Don Quixote* country is the town of **Consuegra** (one hour south of Toledo, www.aytoconsuegra.es). It must

be the La Mancha that Cervantes had in mind. Drive up to the ruined 12th-century castle and joust with a windmill. It's hot and buggy here, but the powerful view overlooking the village, with its sun-bleached light-red roofs, modern concrete reality, and harsh, windy silence, makes for a profound picnic. The castle belonged to the Knights of St. John (12th and 13th centuries) and is associated with their trip to Jerusalem during the Crusades. Originally built from the ruins of a nearby Roman circus, it has been recently restored. Sorry, the windmills are post-Cervantes, only about 250 years old—but you can go inside the Molino de Bolero to see how it works.

# PRACTICALITIES

This section covers just the basics on traveling in Spain (for much more information, see *Rick Steves Spain*). You'll find free advice on specific topics at RickSteves.com/tips.

## MONEY

Spain uses the euro currency: 1 euro (€) = about $1.20. To convert prices in euros to dollars, add about 20 percent: €20 = about $24, €50 = about $60. (Check www.oanda.com for the latest exchange rates.)

The standard way for travelers to get euros is to withdraw money from an ATM (known as a *cajero automático*) using a debit or credit card, ideally with a Visa or MasterCard logo.

Before departing, call your bank or credit-card company: Confirm that your card(s) will work overseas, ask about international transaction fees, and alert them that you'll be making withdrawals in Europe. Also ask for the PIN number for your credit card—you may need it for Europe's "chip-and-PIN" payment machines. Allow time for your bank to mail your PIN to you.

European cards use chip-and-PIN technology; most chip cards issued in the US instead require a signature. European card readers may generate a receipt for you to sign—or prompt you to enter your PIN (so it's good to know it). US credit cards may not work at some self-service payment machines (transit-ticket kiosks, parking kiosks, etc.). If your card won't work, look for a cashier who can process the transaction manually—or pay in cash.

"Tap to pay" cards and smartphone payment apps work in Europe just as they do in the US, and sidestep chip-and-PIN compatibility issues.

To keep your cash, cards, and valuables safe, wear a money belt.

**Dynamic Currency Conversion:** If merchants offer to convert your purchase price into dollars (called dynamic currency conversion, or DCC), refuse this "service." You'll pay extra for the expensive convenience of seeing your charge in dollars. If an ATM offers to "lock in" your conversion rate, choose "proceed without conversion." Other prompts might state, "You can be charged in dollars: Press YES for dollars, NO for euros." Always choose the local currency.

## STAYING CONNECTED

The simplest solution is to bring your own device—mobile phone, tablet, or laptop—and use it just as you would at home (following the money-saving tips below). For more on phoning, see RickSteves.com/phoning. For a one-hour talk covering tech issues for travelers, see RickSteves.com/mobile-travel-skills.

**To Call from a US Phone:** Phone numbers in this book are presented exactly as you would dial them from a US mobile phone. For international access, press and hold the 0 key until you get a + sign, then dial the country code (34 for Spain) and phone number. To dial from a US landline, replace + with 011 (US/Canada international access code).

**From a European Landline:** Replace + with 0 (Europe international access code), then dial the country code (34 for Spain) and phone number.

**Within Spain:** To place a domestic call (from a Spanish landline or mobile), drop the +34 from the phone number printed in this book.

**Tips:** If you bring your mobile phone, consider getting an international plan; most providers offer a simple bundle that includes calling, messaging, and data.

Use Wi-Fi whenever possible. Most hotels and many cafés offer free Wi-Fi, and you may also find it at tourist information offices (TIs), major museums, and public-transit hubs. With Wi-Fi you can use your phone or tablet to make free or low-cost calls via a calling app such as Skype, WhatsApp, FaceTime, or Google Hangouts. When you need to get online but can't find Wi-Fi, turn on your cellular network (or turn off airplane mode) just long enough for the task at hand.

Most **hotels** charge a fee for placing calls—ask for rates before you dial. You can use a prepaid international phone card (*tarjeta telefónica con código*, usually available at newsstands, tobacco shops, and train stations) to call out from your hotel.

## Sleep Code

Hotels in this book are categorized according to the average price of a standard double room without breakfast in high season.

| | | |
|---|---|---|
| **$$$$** | **Splurge:** Most rooms over €170 |
| **$$$** | **Pricier:** €130-170 |
| **$$** | **Moderate:** €90-130 |
| **$** | **Budget:** €50-90 |
| **¢** | **Backpacker:** Under €50 |
| **RS%** | **Rick Steves discount** |

Unless otherwise noted, credit cards are accepted, hotel staff speak basic English, and free Wi-Fi is available. Comparison-shop by checking prices at several hotels (on each hotel's own website, on a booking site, or by email). For the best deal, *book directly with the hotel.* Ask for a discount if paying in cash; if the listing includes **RS%,** request a Rick Steves discount.

## SLEEPING

I've categorized my recommended accommodations based on price, indicated with a dollar sign rating (see sidebar). I recommend reserving rooms in advance, particularly during peak season. Once your dates are set, check the specific price for your preferred stay at several hotels. You can do this either by comparing prices on Hotels.com or Booking.com, or by checking the hotels' own websites. To get the best deal, contact my family-run hotels directly by phone or email. When you go direct, the owner avoids the commission paid to booking sites, giving them wiggle room to offer you a discount, a nicer room, or free breakfast. If you prefer to book online, it's to your advantage to use the hotel's website.

For complicated requests, send an email with the following information: number and type of rooms; number of nights; arrival date; departure date; any special needs; and applicable discounts (such as a Rick Steves discount, cash discount, or promotional rate). Use the European style for writing dates: day/month/year.

In general, hotel prices can soften if you do any of the following: offer to pay cash, stay at least three nights, or travel off-season. Hoteliers are encouraged to quote prices with the IVA tax (value-added tax) included—but it's smart to ask when you book your room.

Room rates are especially volatile at hotels that use "dynamic pricing" to set rates. Prices can skyrocket during festivals and conventions, while business hotels can have deep discounts on weekends when demand plummets. Of the many hotels I recommend, it's difficult to say which will be the best value on a given day—until you do your homework.

## Restaurant Price Code

Eateries in this book are categorized according to the average cost of a typical main course. Drinks, desserts, and splurge items can raise the price considerably.

| | |
|---|---|
| **$$$$** | **Splurge:** Most main courses over €25 |
| **$$$** | **Pricier:** €18-25 |
| **$$** | **Moderate:** €12-18 |
| **$** | **Budget:** Under €12 |

In Spain, takeout food is **$**; a basic tapas bar or no-frills sit-down eatery is **$$**; a casual but more upscale tapas bar or restaurant is **$$$**; and a swanky splurge is **$$$$**.

## EATING

I've categorized my recommended eateries based on the average price of a typical main course, indicated with a dollar-sign rating (see sidebar). By our standards, Spaniards eat late, having lunch—their biggest meal of the day—around 13:00-16:00, and dinner starting about 21:00. At restaurants, you can dine with tourists at 20:00, or with Spaniards if you wait until later.

For a fun early dinner at a bar, build a light meal out of tapas—small appetizer-sized portions of seafood, salads, meat-filled pastries, deep-fried tasties, and so on. Many of these are displayed behind glass, and you can point to what you want. Tapas typically cost around €4. While the smaller "tapa" size (which comes on a saucer-size plate) is handiest for maximum tasting opportunities, many bars sell only larger sizes: the ración (full portion, on a dinner plate) and media-ración (half-size portion). *Jamón* (hah-MOHN), an air-dried ham similar to prosciutto, is a Spanish staple. Other key terms include *bocadillo* (baguette sandwich), *frito* (fried), *a la plancha* (grilled), *queso* (cheese), *tortilla* (omelet), and *surtido* (assortment).

Many bars have three price tiers, which should be clearly posted: It's cheapest to eat or drink while standing at the bar (*barra*), slightly more to sit at a table inside (*mesa* or *salón*), and most expensive to sit outside (*terraza*). Wherever you are, be assertive or you'll never be served. *Por favor* (please) grabs the attention of the server or bartender.

If you're having tapas, don't worry about paying as you go (the bartender keeps track). When you're ready to leave, ask for the bill: "*¿La cuenta?*"

**Tipping:** To tip for a few tapas, round up to the nearest euro. At restaurants with table service, if a service charge is included in the bill, add about 5 percent; if it's not, leave 10 percent. If you're sampling tapas at a counter, there's no need to tip (though you can round up the bill).

## TRANSPORTATION

**By Train and Bus:** For train schedules, visit Germany's excellent all-Europe website (www.bahn.com) or Spain's Renfe (www.renfe.com). Since trains can sell out, and high-speed AVE ticket prices increase as your departure date draws closer, it's smart to buy your tickets at least a day in advance—even for short rides. You can buy them at a travel agency (easiest), at the train station (can be crowded, be sure you're in the right line; you'll pay a five percent service fee at the ticket window), or online (at www.renfe.com). Be aware that the Renfe website often rejects US credit cards—use PayPal; or from the US try Raileurope.com and Petrabax.com (expect a small fee from either), or use the European vendor Trainline.eu. Futuristic, high-speed trains (such as AVE) can be priced differently according to their time of departure. To see if a rail pass could save you money, check RickSteves.com/rail.

Buses pick up where the trains don't go, reaching even small villages. But because routes are operated by various competing companies, it can be tricky to pin down schedules (check with local bus stations, tourist information offices, or the aggregator website Movelia.es).

**By Plane:** Consider covering long distances on a budget flight, which can be cheaper than a train or bus ride. Check the cost of a flight on one of Europe's airlines, whether a major carrier or a no-frills outfit like EasyJet or Ryanair. Kayak is the top site for flights to and within Europe, easy-to-use Google Flights has price alerts, and Skyscanner includes many inexpensive flights within Europe.

**By Car:** It's cheaper to arrange most car rentals from the US. If you're planning a multicountry itinerary by car, be aware of often astronomical international drop-off fees. For tips on your insurance options, see RickSteves.com/cdw. For navigation, the mapping app on your phone works fine for Europe's roads. To save on data, most apps allow you to download maps for offline use. Some apps—including Google Maps—also have offline route directions, but you'll need mobile data access for current traffic.

It's also required that you carry an International Driving Permit (IDP), available at your local AAA office ($20 plus two passport-type photos, www.aaa.com).

Superhighways come with tolls, but save lots of time. Each toll road *(autopista de peaje)* has its own pricing structure, so tolls vary. Payment can be made in cash or by credit or debit card (credit-card-only lanes are labeled "vias automáticas"; cash lanes are *"vias manuales")*. Spaniards love to tailgate; otherwise, local road etiquette is similar to that in the US. Ask your car-rental company for details, or check the US State Department website (www.travel.state.gov, search for your country in the "Country Information" box, then select "Travel and Transportation").

A car is a worthless headache in cities—park it safely (get tips from your hotelier). As break-ins are common, be sure your valuables are out of sight and locked in the trunk, or even better, with you or in your hotel room.

## HELPFUL HINTS

**Travel Advisories:** For updated health and safety conditions, including any restrictions for your destination, consult the US State Department's international travel website (www.travel.state.gov).

**Emergency and Medical Help:** For any emergency service—ambulance, police, or fire—call **112** from a mobile phone or landline. Operators, who in most countries speak English, will deal with your request or route you to the right emergency service. If you get sick, do as the locals do and go to a pharmacist for advice. Or ask at your hotel for help—they'll know of the nearest medical and emergency services.

For **passport problems,** contact the **US Embassy** (Madrid—by appointment only, dial +34 915 872 200, https://es.usembassy.gov) or the **Canadian Embassy** (Madrid—by appointment only, dial +34 913 828 400, www.espana.gc.ca).

**ETIAS Registration:** Beginning in late 2021, US and Canadian citizens may be required to register online with the European Travel Information and Authorization System (ETIAS) before entering certain European countries (quick and easy process, $8 fee, valid 3 years, www.etiasvisa.com).

**Theft or Loss:** Spain has particularly hardworking pickpockets—wear a money belt. Assume beggars are pickpockets and any scuffle is simply a distraction by a team of thieves. If you stop for any commotion or show, put your hands in your pockets before someone else does.

To replace a passport, you'll need to go in person to an embassy (see above). Cancel and replace your credit and debit cards by calling these 24-hour US numbers with a mobile phone: Visa (dial +1-303-967-1096), MasterCard (dial +1-636-722-7111), and American Express (dial +1-336-393-1111). From a landline, you can call these US numbers collect by going through a local operator. File a police report either on the spot or within a day or two; you'll need it to submit an insurance claim for lost or stolen rail passes or travel gear, and it can help with replacing your passport or credit and debit cards. For more information, see RickSteves.com/help.

**Time:** Spain uses the 24-hour clock. It's the same through 12:00 noon, then keep going: 13:00, 14:00, and so on. Spain, like most of continental Europe, is six/nine hours ahead of the East/West Coasts of the US.

**Siesta and Paseo:** Many Spaniards (especially in rural areas) still follow the traditional siesta schedule: From around 14:00 to

**PRACTICALITIES**

17:00, many businesses close as people go home for a big lunch with their family. Then they head back to work (and shops reopen) from about 17:00 to 21:00. (Many bigger stores stay open all day long, especially in cities.) Then, after a late dinner, whole families pour out of their apartments to enjoy the cool of the evening, stroll through the streets, and greet their neighbors—a custom called the paseo.

**Sights:** Major attractions can be swamped with visitors; carefully read and follow this book's crowd-beating tips (visit popular sights very early or very late, or—where possible—reserve ahead). Opening and closing hours of sights can change unexpectedly; confirm the latest times on their websites or at the local tourist information office. At many churches, a modest dress code is encouraged and sometimes required (no bare shoulders or shorts).

**Holidays and Festivals:** Spain celebrates many holidays, which can close sights and attract crowds (book hotel rooms ahead). For more on holidays and festivals, check Spain's website: www.spain.info. For a simple list showing major—though not all—events, see RickSteves.com/festivals.

**Numbers and Stumblers:** What Americans call the second floor of a building is the first floor in Europe. Europeans write dates as day/month/year, so Christmas 2021 is 25/12/21. Commas are decimal points and vice versa—a dollar and a half is 1,50, and there are 5.280 feet in a mile. Spain uses the metric system: A kilogram is 2.2 pounds; a liter is about a quart; and a kilometer is six-tenths of a mile.

## RESOURCES FROM RICK STEVES

This Snapshot guide, excerpted from my latest edition of *Rick Steves Spain*, is one of many titles in my series of guidebooks on European travel. I also produce a public television series, *Rick Steves' Europe*, and a public radio show, *Travel with Rick Steves*. My free online video library, Rick Steves Classroom Europe, offers a searchable database of short video clips on European history, culture, and geography (Classroom.RickSteves.com). My website, RickSteves.com, offers free travel information, a forum for travelers' comments, guidebook updates, my travel blog, an online travel store, and information on European rail passes and our tours of Europe. If you're bringing a mobile device, you can download my free Rick Steves Audio Europe app that features dozens of free, self-guided audio tours of the top sights in Europe (including the Madrid City Walk and Sevilla City Walk), plus radio shows and travel interviews about Spain. For more information, see RickSteves.com/audioeurope. You can also follow me on Facebook, Twitter, and Instagram.

## ADDITIONAL RESOURCES

**Tourist Information:** www.spain.info
**Passports and Red Tape:** www.travel.state.gov
**Packing List:** www.ricksteves.com/packing
**Travel Insurance:** www.ricksteves.com/insurance
**Cheap Flights:** www.kayak.com or www.google.com/flights
**Airplane Carry-on Restrictions:** www.tsa.gov/travelers
**Updates for This Book:** www.ricksteves.com/update

## HOW WAS YOUR TRIP?

To share your tips, concerns, and discoveries after using this book, please fill out the survey at RickSteves.com/feedback. Thanks in advance—it helps a lot.

## Spanish Survival Phrases

| English | Spanish | Pronunciation |
|---------|---------|---------------|
| Good day. | Buenos días. | **bweh**-nohs **dee**-ahs |
| Do you speak English? | ¿Habla usted inglés? | **ah**-blah oo-**stehd** een-**glays** |
| Yes. / No. | Sí. / No. | see / noh |
| I (don't) understand. | (No) comprendo. | (noh) kohm-**prehn**-doh |
| Please. | Por favor. | por fah-**bor** |
| Thank you. | Gracias. | **grah**-thee-ahs |
| I'm sorry. | Lo siento. | loh see-**ehn**-toh |
| Excuse me. | Perdone. | pehr-**doh**-nay |
| (No) problem. | (No) problema. | (noh) proh-**bleh**-mah |
| Good. | Bueno. | **bweh**-noh |
| Goodbye. | Adiós. | ah-dee-**ohs** |
| OK. | Vale. | **bah**-lay |
| one / two | uno / dos | **oo**-noh / dohs |
| three / four | tres / cuatro | trehs / **kwah**-troh |
| five / six | cinco / seis | **theen**-koh / says |
| seven / eight | siete / ocho | see-**eh**-tay / **oh**-choh |
| nine / ten | nueve / diez | **nweh**-bay / dee-**ehth** |
| How much is it? | ¿Cuánto cuesta? | **kwahn**-toh **kweh**-stah |
| Write it? | ¿Me lo escribe? | may loh eh-**skree**-bay |
| Is it free? | ¿Es gratis? | ehs **grah**-tees |
| Is it included? | ¿Está incluido? | eh-**stah** een-kloo-**ee**-doh |
| Where can I buy / find...? | ¿Dónde puedo comprar / encontrar...? | **dohn**-day **pweh**-doh kohm-**prar** / ehn-kohn-**trar** |
| I'd like / We'd like... | Me gustaría / Nos gustaría... | may goo-stah-**ree**-ah / nohs goo-stah-**ree**-ah |
| ...a room. | ...una habitación. | **oo**-nah ah-bee-tah-thee-**ohn** |
| ...a ticket to ___. | ...un billete para ___. | oon bee-**yeh**-tay **pah**-rah ___ |
| Is it possible? | ¿Es posible? | ehs poh-**see**-blay |
| Where is...? | ¿Dónde está...? | **dohn**-day eh-**stah** |
| ...the train station | ...la estación de trenes | lah eh-stah-thee-**ohn** day **treh**-nehs |
| ...the bus station | ...la estación de autobuses | lah eh-stah-thee-**ohn** day ow-toh-**boo**-sehs |
| ...the tourist information office | ...la oficina de turismo | lah oh-fee-**thee**-nah day too-**rees**-moh |
| Where are the toilets? | ¿Dónde están los servicios? | **dohn**-day eh-**stahn** lohs sehr-**bee**-thee-ohs |
| men | hombres, caballeros | **ohm**-brehs, kah-bah-**yeh**-rohs |
| women | mujeres, damas | moo-**heh**-rehs, **dah**-mahs |
| left / right | izquierda / derecha | eeth-kee-**ehr**-dah / deh-**reh**-chah |
| straight | derecho | deh-**reh**-choh |
| When do you open / close? | ¿A qué hora abren / cierran? | ah kay **oh**-rah **ah**-brehn / thee-**ehr**-ahn |
| At what time? | ¿A qué hora? | ah kay **oh**-rah |
| Just a moment. | Un momento. | oon moh-**mehn**-toh |
| now / soon / later | ahora / pronto / más tarde | ah-**oh**-rah / **prohn**-toh / mahs **tar**-day |
| today / tomorrow | hoy / mañana | oy / mahn-**yah**-nah |

## In a Spanish Restaurant

| English | Spanish | Pronunciation |
|---|---|---|
| I'd like / We'd like... | Me gustaría / Nos gustaría... | may goo-stah-**ree**-ah / nohs goo-stah-**ree**-ah |
| ...to reserve... | ...reservar... | reh-sehr-**bar** |
| ...a table for one / two. | ...una mesa para uno / dos. | **oo**-nah **meh**-sah **pah**-rah **oo**-noh / dohs |
| Non-smoking. | No fumador. | noh foo-mah-**dohr** |
| Is this table free? | ¿Está esta mesa libre? | eh-**stah** eh-stah meh-sah lee-bray |
| The menu (in English), please. | La carta (en inglés), por favor. | lah **kar**-tah (ehn een-**glays**) por fah-**bor** |
| service (not) included | servicio (no) incluido | sehr-**bee**-thee-oh (noh) een-kloo-**ee**-doh |
| cover charge | precio de entrada | **preh**-thee-oh day ehn-**trah**-dah |
| to go | para llevar | **pah**-rah yeh-**bar** |
| with / without | con / sin | kohn / seen |
| and / or | y / o | ee / oh |
| menu (of the day) | menú (del día) | meh-**noo** (dehl **dee**-ah) |
| specialty of the house | especialidad de la casa | eh-speh-thee-ah-lee-**dahd** day lah **kah**-sah |
| tourist menu | menú turístico | meh-**noo** too-**ree**-stee-koh |
| combination plate | plato combinado | **plah**-toh kohm-bee-**nah**-doh |
| appetizers | tapas | **tah**-pahs |
| bread | pan | pahn |
| cheese | queso | **keh**-soh |
| sandwich | bocadillo | boh-kah-**dee**-yoh |
| soup | sopa | **soh**-pah |
| salad | ensalada | ehn-sah-**lah**-dah |
| meat | carne | **kar**-nay |
| poultry | aves | **ah**-behs |
| fish | pescado | peh-**skah**-doh |
| seafood | marisco | mah-**ree**-skoh |
| fruit | fruta | **froo**-tah |
| vegetables | verduras | behr-**doo**-rahs |
| dessert | postre | **poh**-stray |
| tap water | agua del grifo | **ah**-gwah dehl **gree**-foh |
| mineral water | agua mineral | **ah**-gwah mee-neh-**rahl** |
| milk | leche | **leh**-chay |
| (orange) juice | zumo (de naranja) | **thoo**-moh (day nah-**rahn**-hah) |
| coffee | café | kah-**fay** |
| tea | té | tay |
| wine | vino | **bee**-noh |
| red / white | tinto / blanco | **teen**-toh / **blahn**-koh |
| glass / bottle | vaso / botella | **bah**-soh / boh-**teh**-yah |
| beer | cerveza | thehr-**beh**-thah |
| Cheers! | ¡Salud! | sah-**lood** |
| More. / Another. | Más. / Otro. | mahs / **oh**-troh |
| The same. | El mismo. | ehl **mees**-moh |
| The bill, please. | La cuenta, por favor. | lah **kwehn**-tah por fah-**bor** |
| tip | propina | proh-**pee**-nah |
| Delicious! | ¡Delicioso! | deh-lee-thee-**oh**-soh |

For hundreds more pages of survival phrases for your trip to Spain, check out *Rick Steves Spanish Phrase Book*.

# INDEX

## Explore Europe

At ricksteves.com you can browse through thousands of articles, videos, photos and radio interviews, plus find a wealth of money-saving travel tips for planning your dream trip. And with our mobile-friendly website, you can easily access all this great travel information anywhere you go.

## TV Shows

Preview the places you'll visit by watching entire half-hour episodes of *Rick Steves' Europe* (choose from all 100 shows) on-demand, for free.

*your travel dreams into affordable reality*

## Radio Interviews

Enjoy ready access to Rick's vast library of radio interviews covering travel tips and cultural insights that relate specifically to your Europe travel plans.

## Travel Forums

Learn, ask, share! Our online community of savvy travelers is a great resource for first-time travelers to Europe, as well as seasoned pros.

## Travel News

Subscribe to our free Travel News e-newsletter, and get monthly updates from Rick on what's happening in Europe.

## Classroom Europe

Check out our free resource for educators with 400+ short video clips from the *Rick Steves' Europe* TV show.

## Rick's Free Travel App

Get your FREE **Rick Steves Audio Europe**™ app to enjoy…

- Dozens of self-guided tours of Europe's top museums, sights and historic walks
- Hundreds of tracks filled with cultural insights and sightseeing tips from Rick's radio interviews
- All organized into handy geographic playlists
- For Apple and Android

With Rick whispering in your ear, Europe gets even better.

## Find out more at ricksteves.com

*Gear up for your next adventure at ricksteves.com*

## Light Luggage

Pack light and right with Rick Steves' affordable, custom-designed rolling carry-on bags, backpacks, day packs and shoulder bags.

## Accessories

From packing cubes to moneybelts and beyond, Rick has personally selected the travel goodies that will help your trip go smoother.

## Save time and energy

This guidebook is your independent-travel toolkit. But for all it delivers, it's still up to you to devote the time and energy it takes to manage the preparation and logistics that are essential for a happy trip. If that's a hassle, there's a solution.

## Rick Steves Tours

A Rick Steves tour takes you to Europe's most interesting places with great

guides and small groups. We follow Rick's favorite itineraries, ride in comfy buses, stay in family-run hotels, and bring you intimately close to the Europe you've traveled so far to see. Most importantly, we take away the logistical headaches so you can focus on the fun.

## Join the fun

This year we'll take thousands of free-spirited travelers—nearly half of them repeat customers— along with us on 50 different itineraries, from Athens to Istanbul. Is a Rick Steves tour the right fit for your travel dreams?

Find out at ricksteves.com, where you can also check seat availability and sign up. Europe is best experienced with happy travel partners. We hope you can join us.

**See our itineraries at ricksteves.com**

## BEST OF GUIDES

*Full-color guides in an easy-to-scan
format. Focused on top sights
and experiences in the most
popular European destinations*

Best of England
Best of Europe
Best of France
Best of Germany
Best of Ireland
Best of Italy
Best of Scotland
Best of Spain

## COMPREHENSIVE GUIDES

*City, country, and regional guides
printed on Bible-thin paper. Packe
with detailed coverage for a mult
week trip exploring iconic sights
and venturing off the beaten pat*

Amsterdam & the Netherlands
Barcelona
Belgium: Bruges, Brussels,
  Antwerp & Ghent
Berlin
Budapest
Croatia & Slovenia
Eastern Europe
England
Florence & Tuscany
France
Germany
Great Britain
Greece: Athens & the Peloponnes
Iceland
Ireland
Istanbul
Italy
London
Paris
Portugal
Prague & the Czech Republic
Provence & the French Riviera
Rome
Scandinavia
Scotland
Sicily
Spain
Switzerland
Venice
Vienna, Salzburg & Tirol

HE BEST OF ROME

e, Italy's capital, is studded with
an remnants and floodlit-fountain
es. From the Vatican to the Colos-
with crazy traffic in between, Rome
derful, huge, and exhausting. The
s, the heat, and the weighty history

of the Eternal City where Caesars walked
can make tourists wilt. Recharge by taking siestas, gelato breaks, and after-dark
walks, strolling from one atmospheric
square to another in the refreshing evening air.

d *Pantheon*—which
st dome until the
y 2,000 years old
y over 1,500).

f *Athens* in the *Vat-*
es the humanistic
e.

ladiators fought
other, entertaining

Rick Steves books are available from your favorite bookse
Many guides are available as ebooks.

## POCKET GUIDES
*Compact color guides for shorter trips*

Amsterdam  
Athens  
Barcelona  
Florence  
Italy's Cinque Terre  
London  
Munich & Salzburg  

Paris  
Prague  
Rome  
Venice  
Vienna  

## SNAPSHOT GUIDES
*Focused single-destination coverage*

Basque Country: Spain & France  
Copenhagen & the Best of Denmark  
Dublin  
Dubrovnik  
Edinburgh  
Hill Towns of Central Italy  
Krakow, Warsaw & Gdansk  
Lisbon  
Loire Valley  
Madrid & Toledo  
Milan & the Italian Lakes District  
Naples & the Amalfi Coast  
Nice & the French Riviera  
Normandy  
Northern Ireland  
Norway  
Reykjavík  
Rothenburg & the Rhine  
Scottish Highlands  
Sevilla, Granada & Southern Spain  
St. Petersburg, Helsinki & Tallinn  
Stockholm  

## CRUISE PORTS GUIDES
*Reference for cruise ports of call*

Mediterranean Cruise Ports  
Scandinavian & Northern European  
  Cruise Ports  

### Complete your library with...

## TRAVEL SKILLS & CULTURE
*Study up on travel skills and gain  
insight on history and culture*

Europe 101  
Europe Through the Back Door  
Europe's Top 100 Masterpieces  
European Christmas  
European Easter  
European Festivals  
For the Love of Europe  
Travel as a Political Act  

## PHRASE BOOKS & DICTIONARIES

French  
French, Italian & German  
German  
Italian  
Portuguese  
Spanish  

## PLANNING MAPS

Britain, Ireland & London  
Europe  
France & Paris  
Germany, Austria & Switzerland  
Iceland  
Ireland  
Italy  
Spain & Portugal

# Photo Credits

Avalon Travel
Hachette Book Group
1700 Fourth Street
Berkeley, CA 94710

Printed in Canada by Friesens
Sixth Edition. First printing January 2021

ISBN 978-1-64171-328-3

For the latest on Rick's lectures, guidebooks, tours, public radio show, and public television series, contact Rick Steves' Europe, 130 Fourth Avenue North, Edmonds, WA 98020, tel. 425/771-8303, www.ricksteves.com, rick@ricksteves.com.

The publisher is not responsible for websites (or their content) that are not owned by the publisher.

**Rick Steves' Europe**
**Managing Editor:** Jennifer Madison Davis
**Assistant Managing Editor:** Cathy Lu
**Special Publications Manager:** Risa Laib
**Editors:** Glenn Eriksen, Suzanne Kotz, Rosie Leutzinger, Teresa Nemeth, Jessica Shaw, Carrie Shepherd, Meg Sneeringer
**Editorial & Production Assistant:** Megan Simms
**Researchers:** Amanda Buttinger, Pål Bjarne Johansen, Robert Wright
**Contributor:** Gene Openshaw
**Graphic Content Director:** Sandra Hundacker
**Maps & Graphics:** David C. Hoerlein, Lauren Mills, Mary Rostad
**Digital Asset Coordinator:** Orin Dubrow

**Avalon Travel**
**Senior Editor and Series Manager:** Madhu Prasher
**Associate Managing Editors:** Jamie Andrade, Sierra Machado
**Indexer:** Stephen Callahan
**Production & Typesetting:** Lisi Baldwin
**Cover Design:** Kimberly Glyder Design
**Maps & Graphics:** Kat Bennett, Mike Morgenfeld

*Although every effort was made to ensure that the information was correct at the time of going to press, the author and publisher do not assume and hereby disclaim any liability to any party for any loss or damage caused by errors, omissions, jamón addiction, or any potential travel disruption due to labor or financial difficulty, whether such errors or omissions result from negligence, accident, or any other cause.*

# Let's Keep on Travelin'

Your trip doesn't need to end.

Follow Rick on social media!